THE WORLDS OF
J. R. R. TOLKIEN

To Lorelei and Jessica,
my fellow adventurers,
with love.

Published in the United States and Canada by
Princeton University Press
41 William Street
Princeton, New Jersey 08540
press.princeton.edu

This book was designed and produced by
Frances Lincoln,
an imprint of the Quarto Group.
The Old Brewery
6 Blundell Street
London N7 9BH

Every effort has been made to trace the copyright holders of material quoted in this book.
If application is made in writing to the publisher, any omissions will be included in future
editions.

This book has been composed in Adobe Garamond Pro and Alice
Printed in Singapore

978-0-691-19694-7

10 9 8 7 6 5 4 3 2 1

JOHN GARTH

THE WORLDS OF J. R. R. TOLKIEN

THE PLACES THAT INSPIRED MIDDLE-EARTH

Princeton University Press

Princeton and Oxford

CONTENTS

INTRODUCTION

'Many reviewers,' Tolkien once lamented, 'seem to assume that Middle-earth is another planet!'[1] It is our own, and takes its name from the Anglo-Saxon term for the known world. It has sun and moon, oak and elm, water and stone. As we travel with Tolkien's characters, we visit places that seem compellingly real.

How Tolkien conjures the spirit of place continues to intrigue. If you google 'places that inspired', 'Tolkien' will appear high among the suggested searches. Yet the answers available are sometimes wildly wrong, and at best unsatisfactory. This book is an attempt to give the question the attention it deserves.

That inspiration is vital for creation should hardly need stating, but some Tolkien devotees feel it is a no-go area. They will quote Gandalf's maxim, 'He that breaks a thing to find out what it is has left the path of wisdom.'[2] Yet even Gandalf, when asked to clear snow with his wizardly powers, protests that he cannot make fire without 'something to work on'.[3] Tolkien, however extraordinary his own imagination, likewise needed fuel. He said, 'I take my models like anyone else – from such "life" as I know.'[4]

Existing discussions of Tolkien's place inspirations are often unsatisfactory. Most boil down to the circular argument that some wood, mountain or river 'must have' inspired him because it looks 'Tolkienesque'. Such assertions say little about Tolkien. Tourist offices and entrepreneurs often ignore or distort the biographical facts to serve local commercial interests, and their assertions acquire the air of fact by being repeated in newspapers or on Wikipedia. At the other extreme, some genuine Tolkien experts are better at identifying possible influences than judging their plausibility, producing a spaghetti of loose ends.

Properly conducted, the search for inspiration can enrich our appreciation of Tolkien's extraordinary creative powers. The investigation helps us understand the world he knew – now rapidly receding into a lost past. It reveals his writings as a reflection of passionately held views and ideas about that world. It also uncovers the many and various means by which he transformed reality for his creative ends.

This book advances many theories of my own about what inspired the Middle-earth 'legendarium', alongside a few of the most cogent and interesting claims made by others. But it does not restrict itself to identifying real locations as the inspiration for particular spots in Middle-earth. The book also looks at places, real and imaginary, that Tolkien knew from his reading. It examines the influences that shaped his imagined cultures and cosmology. It counts place as a combination of location, geology, ecology, culture, nomenclature and other factors. It seeks to show the how and the why.

To the inquiry, I bring a particular interest in biography, history, landscape and language. I observe Tolkien's footsteps closely, consider the context and try to enter sympathetically into his creative thoughts and feelings. I favour conclusions that seem cogent both in themselves and in wider contexts. At times I advance more than one suggestion for the origin of a particular idea – hobbit-holes, for example – and leave it for you to form your own views. Although my intuition will inevitably err at times, everything is weighed on the scales of fact and likelihood, drawing on rich published resources as well as my own extensive researches.

The Worlds of J.R.R. Tolkien is written to be read in order, but also to reward browsing. That goes especially for the panels scattered throughout, each focusing on some topic of special interest related to the main theme of the chapter.

The journey begins, naturally enough, with England and the Shire of the Hobbits. The next chapter, Four Winds, looks at the broad cultural influences behind the peoples, languages and cosmology of Middle-earth, serving meanwhile to outline some of Tolkien's deepest motivations. Chapter Three, The Land of Lúthien, looks at the link he originally made between England and the Elves, tracing its winding thread through several decades of work on his legendarium.

Four topographical chapters follow, covering inland waters, mountains and forests, but starting with The Shore and the Sea – a vital topic, even though it is scarcely touched upon in *The Hobbit* and *The Lord of the Rings*.

The final four chapters deal with places built or shaped by people, ranging from archaeology (Ancient Imprints) to places of defence (Watch and Ward), from battlefields to industrial wastelands.

An appendix tries to clear up a couple of controversies that have dogged debate on Tolkien and the inspiration of place. Some further points of general interest will be found among the notes at the back of the book (flagged in the main text by the asterisked numbers).

Readers who feel unsure about *The Silmarillion* and the creative evolution of the legendarium may wish to bookmark the panel 'Tales that grew in the telling' (p.44) and the Beleriand map (p.55).

THERE AND BACK AGAIN

The first imaginary landscape to meet readers of J. R. R. Tolkien was the gorgeous world of forest, lake and snow-capped mountain he painted for the cover of *The Hobbit*. A road runs up the book's spine and disappears into the mysteries of the biggest, most foreboding peak. Yet this invitation to wonder and adventure comes from a writer who only once travelled in spectacular mountains.

It is the next image in *The Hobbit* that shows us where he was really coming from: *The Hill: Hobbiton-across-the Water*. Poplar, flowering chestnut and other trees dot a sunlit champaign. A watermill in the foreground is one of just a few buildings. A sandy lane bridges the small river and winds between gardens with colourful flowerbeds, up to a cutting on the hillside. And there is the round door to a hole, a home.

The Hill, with its welcoming hobbit-hole, is a cosy mirror of the Lonely Mountain on the cover, where the dragon Smaug lurks in stolen halls. The road from one picture leads to the other. But the Hobbiton image promises that after we have been there, we will come back again.

ABOVE *The Hobbit* jacket illustration by Tolkien, painted in 1937 for the first edition.

RIGHT Tolkien's 1937 illustration *The Hill: Hobbiton-across-the Water*.

The hill : hobbiton~across~the Water

ENGLAND TO THE SHIRE

A FAR GREEN COUNTRY

For Tolkien, England was a land of revelation. Though he had English
parents, he was actually born in the African veldt, in January 1892, and
so it was as a newcomer that he arrived in what became his homeland.
In April 1895 he was brought to stay with relatives as a long break from
torrid Bloemfontein in the Orange Free State, now part of South Africa.
He never saw his father again. Arthur Tolkien died from rheumatic fever
a year later, alone in Bloemfontein. The sharp lesson that nothing is
permanent was to be repeated by later moves and bereavements, and by
much bigger changes.

Meanwhile, the change of scene was profound. Young Ronald Tolkien
had left a land where the summer sun had been so intense that the
curtains remained drawn at Christmas. Now he fell in love with the
West Midlands landscape of elms and small rivers, and with the air of
the country folk.

But he would later reflect that the experience went both deeper and
wider. It left him permanently with 'a very vivid child's view'.[1] In a
sense, all his fictional landscapes stem from this experience. 'The English

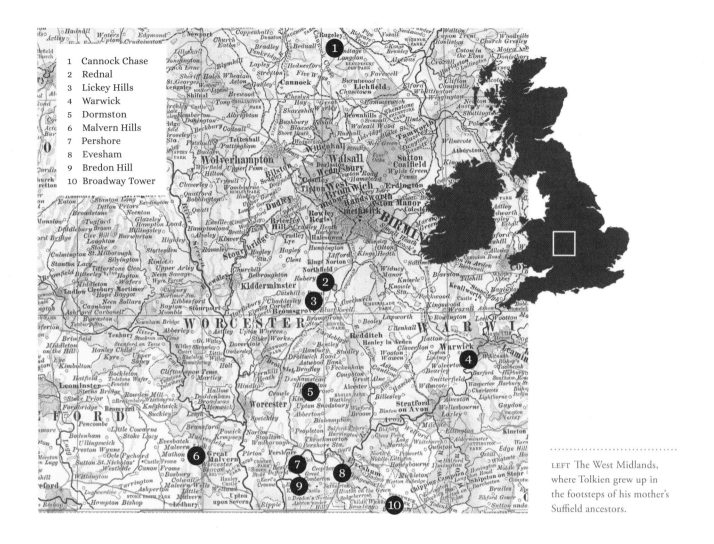

1 Cannock Chase
2 Rednal
3 Lickey Hills
4 Warwick
5 Dormston
6 Malvern Hills
7 Pershore
8 Evesham
9 Bredon Hill
10 Broadway Tower

LEFT The West Midlands, where Tolkien grew up in the footsteps of his mother's Suffield ancestors.

countryside,' he said, 'seemed to me wonderful. If you really want to know what Middle-earth is based on, it's my wonder and delight in the earth as it is, particularly the natural earth.'[2] Reaching far beyond England, it meant the 'North-Western air' of Europe as a whole struck him 'both as "home" and "something discovered"'.[3]

In his own stories, it is remarkable how often the adventurers arrive unexpectedly in havens of rest that are at once both strange and welcoming – Beorn's hall, Lothlórien, Gondolin, Rivendell, the house of Tom Bombadil. Some of his travellers cross the sea and reach a 'far green country' that is founded upon Tolkien's first encounter with England.[4] Here, it would seem, is the source of that acute taste for the sudden, unexpected uplift he found in fairy-stories, a glimpse of 'Joy beyond the walls of the world, poignant as grief'.[5]

The sudden dislocation between old and new worlds also gave Tolkien a kind of visionary superpower. He would always retain a vivid mental picture of a house that never actually existed – an elaborate fusion of his old Bloemfontein home and his grandparents' Worcestershire house in Ashfield Road, Kings Heath. He compared the image to a photographic double exposure. Another process of his imaginative life was forming: the ability to visualize unreal places perfectly, and the tendency to project the world he inhabited onto one he only imagined.

SAREHOLE

The Shire is a reflection of Sarehole, a hamlet that lay about a mile and a half (2.5km) eastward from Kings Heath. It 'was inspired by a few cherished square miles of actual countryside

at Sarehole', he told a newspaper.[6] To his publisher, he said it was 'more or less a Warwickshire village of about the period of the Diamond Jubilee' – Queen Victoria's sixtieth year on the throne, 1897.[7]*

From the summer of 1896, Mabel Tolkien rented 5 Gracewell Road, a new semi-detached cottage that looked downhill to the little River Cole and a mill with a tall chimney and churning waterwheel. Though only five miles (8km) from the centre of booming industrial Birmingham, Sarehole itself stood in a country that was still little altered by the modern age. The horse ruled the roads. On a clear night, the stars ruled the sky. It was a world that had more in common with 'the lands and hills of the most primitive and wildest stories', Tolkien recalled.[8] 'I loved it with an intensity of love that was a kind of nostalgia reversed' – an aching love for a new-found home.[9]

For Bilbo, seeing Hobbiton again after his great adventure, 'the shapes of the land and of the trees were as well known to him as his hands and toes.'[10] Though Tolkien could never return to the Sarehole of his youth, he declared more than sixty years later, 'I could draw you a map of every inch of it.'[11]

No adult gets to know a small area like a child – or indeed like a hobbit, close to the ground and sharply attuned to nature.

Ronald and his brother Hilary, two years his junior, would hang around the watermill (see p.175, Craft and Industry), where swans glided in the willow-encircled pool. They would play in the mill meadow with its huge sentinel oaks, explore the big sandpit just up the road or disappear into a 'wonderful dell' with flowers and blackberries.[12] They called it *Bumble Dell*, from the local word for blackberry. It has been identified as Moseley Bog (see p.114, Tree-woven Lands).

Tolkien once said he 'took the idea of the hobbits from the village people and children'.[13] He mixed with the local boys, 'fascinated by their dialect and by their pawky ways'.[14] Among other things, the dialect word *pawky* means impudently inquisitive. It is the kind of attitude he would attract effortlessly, with his long hair, his 'Little Lord Fauntleroy costume' and his educated air.[15] He was a Baggins among Gamgees.

There would also be visits to an uncle two miles (3km) away in Acocks Green, and walks further afield.[16] 'Children walked long distances in those

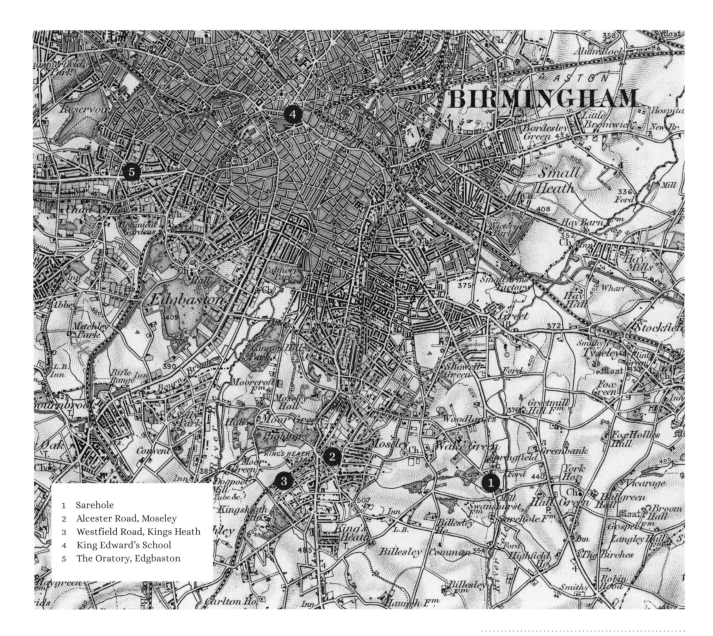

1 Sarehole
2 Alcester Road, Moseley
3 Westfield Road, Kings Heath
4 King Edward's School
5 The Oratory, Edgbaston

ABOVE Tolkien's Birmingham. From 1902 to 1911 he lived mostly in a succession of lodging houses near the Oratory.

RIGHT At seven, in wide-brimmed hat, with his brother Hilary, five.

days,' said Tolkien.[17] They also told tall tales. No doubt it was Ronald who convinced Hilary that a black witch lived in the nearby windmill and a white witch in the cottage sweet shop.[18] He was already getting into his stride, making the familiar landscape into a perilous realm.

What Sarehole did for his books was the exact opposite. Within the vast and ancient world of dangers and enchantments, it conjured a place where you could have tea, check the clock on the mantelpiece and stroll to the post office or play on the green.

The Hobbit was begun in 1928 or more likely 1929, when Tolkien's sons turned twelve, nine and five – his own age at Victoria's Diamond Jubilee. He was inviting them to join him in his own childhood world, not too distant from theirs, to set them on the road to distant lands of adventure.

END OF AN ERA

The Sarehole idyll ended quickly. At eight, Ronald won a place at King Edward's School in Birmingham. It was an eight-mile (13km) round trip from the village, half of it on foot. Nor was it much easier getting to the city-centre church that they now attended since Mabel had embraced Catholicism. So from 1900

they moved into a succession of houses closer to the city with its crowds, noise and smoke.

A brief return to the countryside came four years later after Mabel fell seriously ill with diabetes. A Catholic priest friend from the Birmingham Oratory arranged for her to convalesce with the village postman and his wife at Woodside Cottage, Rednal, near the Oratory retreat south of Birmingham. Ronald and Hilary, sent elsewhere while their mother was in hospital, now rejoined her. In glorious weather, they had the best holiday of their lives, flying kites with Father Francis Morgan, picking bilberries, sketching and climbing trees (see pp.114–5, Tree-woven Lands). The Oratory property backed onto the wooded Lickey Hills, where the boys could roam freely. They looked '*ridiculously* well compared to the weak white ghosts that met me on the train 4 weeks ago,' wrote their mother.[19]

In November 1904, Mabel Tolkien died. Tolkien once said that his writing about hobbits 'began partly as a *Sehnsucht*' – a wistful yearning – 'for that happy childhood which ended when I was orphaned'.[20]

Sarehole itself would not last for long. Absorbed into busy suburban Hall Green, it has lost even its name (see pp.181–2, Craft and Industry). Moseley Bog is now on a 'Tolkien trail' running through what has been renamed the Shire Country Park – a thin ribbon of green along the Cole. A Middle-earth Weekend takes place annually, centred on Sarehole Mill – a gentle tribute to Tolkien's 'lost paradise' of all-year-round green horizons.[21]

LAND OF BLISS, AND OTHERS

Tolkien did not copy Sarehole as Hobbiton. Hobbiton has no wildwood. Sarehole has no high hill. His instinct was to dip, mix and layer, drawing from personal experience, reading and imagination – a touch from here, a hint from there, a flourish out of nowhere. He also said the Shire was based on his memories of visiting the Worcestershire smallholding that Hilary bought after the First World War, or the Great War as their generation knew it.[22]

Tolkien felt an umbilical connection with the Vale of Evesham, ancestral home of their mother's family, the Suffields. As he grew up, and during his undergraduate years at Oxford (1911–15), he delighted in train journeys here. Later he would take his children to see their uncle and cousins at the farm, at Blackminster near Evesham, where they would fly kites or help to pick plums. The River Avon winds lazily through heavy soil ideal for fruit, so the whole vale thronged with market gardens and orchards like Hilary's.

During a summer visit in 1923, Tolkien convalesced from severe pneumonia and turned again to the mythology he had begun to create during the war. In the following years he would also begin to write for his children, weaving familiar landmarks and place-names into the stories. In one, *Roverandom*, a wizard asking for directions home to Persia is misdirected to Pershore, near Evesham, and becomes a fruit-picker.

Another tale, *Mr. Bliss*, features a hair-raising motor tour among fields and hills, country inns, church spires, walled kitchen gardens and a picturesque village. Tolkien's delightful illustrations make it

all look much like the Cotswold Hills, between Oxfordshire and the Vale of Evesham. A hilltop panorama looks past a nestling village and across a broad valley to distant hills. Such views can be had from the western edge of the Cotswolds around Broadway Tower, looking across Hilary country towards Bredon Hill and the heights of the Malverns and Wales. Wayne Hammond and Christina Scull suggest *Mr. Bliss* may have been created during a visit to Hilary's. (By one account, it was inspired by a 1932 trip there, when Tolkien managed to damage a dry-stone wall with his new Morris Cowley. Another

'The Little Kingdom' around Tolkien's Oxford home, and the setting for *Farmer Giles of Ham*.

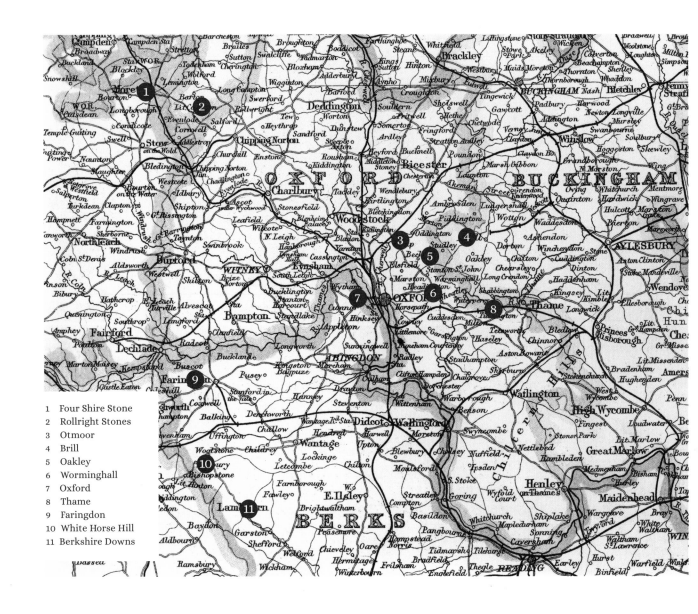

1   Four Shire Stone
2   Rollright Stones
3   Otmoor
4   Brill
5   Oakley
6   Worminghall
7   Oxford
8   Thame
9   Faringdon
10 White Horse Hill
11 Berkshire Downs

account puts it four years before they bought the car, which would make Mr Bliss's driving rather prophetic.)

Oxford had already made its mark on Tolkien's writing while he was an undergraduate (see pp.147–9, Watch and Ward) and in the first of his mythological *Lost Tales* (see pp.105–6, Rivers, Lakes and Waterlands). After he returned from Leeds to Oxford in 1925, family walks or drives were fuel for his imagination. So Tom Bombadil sprang into being. The name first belonged to a jointed wooden doll, one of the Tolkien children's toys, but escaped into much larger life.[23]* *The Adventures of Tom Bombadil*, a poem of 1931 or earlier, has him gallumphing from hill to dale to water meadow, among water-rats and bumblebees, laughing in sun and rain alike.

Bombadil was not yet part of Middle-earth. In 1937, desperate for something to follow up *The Hobbit*, Tolkien offered him to his publisher as a standalone figure embodying 'the spirit of the (vanishing) Oxford and Berkshire countryside'.[24] But if Bombadil is a *genius loci* or guardian spirit of place, as Tom Shippey says, then he is also merrily at odds with his neighbours. He masters them all – badgers, barrow-wights, Willow-man, and River-woman's daughter (see pp.105–6, Rivers, Lakes and Waterlands). He delights in nature like a child immune to its dangers, or like a Thames Valley Adam. When Tolkien absorbed him into *The Lord of the Rings*, he tied Bombadil's power to song and made him 'Eldest' – like the primal Finnish hero Väinämöinen, I suggest, 'but perhaps with a bit of Oxfordshire ploughman thrown in,' adds Oxford medievalist Maria Artamonova.[25] And though his countryside might be vanishing, Bombadil carries no trace of the kind of melancholy or portentousness that Tolkien expressed elsewhere, such as Lothlórien.

Tom had first appeared in a rowing song with real and concocted English place-names, and in a story fragment set in Britain under a pseudo-historical King Bonhedig. It sets the tone for another tale inspired by the counties around Oxford, *Farmer Giles of Ham*.[26]* Here, the country around Oxford belongs to a 'Little Kingdom', in what Tolkien called 'a no-time in which blunderbusses or anything might occur', though it is between the Romans and King Arthur.[27] The tale refers to real places – Thame, Oakley, Otmoor, the standing stones of Rollright (see pp.*137*, 139, *141,* Ancient Imprints). Yet the fictional topography is as pick-and-mix as the era, so that even though the named locations still exist, 'there is little point in visiting them looking for Gilesian landmarks,' as Brin Dunsire says.[28]

Farmer Giles of Ham is really about place-names rather than places – a frolic through the mistaken folk etymologies that

Tom Bombadil with Goldberry, the River-woman's daughter, as seen by Pauline Baynes.

Otmoor, Oxford's
local wetland and the
northern limit of the
'Little Kingdom' in
Farmer Giles of Ham.

frequently attach to obscure names. Tolkien said it
came out of a 'local family game played in the country
just around us'.[29] The whole story is an elaborate false
explanation for the name of the Buckinghamshire
village of Worminghall, a few miles from Oxford.
Tolkien makes it the hall of the Wormings,
descendants of a farmer who tamed a dragon or *worm*.
This is entertaining nonsense (it originally meant the
field belonging to someone called Wyrma).

A much later story, *Smith of Wootton Major*, features
unexplained, but equally convincing, place-names.
England has an embarrassment of Woottons, with
three in Oxfordshire alone. This 1960s story surely
refers to none of them. *Wootton*, simply meaning
'settlement in a wood', marks the fictional village as
utterly ordinary – though it is a hidden gateway to
the forest of Faërie. When Smith's fame spreads from
Far Easton to the Westwood, Tolkien is punning on
eastern and *westward*.

HOBBIT-LANDS AND NAMES

Tolkien compared the Shire with Warwickshire
and Worcestershire, yet said his 'patriotism' for

the March-counties bordering Wales had 'some
bearing on the placing of Hobbiton … in the
West Farthing'.[30] And his love of Oxfordshire and
Berkshire surely ran into the Shire too. He meant
it to be understood as none and all of these English
shires. It is Everyshire.

With the few names he devised for the 'hobbit-
lands' of *The Hobbit*, Tolkien was aiming for
something even more evidently universal and
primal than *Wootton*.[31] He once said,

> *If a story says 'he climbed a hill and saw a river in the
> valley below,' … every hearer of the words will have
> his own picture, and it will be made out of all the hills
> and rivers and dales he has ever seen, but especially
> out of The Hill, The River, The Valley which were for
> him the first embodiment of the word.*[32]

So Bilbo's hill is 'the Hill', his river is 'the
Water'; the hobbits' town is *Hobbiton* and
its neighbour is *Bywater*. Tolkien knew that
many genuine place-names originally had
the same simplicity (see p.108, Rivers, Lakes
and Waterlands).

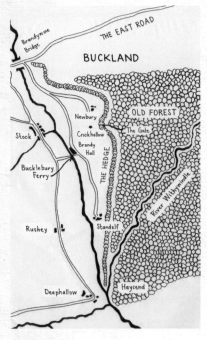

Besides England's many Bucklands, there is a Buckland estate in South Wales that looks surprisingly like Tolkien's. Though much smaller, the shape, orientation and layout all match well, with a hall between river and wooded upland.

Seamus Hamill-Keays has turned up several other similarities between this Powys estate (formerly in Brecknockshire) and *The Lord of the Rings*. Tolkien's Buckland has the Bucklebury Ferry across the Brandywine, where Frodo Baggins's parents drowned in a boating accident. Buckland on the River Usk once had a ferry too and was the scene of a nineteenth-century boating tragedy.

Yet the claim for inspiration depends on the idea that Tolkien visited this private estate as a child, which is not known. Hamill-Keays' careful research has shown only that the necessary social connections – via Father Francis Morgan's ancestors and the wine trade – *may* have existed for such a visit.[1]

Coincidence cannot be ruled out. Tolkien picked the name Buckland after trialling others, perhaps for good literary reasons that have nothing to do with any specific real Buckland (see pp.126–8, Tree-woven Lands).

The Shire, only named and fully fleshed out in *The Lord of the Rings*, grew right alongside the Little Kingdom of *Farmer Giles of Ham*, which Tolkien was simultaneously expanding in early 1938. Both take the same pleasure in place-names and in gentle mockery of English foibles. Tolkien saw the toponymy of the Shire as 'a "parody" of that of rural England, in much the same sense as are its inhabitants: they go together and are meant to'.[33]

Tolkien felt free to dot the Shire with real English place-names, such as Bucklebury (Berkshire), Stock (Essex, Yorkshire and Somerset) and Newbury (Berkshire and four other counties). Few, if any, of these real places will tell you anything about their Shire namesakes, though some might tell you a little about the Shire generally.

The game stretches to Bree, east of the Shire, too. In *The Lord of the Rings*, *Bree* is simply 'hill', like Welsh *bre*. *Bree-hill* translates itself, as does the slightly more compressed *Brill*, the name of a village near Oxford. *Brill* conveys a history – named by Celts

and renamed by the Anglo-Saxons who displaced them. The names *Bree-hill* and *Chetwood* (British-English 'wood-wood') are meant to whisper a similar story of forgotten migrations passing through Tolkien's Eriador.

With Bree and Brill there may be more behind the inspiration than just the name. The real village stands on a hill nearly four hundred feet above the Buckinghamshire fields, whereas Tolkien's Bree nestles at the foot of Bree-hill; but Brill is east of Oxford, the same direction as Bree from Hobbiton. Edmund Weiner, one of Tolkien's latter-day successors at the *Oxford English Dictionary*, is convinced there is some influence. 'Brill has an extraordinarily magical atmosphere, and the sort of view you would have got from Weathertop.'[34]

Other Shire names, such as *Overbourne*, *Longbottom* and *Rushey*, are pure invention. They seem familiar because they are built out of genuine place-name elements by an expert – Tolkien was a member of the English Place-Name Society from its launch in 1923. Some names, including *Nobottle*, were actually invented

(with permission) by his son Christopher in drawing the Shire map, not by Tolkien senior.[35]*

There was often a degree of private game-playing, to amuse others or just himself. The Shire's *Frogmorton* sounds like a joking or juvenile mispronunciation of *Throckmorton* (near Evesham). Privately meaningful allusions probably abound. Bag End was named after the home of Tolkien's aunt Jane Neave (Mabel's sister), at Dormston in Worcestershire. Sam Gamgee's sweetheart Rosie Cotton gets her surname from Cotton Lane in Moseley, Birmingham, the home of Tolkien's Suffield grandparents from 1904. Tolkien called it 'a purely private jest, of no importance to the tale' but said, 'It belongs to childhood memories which are a large ingredient in the make-up of the Shire.'[36]*

A more serious personal reference may underlie Long Cleeve, home of Pippin Took's wife, Diamond. The Cotswolds' highest summit, Cleeve Cloud, gives astonishing views across the Vale of Gloucester to the Bristol Channel. At its feet lies Cheltenham, where Tolkien proposed to Edith Bratt in 1913 (see p.48, The Land of Lúthien).

He never expected readers worldwide to pick up local or personal references. He never expected readers worldwide, full stop. Tolkien wrote firstly to entertain himself and those close to him. For *The Hobbit* and *The Lord of the Rings*, that mostly meant his family and the Inklings, the Oxford circle of friends who would read to each other weekly. In-jokes and sly (or not-so-sly) allusions would sit well enough in the hobbit-lands, which were meant to seem familiar.

A goodly crop of Middle-earth inns seem to recall real ones. The Ivy Bush evokes the ancient vintners' symbol that gives England many pubs of the same name; but Tolkien cannot have forgotten the Ivy Bush on the Hagley Road, Edgbaston – within half a mile (0.8km) of his various Birmingham lodgings from 1902. Hobbiton's other inn, the Green Dragon, shares its name with one that stood in St Aldates, Oxford, when he was an undergraduate there from 1911.

Tolkien originally called the Prancing Pony at Bree 'the White Horse', the name of an Inklings watering hole in the heart of Oxford. The Golden Perch, where Pippin longs to taste the Eastfarthing's best beer, suggests the Perch in Binsey, just upstream from Oxford. Straying from beer to buns, Boffin's Bakery was Oxford's grandest cake shop – fit inspiration for the surname of the prominent hobbit family. The final Saturday of the Oxford term would see over-excited students hurling bread rolls and butter-pats across Boffin's first-floor dining room.

Landmarks further afield must have featured, too – known from country walks and days out in the car. It seems a safe bet that the Four Shire Stone, a pillar marking the juncture of Oxfordshire, Gloucestershire, Warwickshire and Worcestershire, suggested the Three Farthing Stone, meeting-point of all but one of the Shire's four divisions or farthings. The term *farthing* is good English for 'fourth part, quarter', and Tolkien modelled its Shire usage directly on *riding* ('third part', from *thriding*), the old word for any of the three regions of Yorkshire.[37] It is also a pun – in the pre-decimal system current when he was writing, a farthing was a quarter of a penny. 'The name would have neatly associated the small people of the Shire with the smallest British coin in circulation,' say Peter Gilliver and colleagues from the *Oxford English Dictionary*.[38] Either that or it is a satirical dig – the Shire amounts to virtually nothing.

Artamonova, who regularly walks Tolkien's old turf, believes he often took his scenery from observation. 'It's just so detailed, it feels like a real portrait of a real landscape,' she says.[39] Walking while listening to *The Lord of the Rings*, she has sometimes been struck by the uncanny sense of being inside the scene described. Tolkien's stories have been described as 'elaborate fantasy tramping tales' aimed at the Inklings.[40] This can never have been truer than in the journey across the Shire, written when Tolkien had little idea where the plot of his *Hobbit* sequel was going. C. S. Lewis was reading the story as it unfolded. Their walking tour in Somerset's Quantock Hills the previous April surely lent colour and detail to some of Tolkien's finest landscape writing.

HOBBIT-HOLES

Hobbits come out of hobbit-holes, but where hobbit-holes came from is a moot point. Bob Blackham points to old forges with horseshoe-shaped doors, like one at Claverdon, Warwickshire. Archaeological explanations offer themselves (see pp.134–6, Ancient Imprints), as well as an enticing seaside folklore one (see p.72, The Shore and the Sea).

Pressed by a journalist about hobbit-holes, Tolkien mentioned the surprising comforts of trench dugouts (see pp.163–4, Places of War) and the enduring popularity of thatched houses. His sketchbooks show

SAM AND OTHER SKETCHES FROM LIFE

A small minority of Tolkien's fictional characters can be traced to Sarehole and elsewhere.

The Sarehole miller and his son, both named George Andrew, were 'characters of wonder and terror' to the young Tolkien brothers.[1] The son, whom they nicknamed the White Ogre because of his sharp eyes and dusty face, would yell at them if they strayed too close to the mill machinery or into his crops. Tolkien made his fictional millers small-minded and mean. The miller in *Farmer Giles of Ham* is 'bosom enemies' with the hero, much as the Hobbiton miller's son, Ted Sandyman, is with Sam Gamgee.[2]

Sam's father goes back to 'a curious local character, an old man who used to go about swapping gossip and weather-wisdom and such like' in Lamorna Cove, Cornwall, where the Tolkiens holidayed in 1931. Tolkien nicknamed this Cornishman *Gaffer* ('grandfather') *Gamgee* (a kind of cotton wool named after its Birmingham inventor). It became the standard family nickname for 'old chaps of the kind', one of whom appears briefly in *Mr. Bliss*.[3]* When such a figure popped up in Hobbiton, the name attached to him and stuck.

Sam combines qualities of Sarehole lads and the ordinary soldiers of the Great War, particularly the servants or 'batmen' assigned to Tolkien as a junior officer. Sam, he wrote, is 'largely a reflection of the English soldier – grafted on the village-boys of early days, the memory of the privates and my batmen that I knew in the 1914 War'.[4]

Sarehole also had a Black Ogre, a farmer who once chased Ronald for picking mushrooms. He is remembered in Frodo's youthful escapade on the land of Farmer Maggot. In the published book, Maggot is wise and welcoming, but in one experimental draft he is a violent, threatening figure.

Tolkien saw the name *Barnabas Butter* 'on an old grey stone in a quiet churchyard in southern England'.[5]* Several generations of men with this distinctive name lived around Sidmouth in Devon, where the Tolkiens holidayed later in the 1930s. It popped back into Tolkien's mind when he was drafting the Bree chapters there in 1938, leading to Barliman Butterbur, innkeeper at the Prancing Pony.

Were hobbits inspired by tales of Kentucky folk? So it is claimed in an early, unauthorized biography of Tolkien by Daniel Grotta and in articles by journalist Guy Davenport. Allen Barnett, an American friend of Tolkien's from undergraduate years at Oxford, is said to have told a fascinated Tolkien 'about the Kentuckians, their contempt for shoes, their fields of tobacco, their countrified ancient English names like Proudfoot and Baggins'.[6]

Barnett, from Shelbyville, died in 1970, and most of his papers are lost. Occasional exchanges with Tolkien, from the 1940s and later, say nothing about hobbits or Kentucky.[7]

A claim by Davenport that every hobbit name appears in Shelbyville or Lexington phonebooks has been carefully debunked by David Bratman. Among very few hobbit surnames clustering in Kentucky was *Cotton* – for which we know Tolkien had a Birmingham inspiration. Bratman comments, 'It's not impossible that Barnett's tales contributed a soupçon to Tolkien's cauldron of story, but he isn't the secret key to the Shire.'[8]

that these caught his eye – and perhaps enough to be drawn into fantasy. There are the cottages he sketched in 1912 at Eastbury, Berkshire, their windows peeping from beneath unruly thatch.[41] Umbrella Cottage, a picture-postcard landmark in Lyme Regis, has been suggested as an inspiration for his untitled 1914 drawing of a fantasy house, later reworked for pictures of Father Christmas's houses at the North Pole.[42]

Yet closer to hobbit-holes are the turf houses of Iceland, as Lorelei Garth suggests. Tolkien was deep in Icelandic lore, and *The Hobbit* was begun at a time when Icelandic au pairs looked after the boys. They told them about trolls, so perhaps the au pairs also piqued their interest in turf houses, many of which could still be seen in Iceland. The house set up for Frodo at Crickhollow in Buckland sounds almost exactly like one of these – 'as much like a hobbit-hole as possible: it was long and low, with no upper storey; and it had a roof of turf'.[43]

BEGINNINGS AND BORDERLANDS

Looking from the Shire into the dim distance – present or past – it is clearer still that we are standing in a kind of England. Both the Shire and England are reputedly founded by brothers whose names mean 'horse' and 'horse' – Marcho and Blanco for the hobbits and Hengest and Horsa for the Germanic peoples. Both settlements involved three peoples – the hobbit Fallohides, Harfoots and Stoors and the Germanic Angles, Saxons and Jutes. It all happened fourteen centuries ago from the perspective of the War of the Ring or Victoria's Diamond Jubilee.

There is one big difference. The Anglo-Saxons had to deal with the Celts who already lived in Britain. The hobbits found the Shire uninhabited (though the former royal cornlands and vineyards of Arnor make it a 'fortunate land' (see pp.68–9, The Shore and the Sea). Nonetheless, a far older people still haunts the Shire. It retains traces of their enchantment, though few hobbit residents of Woodhall are likely to know that elves use a nearby glade as a feasting place. Similarly, Oxfordshire has an Elvendon, though few know the original meaning of the name, 'hill of the elves'.[44]*

Westward, both England and the Shire look towards lands still occupied by the peoples who preceded them. The western English counties bordering Wales were blessed, Tolkien felt, with a particular enchantment rooted in long contact between two cultures he loved. Once this had been the kingdom of Mercia, inspiration for Tolkien's reimagining of Anglo-Saxon culture, Rohan (see p.32, Four Winds). The *March-counties* may be reflected in the Shire's Westfarthing (as he said), but they are yet more clearly reflected in the region beyond. This is the *Westmarch*, home of Sam Gamgee's descendants and the Red Book; the part of the Shire closest to elven Lindon (see p.59, The Land of Lúthien).

THE HILL

When Tolkien depicted the Hill at Hobbiton, he produced what is now an iconic image, indeed an archetypal one. It has been likened to views of Bredon Hill five miles from Evesham.[1] Andrew Ferguson has pointed out similarities with *German Planes Visiting Cassel, 1917* by Sir William Orpen.[2]

I see a closer kinship with a picture of a new and controversial landmark near Oxford – an image that was highly visible in the months before Tolkien first drew the Hobbiton view in January 1937.[3*] A painting of Faringdon Folly (below) by owner Lord Berners was used prominently in 1936 advertising on the sides of Shell's oil and petrol delivery lorries. Despite some obvious differences (one is wide, the other tall), the angles, proportions, shapes and arrangement of Tolkien's and Berners' pictures are strikingly similar, from the foreground building to the tree-crowned hill.

Other pictures for *The Hobbit*, such as *Beorn's Hall* (see p.137, Ancient Imprints), were closely modelled on published precedents.[4] Tolkien certainly took note of Shell's 1930s advertising strategy, aimed at persuading motorists to visit the countryside and heritage sites (see p.180, Craft and Industry). And there are other reasons to think that he took an interest in Faringdon Folly (see pp.156–7, Watch and Ward).

FOUR
WINDS

'What news from the North, O mighty wind…?' sings Aragorn in *The Lord of the Rings*. In this song at the falls of Rauros, the North wind is by far the strongest. 'Clear and cold … its loud horn calls.'[1] The same is true for Tolkien's imagination: the North – which meant for him especially the Germanic past – was a primary inspiration, even shaping his fundamental interests, aims and methods. Before delving further into the influence of specific places, it helps to understand such cultural influences. And it will be seen that each of the four winds helped breathe something into the cosmology and cultures of Middle-earth.

It has gradually become clear how much he owed to the West, too – to Celtic traditions of Faërie. The influence of the classical South, Greece and Rome, is still almost unexplored, even though it dominated his own cultural era. Then there is the East, which reached him primarily through Anglo-Saxon wonder-tales. All this is so superbly fused in his invented world that it feels both unique and original.

I. NORTH
News from the North

As a child, Ronald Tolkien was spellbound by the tale of Sigurd in Andrew Lang's 1890 collection, *The Red Fairy Book*. He never forgot

Sigurd battles the dragon Fáfnir in carvings on the doorposts of a twelfth-century church in Hylestad, Norway.

its opening line: 'Once upon a time there was a King in the North who had won many wars, but now he was old.'[2]* Tolkien enjoyed stories from other lands, but 'best of all the nameless North'.[3] During his formative years, the immense influence of this North would help lay the foundations for Middle-earth.

It was the Germanic North, inhabited a millennium and more ago by Anglo-Saxons, Vikings, Icelanders and others. During the three centuries before Tolkien, this Old North had been a frontier-land, explored by a growing posse of enthusiasts. Thomas Gray, who has been described as 'northern antiquity's most persuasive eighteenth-century advocate', had first turned Old Icelandic poetry into English of matching power.[4] Even then, many medieval writings remained obscure and troublesome thanks to the way their languages had shifted in shape over time.

Then came the rise of comparative philology (now called historical linguistics) – a quantum leap in the understanding of how languages change. In the nineteenth century, the 'comparative method' unlocked the medieval word-hoard. Scholars deciphered the languages and brought ever-clearer light to bear upon the myths of Asgard; Old Norse sagas such as the one about Sigurd the Volsung; and Old English poetry including the epic *Beowulf.*

At a time of nation-building, these myths and legends were prized as an ancestral and national heritage. The Victorian polymath William Morris – whose works left a deep impression on Tolkien – said that for English people, the *Völsunga Saga* should be 'what the Tale of Troy was to the Greeks'.

In his teens, Tolkien's genius for language led him to explore Old English, Old Icelandic (or Old Norse) and their easterly cousin, Gothic. He was thrilled by the way philology could reconstruct words – even whole languages – that had never been written down. His hobby was inventing languages, and now he imaginatively 'reconstructed' a lost Germanic language.

In 1911, he went to Oxford University to study Latin and Greek (the norm for a talented linguist), but after two years he ditched these classical studies for English, a course steeped in Germanic philology.

This was a road into a past littered with the mythological or 'faëry' remnants of pre-Christian belief, and Tolkien now found himself deeply interested in 'fairy-stories'. In the fourteenth-century Middle English poem *Sir Gawain and the Green Knight*, England's wild places are the haunt of enchanters, trolls and mysterious *woodwos* (see p.116, Tree-woven Lands). In *Beowulf* and the *Völsunga Saga*, heroes with superhuman abilities face dragons and fatal fay-women. Philologists realized that such interrelated traditions must descend from older Germanic stories that were now lost.

Northern language and literature would become the core of Tolkien's professional life. He would achieve a first-class degree in English in 1915, return from war service in 1918 to work at the *Oxford English Dictionary*, and spend five years to 1925 teaching at Leeds University. Back in Oxford, he would be Rawlinson and Bosworth Professor of Anglo-Saxon until 1945 and finally, until 1959, Merton College Professor of English Language and Literature.

But before any of this, around the end of 1914 the surging wind from the North helped to thrust open the doors into Middle-earth.

The Germanic spark

If a lost language could be recreated, so could a lost tale. In his academic conjectures about lost beliefs, Tolkien would always stick scrupulously close to the philological evidence.

In private, his imagination could barely be restrained. It took one spark to set him off.

He was fascinated by the Old English name for the Evening Star, *Éarendel*. Some philologists, pointing out that Old English *ear* can mean 'sea, wave', argued that Éarendel originated as a forgotten Germanic mariner hero. These ideas of sea and sky seem contradictory, but not if you have Tolkien's imagination. In September 1914, he wrote a poem in which the mariner Éarendel sails off the edge of the world into the night sky – an origin myth for the Evening Star, Venus (see pp.64–5, The Shore and the Sea). At just twenty-two, and without knowing what was to come, he had invented the first hero of Middle-earth.

WHERE IT ALL BEGAN

Tolkien called his mythology an attempt to 'rekindle an old light in the world'. Aptly, it began at Phoenix Farm, named after the mythological bird reborn from the ashes.[1] This was the home of his aunt, Jane Neave, in Gedling, Nottinghamshire, where he wrote *The Voyage of Éarendel the Evening Star* on 24 September 1914.

The area around Gedling seems to be remembered in the name of the hero of a story written three decades later. *The Notion Club Papers*, about a literary circle much like his own Inklings, comes close to describing the literary and linguistic inspiration for Tolkien's poem. One club member, Lowdham, recalls first seeing the name *Éarendel* in lines from the Old English poem *Crist*. Seeing the words gave him 'a curious thrill, as if something had stirred in me half wakened from sleep', he says.[2]* Evidently, he describes Tolkien's own memory. And his name is significant. Lowdham is also the name of a village just a pleasant walk away from Gedling.

Phoenix Farm (known in Gedling as Lamb's Farm), drawn by Tolkien probably in 1913. Here, in 1914, he wrote the poem that launched his mythology.

Pondering Éarendel's earthly voyage before he sails into the sky, Tolkien decided the mariner would go from Iceland to Greenland and into the West – like Thorfinn Karlsefni, the hero of an Icelandic saga about the discovery of Vinland that Tolkien was studying at the time (see pp.67–9, The Shore and the Sea). When Bilbo sings about the star-mariner at Rivendell in The Lord of the Rings – a poem Tolkien wrote in the 1940s – his voyage has some of the same waypoints. He reaches Eldamar or Elvenhome, and even divine Valinor. But the 1914 outline is undisguisedly set in our own world, with no elven background and no Elvish names. These came in with Tolkien's next big step.

Fuel from Finland

The inspiration for Tolkien's first Elvish language also came from the North – but not the Germanic one. For the past three years Tolkien had been exploring the legends and folk tales of the Kalevala or 'Land of Heroes', the Finnish verse epic. Pieced together from folk songs still sung among the forests and lakes of Karelia in Finland, the Kalevala pulsed with stories passed down since pre-Christian times.

Reading it was like crossing a gulf into a new world, Tolkien enthused. Stories and names alike enchanted him. In 1914 he had begun retelling a Kalevala tale about the troubled, doomed youth Kullervo – Tolkien's earliest known story. Much more idiosyncratically, he had also been trying to distil the essence of the Finnish language – its characteristic sounds – into an invented tongue of his own.

But what especially struck him was how the Finnish names suited the Finnish tales, and how the tales breathed life into the names. He saw a symbiosis of language and legend. It prompted him to try a curious experiment. In his Story of Kullervo, he used names from his new Finnish-sounding tongue, such as Telëa for Karelia, Kemenúmë for Russia and Ilu for God.

For the first time, he was giving one of his invented languages a home inside a story. Yet adding essence-of-Finnish to a Finnish story was like switching salt for salt, and he soon abandoned the experiment.

Instead, he decided to use his new language to season 'lost tales' such as the Éarendel plot that was now simmering. This great turning point on his creative journey seems to have come after talking with friends that December.

Crucially, Tolkien had to decide who would speak this newly invented language and tell these 'lost tales'. It would not be the Finns, nor the early Germanic peoples. The speakers would need to be far more ancient than any of us, witnesses to the events that are now only remembered in Europe's garbled and fragmentary legends. He decided that they would be a half-forgotten people whose very existence had become a matter of fairy-story – the fairies themselves.

Tolkien's May 1915 painting The Shores of Faery shows his earliest conception of Valinor, with the trees of Sun and Moon framing the elven city of Kôr.

ELVES, FINNS AND ENGLAND

A recent insight suggests that Tolkien took some of his inspiration for the Elves from medieval Norse beliefs about the Finns – the people whose language inspired Quenya.

The Germanic Scandinavians considered their neighbours the Finns – or Kvæns, as they called them – to be elves and enchanters. The Old English equivalent Cwénas, singular Cwén, appears in King Alfred's account of a conversation with a Norse mariner, which Tolkien was studying in 1914. All this leads Andrew Higgins to argue that the language-name Quenya and Quendi 'Elves' were modelled on Cwén, Kvæn – 'Finn', or in other words 'elf'.[1]

Cwén also happens to be Old English for 'woman', and Tolkien uses it as the name of the wife of Eriol, the mariner who hears the elven Lost Tales. Higgins suggests it is a pun to imply she is Finnish and that their sons Hengest and Horsa, England's legendary founders, have a streak of Finnish in them too (see p.28, Four Winds).[2] It does sound Tolkienian. But antiquarian Thomas William Shore had already argued in 1906 that English place-names such as Queninstone, Quinton, Finningham and Finborough could mean that 'Cwéns or Quéns' or Finns had been intermingled with the Germanic settlers of England.[3]

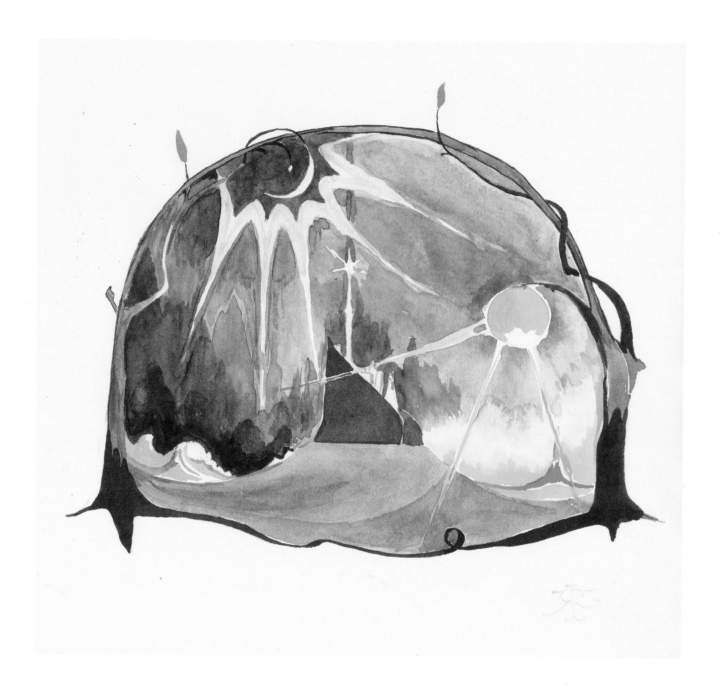

Fairies, or elves, are widespread in Germanic and Celtic traditions, but in Tolkien's England they had been reduced by Shakespeare and others to pretty little winged things. Theirs was a lost tale ripe for rediscovery.

Soon, Tolkien was using his Elvish language, Quenya, to furnish the names for what he came to call his *legendarium*. A poem from summer 1915, *The Shores of Faery*, names Valinor, its holy mountain Taniquetil, and *Eärendel*. Tolkien had turned the mariner's Old English name into a Quenya one, containing an invented word *eären* 'eagle'.

Vast invention lay ahead – and vast changes (see p.44, The Land of Lúthien). To take one tiny detail, Tolkien later decided *eären* meant 'sea' and the star-mariner's name was *Eärendil* (the familiar *Lord of the Rings* spelling that this book will generally use), meaning 'sea-lover, mariner'.

A HOSTILE WORLD

More than fancy or blind preference made Tolkien
want to emulate the early Anglo-Saxon cosmology. 'It
transcends astronomy,' he said.[1] To him, the modern
scientific universe had none of its poetic richness.

To the pagan Anglo-Saxons there was no heaven above,
just 'the sky's inaccessible roof'. They pictured their
world hemmed about by danger and darkness, as if in 'a
little circle of light about their halls'. Lacking Christian
assurance of victory over evil, they expected in the end to
lose against 'the offspring of the dark', as the Norse gods
do at Ragnarok.[2] Tolkien found this poignant, and he
greatly admired the indomitable spirit displayed by heroes
such as Beowulf, which he called 'Northern courage'.[3]

A world of danger surrounds the few safe spots in
Middle-earth, and many of the perils are straight out
of Germanic tradition – dragons, trolls, barrow-wights
(from Icelandic saga) and orcs (from *orcnéas*, a word in
Beowulf that Tolkien translated 'haunting shapes of hell').[4]

As a Christian, Tolkien gave his own mythology a
Creator, Ilúvatar, with a providential plan for final victory
over evil. Yet for several reasons this does not ease matters
for the peoples of Middle-earth. Ilúvatar is outside the
world. His servants, the Valar, largely withdraw into the
West, leaving their great enemies, Morgoth and Sauron,
to wreak havoc. The Elves, though immortal by human
standards, seem fated to be snuffed out body and soul
when the world ends. Mortals seem largely unaware
of Ilúvatar, of Providence, and of the fate of their own
souls after death. So the Anglo-Saxon ideal of 'Northern
courage' fits very well in Middle-earth. Elven or mortal,
Tolkien's heroes face almost certain defeat – unbowed.

Yggdrasil, the World Tree, cradles
Midgard (Middle-earth) in a Victorian
visualization of Norse cosmology.

Strong threads nevertheless run through the ever-changing
tapestry. *The Book of Lost Tales*, begun during the Great War, was
abandoned by the early 1920s. But much of its material was
reshaped as the *Silmarillion* – on which Tolkien was still working
when he died in 1973. Even elements of pre-legendarium names
Telëa, *Kemenúmë* and *Ilu* can be seen in *The Silmarillion*'s *Teleri*
(an elf kindred), *Kementári* (surname of the divine earth-mother
Yavanna), and *Ilúvatar* (the Creator, God). Eärendil, Taniquetil
and Valinor are all there too.

A Northern worldview

Long before *The Lord of the Rings*, Tolkien wanted to build
a mythology of England. That meant two things. It was
counterfactual, built out of discarded beliefs in fairies, an
earth-centred cosmos, and so forth. And it was English rather
than British – ostensibly it had nothing to do with the Celts
who lived in Britain before the Anglo-Saxons arrived.

He set the mythology in an imaginary deeper past, when
Britain is called the Lonely Isle and is ruled by Elves (see

pp.46–52, The Land of Lúthien). A mortal traveller called Eriol hears the elven Lost Tales, writes them down in Old English and passes them on to his Anglo-Saxon descendants. So although the Elves eventually sail away or go into hiding, their 'true tradition' is preserved by the English.[5]

Technically, Tolkien should have used Anglo-Saxon beliefs and nothing else. But that would have required listening in on storytellers who had died around a millennium and a half earlier. The real English mythology, which they had told in their feasting halls, had been consigned to oblivion by the only people who could have written it down – Christian monks. Mere shreds remain.

Tolkien salvaged what he could. As he would later tell his students, the early Anglo-Saxons imagined the earth was a flat disc on which the habitable lands were surrounded by 'the shoreless sea' and then by a great wall.[6] When the sun sank, they thought it travelled in 'the dark underworld' before rising again in the east.[7] This is precisely the cosmology of *The Book of Lost Tales* and *The Silmarillion*. Tolkien set the main action of his legendarium in what the Anglo-Saxons called *middangeard*, 'Middle-earth', between western and eastern seas, between southern heat and northern ice.

Where Anglo-Saxon sources were silent, Tolkien could turn to the better-preserved mythology of their Scandinavian cousins. In making the utter North the realm of Morgoth, the satanic Enemy, he adapted the Norse idea that it was the home of Hel, queen of the dead. The placement of Elvenhome beside divine Valinor borrows from the Norse idea of Asgard (see p.66, The Shore and the Sea). Bifröst, the rainbow bridge joining Asgard with mortal Midgard, was borrowed wholesale in the *Lost Tales*, then scrapped, but later reintroduced in a far subtler form as the Straight Way (see pp.80–1, The Shore and the Sea). But Tolkien never made use of Norse ideas that Asgard lies in a heaven above, or at the centre of Midgard, or at one of the roots of a vast World Tree. Instead, he situated his divine land west over the sea.

Tolkien was certainly moved by a hint in *Beowulf* that the Anglo-Saxons and Scandinavians believed in a paradise in the West. But there is reason to think that when he created Valinor, he had also heard a trumpet-blast of controversy about medieval ideas of the West. Vinland, a region named in sagas about Icelandic exploration westwards, is generally considered to represent a real place in America. But world-famous explorer Fridtjof Nansen had made news by arguing that it was a literary fable, a fairyland (see pp.67–8, The Shore and the Sea).

What were the Elves like? A few notable Anglo-Saxon words and names implied they were creatures of wonder and wisdom – *ælfscýne* 'elf-fair', *Ælfred* 'elf-counsel', *Ælfwine* 'elf-friend'. Old English translations from Latin furnish a bare list of elf types – wood-elves (dryads), sea-elves (naiads) and more. Norse mythology gives a clearer picture of the Liós-álfar, 'Light Elves' who are more beautiful than sunlight and who serve the gods of fertility and magic.

For the real *craic* about Faërie and faëry folk, however, Tolkien would need to consult the Celts.

Entire Middle-earth cultures carry the stamp of 'Northernness'. It marks the landscape, from the Moot-ring of First-Age Brethil to Beorn's equally Norse hall (see pp.137, 142, Ancient Imprints).[1] Most pervasively, it appears in names. In *The Hobbit*, Tolkien conveniently took the dwarf names *Thorin*, *Bifur*, *Glóin*, etc., from the Norse mythological *Poetic Edda*. Making this part of a larger conceit, *The Lord of the Rings* poses as a translation into English from the Common Speech or Westron used by hobbits, with other Germanic languages representing tongues related to that. So it gives Norse names to the Men of Dale; Gothic names to the Northmen of old Rhovanion; and Old English names to the people of the Vale of Anduin.

Most prominently, the Riders of Rohan use Old English. Tolkien insisted this did not mean 'that the Rohirrim closely resembled the ancient English otherwise', but it will not wash.[2] The hall of Meduseld and the whole scene leading up to it come from *Beowulf* (see p.152, Watch and Ward). *The Mark*, the Riders' name for Rohan, is what Anglo-Saxons in Tolkien's West Midlands and Oxfordshire would have called their own kingdom, which we know by its Latin name, *Mercia*. That suggests he made a personal investment in their Englishness. As Tom Shippey says, Théoden's people resemble Anglo-Saxons 'down to minute details'.[3]

The one big difference is that the Riders are riders and the Anglo-Saxons reputedly were not (notoriously losing to the Norman cavalry of William the Conqueror in 1066). As elsewhere, Tolkien's model was not history but ancient belief, and he founded Rohan on signs that the Anglo-Saxons remembered a time when they were horsemen. The edge of Mercia was perhaps marked by the giant White Horse carved in chalk at Uffington, Berkshire (see pp.*137, 144*, 145, Ancient Imprints). The names *Hengest* and *Horsa* for the legendary founders of England both mean 'horse'. The emblem of continental Saxony, home of the Old Saxons, was a horse. Shippey suggests the Rohirrim are what the Anglo-Saxons would have been if they had lived on the steppes rather than an island.

The Riders of Rohan in battle at Minas Tirith, as seen by Alan Lee. Horses aside, they are Anglo-Saxon to the core.

II. WEST
'Celtic things'

Tolkien's debt to the Celtic West has long been severely underrated – mostly thanks to his own comments. He once said that 'Celtic things' were 'like a broken stained glass window reassembled without design … in fact "mad"'.[8] A note for *The Book of Lost Tales* says the Irish and Welsh only know 'garbled things' about the Elves.[9]*

The 'mad' comment is the outburst of a wounded man, made in 1937 just after his *Silmarillion* and other mythological writings had been rejected as a follow-up to *The Hobbit*. The publisher's reader had complained that Tolkien's epic histories and poems had 'that mad, bright-eyed beauty that perplexes all Anglo-Saxons in face of Celtic art'.[10] In calmer moods, Tolkien spoke otherwise of Celtic things. And the 'garbled' comment is not genuine opinion at all – it is fiction. For Tolkien as a philologist, garbled things were his field; and as an imaginative writer, they were his inspiration. For his imaginary Anglo-Saxon 'true tradition of the fairies', he needed to quarry Celtic material – and no doubt he did it gladly.[11]

As a child he had yearned for the Britain of Arthur and Merlin. From eight or nine, he was enchanted by Welsh, glimpsed in names on coal trucks behind 86 Westfield Road, Kings Heath, Birmingham, where the Tolkiens lived for a year or so. On an early train journey into Wales, he spotted the name *Ebbw* and 'just couldn't get over it. Not long afterwards, I started inventing my own languages.'[12] As an Oxford undergraduate he delved into the Welsh legends in *The Mabinogion*, and into Welsh philology. At Leeds University in the early 1920s, he taught Medieval Welsh besides English. Later he lent his Celtic philological expertise to Oxford colleagues and a national archaeological dig at Lydney Park in Gloucestershire (see pp.188–9, Appendix). His landmark 1955 talk on *English and Welsh* expressed the importance of Welsh to England, especially to his beloved West Midlands. Holidays took him to the West Country, Wales, Scotland and Brittany. For work and pleasure, he visited Ireland often from 1949

ELVISH AND WELSH

Tolkien's Welsh-inspired language was first crafted as 'Gnomish', for the Noldor of *The Fall of Gondolin* in 1917. But late in writing *The Lord of the Rings*, Tolkien decided to take it off them and give it to the Sindar or Grey Elves. Sindarin might look and sound much the same as Noldorin as Tolkien had developed it by that time, but its fictional history is very different (mainly because unlike the Noldor, the Sindar never went to Valinor).

Even so, Tolkien stuck to one point. Noldorin or Sindarin is a living language in Middle-earth, whereas Quenya is a book-language, only actually spoken across the sea in the Undying Lands. This deliberately mirrored the way Latin and British (the ancestor of Welsh) were used in Celtic Britain after the occupying Romans had withdrawn across the Channel to the continental mainland. Sometimes Tolkien actually refers to Quenya as *Elf-latin*; and over the years he made Noldorin/Sindarin ever more similar to Welsh in sound and grammar.

Welsh was an underpinning inspiration for *The Lord of the Rings*, Tolkien said – and he thought his Welsh-inspired language Sindarin had 'given perhaps more pleasure to more readers than anything else in it'.[1]* That was surely wishful thinking. But I can vouch that *Gondor*, *Anduin*, *Lothlórien* and other names on his maps drew me into his epic at nine as surely as *Senghenydd* or *Tredegar* on coal trucks drew Tolkien into Welsh.

(though too late to influence *The Lord of the Rings*).[13]*

In the early 1930s, Tolkien directly adapted a Breton legend as *The Lay of Aotrou and Itroun* and worked long on an epic *Fall of Arthur*. In two unfinished novels, *The Lost Road* (1937) and *The Notion Club Papers* (1946), he planned to link Celtic legends explicitly with his legendarium. But he had quietly been weaving Celtic threads into it from the outset.[14]

Wonders of the West

To put it bluntly, Celtic tales about voyages of wonder are more wonderful than any Scandinavian equivalent. Because such tales continued to develop in the Christian era, the West that they envision carries hints of something eternal that goes well beyond pagan belief. That especially suited Tolkien's worldview, in which the Valar are angelic beings sent down to Earth by one true God. The most famous Celtic wonder-voyage or *imram* (Irish, 'voyaging') is the *Navigatio* of St Brendan. Tolkien retold it in a poem titled *The Death of St Brendan*, later published as *Imram*. He wrapped it into *The Notion Club Papers* so that it would seem to recount, in Celtic terms, a voyage towards his own Undying Lands (see pp.66, 80–1, The Shore and the Sea).

Legends of a western island paradise can be found across Europe, but especially in the Celtic world – and the poets of medieval Ireland win the fantasy island contest hands down. Facing the mystery of the seemingly shoreless Atlantic, they dreamed up an archipelago's worth of isles of bliss, from Tír na nÓg, 'Land of the Ever Young', to Hy Breasail, 'Fortunate Isle'. Tolkien imagined an elven Lonely Isle, Tol Eressëa, as the first enchanted place to be reached sailing west. From Welsh and Arthurian legend, he borrowed *Avallon* as an Elvish byname for the Lonely Isle. His Tol Eressëa floats around, like several islands in Irish legend (see p.66, The Shore and the Sea).

Meanwhile, coastal Celtic traditions of sunken lands contribute to his stories of the drowning of Beleriand, land of the elf-wars in the First Age, and of Númenor, a mighty naval power during the Second Age (see pp.77–8, The Shore and the Sea). Of course, even while his legendarium borrows from such traditions, it poses as their 'true' origin.

Celtic Faërie

Tolkien's Elves most resemble the Tuatha Dé Danann of Irish mythology, also known as the *Áes Sídhe* or People of the Mounds. They are both godlike and faëry; they arrive in mortal lands from an enchanted land over the sea; and they vanish back over the sea or dwell underground.

The Riders of the Sidhe, a 1911 painting by John Duncan, shows Celtic fairies much as Tolkien imagined his own Elves.

All this goes for the Noldor or Gnomes, most illustrious of elf kindreds, whose marvellous achievements include the holy jewel-like Silmarils and paradisial Lothlórien. The subterranean elf-citadels of Nargothrond, Menegroth and Mirkwood all share features with the fairy mounds of the Sídhe (see pp.134–5, Ancient Imprints). If Tolkien needed inspiration in contemporary art, he could have looked to the tall, beautiful and noble figures of John Duncan's 1911 *The Riders of the Sidhe*.

'The Celts,' says Marjorie Burns, 'were less inclined to speak of inaccessible distance when it came to housing their otherworldly beings.' She hypothesizes that this was because of the clement climate and landscape of the British Isles.[15] Likewise, most of Tolkien's elven demesnes may be reached via natural thresholds – running water, shadowed descents, archways of trees – so that entry is swift and almost imperceptible.

Once inside, the wayfarer may be liberally entertained and fed. Like a house described in the Irish story of the birth of Cú Chullain, Tol Eressëa's Cottage of Lost Play (where Eriol hears the Lost Tales) looks small yet miraculously fits many guests. But mortals may also find themselves imprisoned, as the dwarves are in Mirkwood – or like Robert Kirk, seventeenth-century Scottish author of *The Secret Commonwealth of Elves, Fauns and Fairies*, reputedly carried off into the Fairy Knowe at Aberfoyle.

Time moves strangely in Faërie. Oisín returns from what seemed three years in Tír na nÓg to find three hundred have passed in Ireland. After Lothlórien, Sam finds the moon out of phase, 'as if we had never stayed no time in the Elvish country'.[16]

Tolkien's own gateway to Celtic Faërie was through the stories of King Arthur. He made a valiant attempt to distance himself from the Arthurian world, declaring it too British (rather than English), too explicitly Christian and 'too lavish, and fantastical, incoherent and repetitive'.[17] Yet he underpinned *The Lord of the Rings* with the idea of the king who will return, centred it on a fellowship on a perilous quest, and ended it by sending the wounded hero to Faërie for healing. For a long time, he called Beleriand *Broseliand*, recalling Broceliande, the enchanted forest in Arthurian tales (see p.78, The Shore and the Sea).

Even the similarity between *Mordor* and *Mordred*, the name of King Arthur's nemesis, may be more than chance. *Mordor* and the unarguably Arthurian *Avallon* were both coined in a single short piece of writing in 1937, as David Doughan has pointed out. At that time, Tolkien still hoped to finish *The Fall of Arthur*, in which Mordred is a power-hungry tyrant and destroyer not unlike Sauron (see p.184, Craft and Industry).

Longfellow's hero Hiawatha (depicted here by N. C. Wyeth in 1911) was a key early influence on Tolkien.

A suppressed Arthurian element 'keeps on breaking through' into the legendarium, says Doughan.[18]*

The other West

Besides Celtic, Tolkien was inspired by another West – America. In childhood, only the tales of Arthur's Britain and Sigurd's North seemed more exciting than stories about 'Red Indians' (as he called the indigenous Americans, in the parlance of the era). 'There were bows and arrows … and strange languages, and glimpses of an archaic mode of life, and, above all, forests in such stories,' he recalled.[19]

Even on a cursory reading, Henry Wadsworth Longfellow's *Song of Hiawatha* helped Tolkien towards the brink of Middle-earth in autumn 1914. He surely noted Hiawatha's departure by canoe into 'the portals of the Sunset', so much like the westward flight of his own Éarendel. Researching the word *wampum* for the *Oxford English Dictionary* a few years later, Tolkien went to Oxford's Bodleian Library 'to read *Hiawatha*, and to pass on to early descriptions of Algonkin languages, and early accounts of racial contacts, in war, language or trade, on the east seaboard of N. America'.[20] Perhaps at some point he also explored Longfellow's chief source, Henry Rowe Schoolcraft's *Algic Researches*, or (as Roger Echo-Hawk argues) other folklore collections such as the 1904 *Traditions of the Skidi Pawnee*. The natural worlds of Longfellow and Tolkien are alike in their animism – their rivers imbued with spirit, and their trees with speech. Touches of *Hiawatha* can also be observed in the Dead Marshes and in Hithlum (see pp.102–3, 109, Rivers, Lakes and Waterlands), in the Misty Mountains and even upon Taniquetil (see p.90, Roots of the Mountains).[21]

When Tolkien needed to depict the most hidden or remote Middle-earth cultures, indigenous North America was one touchstone – heard in the distant drumbeats of Drúadan Forest (see p.116 panel, Tree-woven Lands) and seen among the Inuit-like Lossoth of the frozen north. Shippey sees shades of James Fenimore Cooper's 'Leatherstocking' *Last of the Mohicans* series in the Great River journey (see p.111, Rivers, Lakes and Waterlands) as well as in Rohan – its prairies and its Riders, like 'mail-shirted Sioux or Cheyenne'.[22] The passion for 'bows and arrows' surfaces wherever a woodcrafty archer picks off an enemy in Middle-earth's vast forests (see p.117, Tree-woven Lands) or beside its great rivers. Elves such as Beleg and Legolas, with their acute senses, their silent tread and their reverence for nature, seem more Iroquois than Tuatha Dé Danann.

III. SOUTH
A classical world

Tolkien refuted the idea that the North was 'a sacred direction' for him – a claim made by W. H. Auden.[23] A thorough grounding in classics shaped his imagination even before he looked northward to fresher fields.

He loved Latin, and a truly precocious bid to distil 'the Greekness of Greek' – in a language invented around the age of ten – was the first forerunner of how he used Finnish and Welsh to create his Elvish tongues. By twelve he had read every classical book deemed fit for a boy of his age. 'I was brought up on the classics,' he wrote, 'and first discovered the sensation of literary pleasure in Homer.'[24]

Reading Caesar's *Gallic Wars* for school, he first encountered the Hercynian Forest, Europe's real 'Mirkwood' (see pp.123, 126 panel, Tree-woven Lands). Homer's Odysseus and Virgil's Aeneas must have been his first guides to the underworld of the dead. Elysium and the westward Garden of the Hesperides were probably the first lands of bliss he visited.

Even after Tolkien dropped classics for English at Oxford, he looked for classical resonances in Northern literature. His notes on *Beowulf* highlight 'Homeric reminiscences' in descriptions of the sea.[25] So when he read a philological theory that the original Germanic Éarendel must have been an Odysseus for the North, he was primed to turn it into an epic narrative of his own.

Though he aimed for his English mythology to
be 'redolent of our "air" … not Italy or the Aegean,
still less the East', he was able to borrow classical
ideas without borrowing the atmosphere. He
was not the first to do this – the Middle English
Sir Orfeo, which he knew well, transforms the
Greek Orpheus myth into a Celtic-tinged tale of
Faërie. Classical myth, which had been massively
developed by literary cultures at their zenith,
was also a yardstick for Tolkien's never-ceasing
ambition to depict a large, detailed geography
and vast timescales.

Gods and heroes

On Taniquetil, the chief Valar, Varda and Manwë,
occupy a version of Mount Olympus. But what with
the Valar of water, earth, green nature and so forth,
and with a multitude of lesser spirits too, Tolkien's
world is filled with natural divinities as diverse as
those in classical myth. His major innovation is that

all of these are beings made by one Creator beyond
and before the world. Though the Valar are often
referred to as gods, in the divine hierarchy they are
more like Judaeo-Christian angels.

The Troy of Homer's *Iliad* and Virgil's *Aeneid*
makes a broad imprint in the legendarium. The
long, grim Greek war against Troy has stiff literary
competition indeed in the Elves' tragic and reckless
campaign to recover the Silmarils. Echoes of the
siege of Troy have been noted in the fall of the
elven city of Gondolin. Like Troy in the medieval
imagination, it is the wellspring of later dynasties
and realms (see pp.150–1, Watch and Ward).

Tolkien called Númenor itself 'my own use
for my own purposes of the *Atlantis* legend'. His
account of its downfall builds from Plato's account
of the powerful western sea-empire destroyed by
hubris (see pp.78, 80, The Shore and the Sea).[26]

At Minas Tirith, Tolkien created what he called
a 'Homeric catalogue' of forces arriving from

Gondor's Outlands, inspired by the *Iliad*'s list of Greek forces assembling against Troy.[27] Indeed, it is for this catalogue that he first named or invented the regions of Lamedon, Pinnath Gelin, Ringló Vale and coastal Anfalas.

Gondor's relations with the Northmen and their Rohirrim descendants echo the long entanglements between Rome and the Goths – who sacked the city in AD 410. However, the outcome differs – the restoration of peace and power with the help of the barbarian-like Riders. The history of Minas Tirith has been well described as 'the story of the fall of Rome with a happy ending'.[28]

Yet even Rohan, ostensibly the most Germanic of creations, seems to have germinated from a classical seed. Its Riders first appear in Tolkien's notes as *Hippanaletians* and *Anaxippians*, Greek words for 'horse-lords', implying that he was thinking of classical accounts of the fearsome Scythians who could shoot from horseback. He persisted in calling them 'heroic "Homeric" horsemen', one of several peoples 'in a simple "Homeric" state of patriarchal and tribal life'.[29]

The hot South

Middle-earth affords occasional glimpses of another, more distant South – hotter climes with exotic islands, cities, warriors and war-beasts. In the very first plot outline, Éarendel is blown southward to encounter wonders – 'Tree-men, Sun-dwellers, spices, fire-mountains, red sea'.[30] Perhaps looking far ahead to Fangorn and Mount Doom, this may also look back to the volcanic islands that Tolkien saw in early childhood en route to England (see pp.62, 65, 66, The Shore and the Sea).

The impact of Africa itself on Tolkien's work goes beyond priming him to fall for green England (see pp.11–12, England to the Shire).[31] He had no recollection of the time he was bitten by a tarantula in the garden of Bank House, Bloemfontein, but he did remember the long, dry grass that he ran through in terror before his nurse snatched him up and sucked out the poison. In his first Elvish lexicon, Africa is *Salkinor* 'Grass Land' and *Andisalkë* 'Long Grass'.

Tales of Africa never failed to move him deeply with 'a curious sense of reminiscence', he wrote in 1944 to his son Christopher, who was training with the Royal Air Force in South Africa.[32] He read books on African exploration and loved some of Henry Rider Haggard's ripping yarns about lost civilizations in the unmapped interior. The city of Kôr and its queen Ayesha in Haggard's 1886 romance *She* make a clear impression on

A war elephant or 'Oliphaunt' in a Middle-earth manuscript, as imagined by Jay Johnstone.

A contemporary postcard captures the torrid climate of Bloemfontein in the Orange Free State, southern Africa, the birthplace Tolkien never forgot.

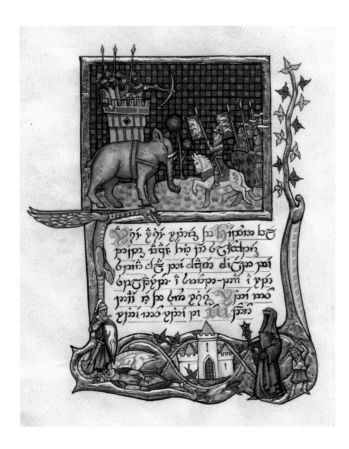

of the 'swarthy men', Sam Gamgee is filled with pity for an enemy he sees as much like himself:

> He wondered what the man's name was and where he came from; and if he was really evil of heart, or what lies or threats had led him on the long march from his home; and if he would not really rather have stayed there in peace…[35]

Sam's insight follows plainly from Tolkien's recent comments to his son about race.

Simultaneously, the story sticks to his overarching method – portraying remote peoples and places as medieval Europeans believed them to be, rather than as they actually were. The elephant, or 'Oliphaunt', is straight out of medieval bestiaries. For better or worse, the Men of the Harad are portrayed much as the remoter peoples of South and East were in early medieval writings.[36] Drafts of *The Lord of the Rings* call them *Silharrows*, a modernized form of *sigelhearwan*, the term used in the Old English *Exodus* and elsewhere for Ethiopians. In the 1930s, Tolkien had published a close analysis of the word and its obscure origins. Back at the outset of his world-building, *sigelhearwan* probably underlies the enigmatic reference to the 'Sun-dwellers' of the South in the earliest Éarendel outline.

Tom Shippey thinks a far deadlier, utterly implacable Tolkienian foe may have sprung from this ancient word. Tolkien's study of *sigelhearwan* reaches a remarkable conclusion. Formed of *sigel* 'sun' and *hearwa*, which is linked with words for 'coal, soot', it must date back to pagan times when the Germanic peoples knew nothing of Africa. If it did not originally mean Ethiopians, argues Tolkien, perhaps it meant the sons of Múspell (the demonic fire giant of Norse myth), 'with red-hot eyes that emitted sparks, with faces black as soot'.[37] This, says Tom Shippey 'gave Tolkien Durin's Bane, the Balrog'.[38]

IV. EAST

When Aragorn and Legolas have sung the songs of the North, West and South winds, Gimli refuses to provide the song of the East. Gandalf says 'To the East I go not.'[39] This fits within the story, in which Sauron holds sway over the East. Tolkien himself was not immune to Eastern influences, although his sources seem to stem from the Middle East or the European medieval tradition, not from Indian, Chinese or Japanese myth.

'As one interested in antiquity and notably in the history of languages and "writing",' Tolkien said, 'I knew and had read a good deal about Mesopotamia.'[40]* Indeed, his creation story of

Elvenhome and Lothlórien (see pp.118, Tree-woven Lands; 148, 154, Watch and Ward).

Tolkien said he could remember his mother Mabel talking about the mistreatment of South Africa's black majority and had taken 'a special interest' ever since. 'The treatment of colour nearly always horrifies anyone going out from Britain,' he told Christopher.[33] Yet hearing about Africa from his son sharpened Tolkien's lifelong desire to see it again, and he wished he were there too.

Perhaps, through his writing, he was. New chapters sent out to Christopher described the exotic landscape of Ithilien – not a dry veldt, to be sure, but filled with 'fir and cedar and cypress', the same trees his father Arthur had planted in the old garden in Bloemfontein.[34]* It is here, too, that a gargantuan elephant bursts suddenly into view with a war band from the Harad, the hot South.

Tolkien is often criticized for moral simplicity and alleged racism. Yet in the midst of the scene where the men of Harad are ambushed by those of Gondor, the divisions of enmity and race vanish in a puff of empathy. Witnessing the death of one

the Music of the Ainur appears to be founded upon an Assyrian myth – construed in the 1870s from a cuneiform tablet found at Nineveh – in which God (Akkadian *Ilu*) thrice begins a hymn for his angels to sing, but a satanic rebel brings discord to the music.[41]

Medieval legends of Alexander the Great and his eastward campaigns furnished a key part of Tolkien's own world-building. When he was asked whether his Two Trees reflected the Norse World Tree Yggdrasil, he replied, 'No, no, they're not like it: they're much more like the Trees of the Sun and Moon discovered in the Far East, in the great Alexander stories.'[42] The Nowell Codex, containing the original manuscript of *Beowulf*, also contains a descriptive *Wonders of the East* and a letter supposedly written by Alexander to his tutor Aristotle.

Here, Alexander says he found the two sacred speaking trees in a Paradise beyond India; they drip a marvellous balsam and they prophesy that he will die in Babylon. The sun tree became widespread in fairy-tale and myth, and W. B Yeats wrote memorably of a place of eternal youth with

> *The silver apples of the moon,*
> *The golden apples of the sun.*[43]

East or west, the land of bliss had much in common – if you could penetrate its protecting shadows. So it was natural for Tolkien to transplant the trees of sun and moon into the Undying West, and with them the lakes of sun and moon from the Old English *Wonders of the East*. His Two Trees exude liquid light rather than balsam. They do not make any prophecies of death, but their own deaths herald

The mystical trees of sun and moon in the medieval legends of Alexander the Great, visualized here in a medieval bible and cited by Tolkien as inspiration for the Two Trees of Valinor.

the era of mortality. Their final fruit and flower
become sun and moon, at whose rising mortal Men
are born in Middle-earth.

Alexander's journey to Paradise seeking endless
life is mirrored in the assault on Valinor by Ar-
Pharazôn the Golden of Númenor, egged on by
his adviser Sauron (see pp.78–9, The Shore and
the Sea). As Nansen puts it in his conclusion to *In
Northern Mists*, Alexander was said to have tried 'to
scale the walls of Paradise itself – there to be checked
for the first time: "Thus far and no farther."'[44]

Tolkien planted multiple flags of biblical portent
in his story of Númenor. Its kings are as long-lived
as biblical patriarchs, yet give more thought to
their tombs than to their palaces, like Egyptian
pharaohs (see p.143, Ancient Imprints). Adunaic,
its language, is Semitic in form and Akkadian in

flavour.[45]* Sauron's Adunaic name *Zigûr* ('Wizard')
suggests *ziggurat* (Akkadian 'height, pinnacle, top of
a mountain, temple-tower'), and his construction of
a temple to Morgoth on Númenor's holy mountain
is as hubristic as the Tower of Babel (see pp.*150*,
151, Watch and Ward). Finally, only cataclysm
can sweep away the corruption. Tolkien described
Elendil's voyage out of ruin to found a new dynasty
as 'Noachian' – Noah-like.[46]

In Gondor, the Egyptian obsession with
mortuary architecture continues. The White Tree,
standing withered until the return of the king, has
been compared to the Dry Tree in the fourteenth-
century *Travels of Sir John Mandeville*. Bare since
Christ's crucifixion, the Dry Tree is prophesied to
flower anew when 'a prince of the west side of the
world' should sing a mass beneath it.[47]

THE LAND
OF LÚTHIEN

FROM FAËRIE TO BRITAIN

In the Third Age of Middle-earth, Hobbits lived in 'the North-West of the Old World, east of the Sea', Tolkien wrote in *The Lord of the Rings*. He meant the north-westerly extremity of Europe, facing the Atlantic, where the British Isles now stand and where hobbits 'still linger'.[1] It is a tantalizing notion. Yet it is the merest echo of a bold idea that went back to his youth, long before he even thought of hobbits. Tracing it means digging deep into the origins of his *Silmarillion* – the *Book of Lost Tales* that he once imagined as a mythology for England.

The vast span of Middle-earth on the Third Age map in *The Lord of the Rings* – from the Gulf of Lhûn to the Sea of Rhûn, from the snows of Forodwaith to torrid Haradwaith – is as familiar as any imaginary geography. *The Silmarillion*, set in a yet more ancient past, explores other regions that had once existed. These – the drowned lands of Beleriand in the First Age and Númenor in the Second Age – are explored in *The Silmarillion*. And there are Valinor, Eldamar and Tol Eressëa – the Undying Lands that once stood west of the Great Sea but from the perspective of the Third Age exist in a kind of otherworld that only elven ships can reach.

'The grey bridge at Tavrobel': Essex Bridge in Great Haywood, the Staffordshire village where Tolkien began writing *The Book of Lost Tales* and which he incorporated in his elven mythology.

An evolving world-picture

All this adds up to a world-picture so rich, elegant and self-consistent that it invites something like the belief we attach to the real, primary world. Tolkien calls it *secondary belief*. The story-maker 'makes a Secondary World which your mind can enter. Inside it, what he relates is "true": it accords with the laws of that world. You therefore believe it, while you are, as it were, inside.' A devout Christian, Tolkien considered the making of secondary worlds to be an act of *sub-creation* inspired by God's creation of the primary world.

TALES THAT GREW IN THE TELLING

The first map that Tolkien drew for *The Lord of the Rings*, in 1940–2, is a mass of alterations, minor and major, as the geography and names unfolded in his work on the story. Some regions changed so much that he glued new paper on top to start them afresh. Other lands had to be accommodated by taping extra sheets to the edges.

It was probably at the back of his mind when he wrote his 1942 story *Leaf by Niggle*. Niggle, whose picture of a leaf has expanded into a whole tree and landscape, is constantly 'putting in a touch here, and rubbing out a patch here', and tacks other, originally separate pictures onto the edge.[1] Both the story and the map illustrate how Tolkien crafted his legendarium.

For many years of Tolkien's work on his legendarium, he wrote solely about the Undying Lands and war-torn Beleriand during the Elder Days. This is the era from creation to the overthrow of the satanic Morgoth, marking the end of the First Age. The mythology emerged during the Great War in *The Book of Lost Tales*. But in the 1920s Tolkien began major verse retellings of two tales: the alliterative *Lay of the Children of Húrin*, about Túrin the dragonslayer, and the rhyming *Lay of Leithian*, about lovers Beren and Lúthien. In 1926 he scrapped the outdated *Book of Lost Tales* and wrote a much briefer so-called *Sketch of the Mythology* (1926). This he then expanded as the austere chronicle we call the *Silmarillion* – in three successive versions, around 1929–31, in 1937–8, and from the 1950s until his death in 1973.

We would probably never have heard of Middle-earth but for *The Hobbit*, the story that Tolkien began for his children in the late 1920s. Rather casually, he set Bilbo Baggins's adventures in a later era of the same world – in a newly invented area, Wilderland, but with Morgoth's old servant the Necromancer lurking in the forest of Mirkwood. Only a surprise publishing deal for *The Hobbit* spurred Tolkien to think seriously about what must have happened since Morgoth was overthrown.

Now, in 1936–7, Tolkien created the Atlantis-like Númenor, an island utopia for mortal Men. It is brought to its own destruction by the wiles of the Necromancer, whom Tolkien now called Sauron. Survivors from Númenor ally with the Elves in Middle-earth to drive Sauron from his realm of Mordor into Mirkwood. This marks the end of the Second Age – still long before the era of Bilbo's adventures.

The success of *The Hobbit* in 1937 prompted a sequel, *The Lord of the Rings*, published in 1954–5. For this Tolkien devised a history of Sauron's long wars against the post-Númenórean realms of Gondor and Arnor. He determined that the hobbits' Shire was just over the Blue Mountains from where Beleriand had once stood. He fixed *The Hobbit* and *The Lord of the Rings* at the end of the Third Age.

Besides annals, languages, calendars, genealogies and artwork, Tolkien produced two unfinished novels about time-travel between present-day England and ancient Númenor, *The Lost Road* (1937) and *The Notion Club Papers* (1945–6).

But it was left to his son Christopher to edit *The Silmarillion* (1977) from his papers. He has since published and analysed his father's many drafts in a twelve-volume *History of Middle-earth* (1983–96), with further material in *Unfinished Tales* (1980); as well as three editions of individual stories from the Elder Days, *The Children of Húrin* (2007), *Beren and Lúthien* (2017) and *The Fall of Gondolin* (2018). A *History of The Hobbit*, by John D. Rateliff, was published in 2007.

Even this brief summary gives a false sense of consistency. Countless details changed in six decades' work on the legendarium. Elves were originally also called *fairies* and *gnomes*. *Beleriand* was originally *Broseliand*. The wider lands east of the Great Sea were only renamed *Middle-earth* in about 1936. *The Shire* and *the Elder Days* were only given these names in 1938; the *First*, *Second*, *Third* and *Fourth Ages* were not actually classified by name until 1950.

But Tolkien described himself as 'a natural niggler', and he had actually put in years of creative work before arriving at the familiar world-picture just described.[2]

But it was more than mere niggling, and the legendarium was not a single, continually evolving, expanding work. Until *The Lord of the Rings* finally fixed it in print, Tolkien began his literary world-picture afresh several times. He did not scrap everything, but each time he rebuilt on a new foundation of thought. As we might say today, he put his legendarium through several reboots.

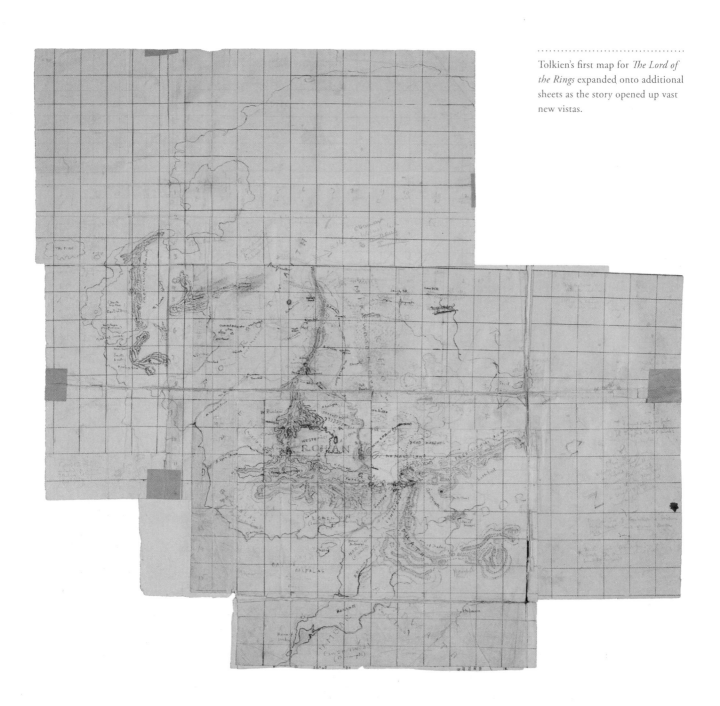

Tolkien's first map for *The Lord of the Rings* expanded onto additional sheets as the story opened up vast new vistas.

Tolkien wanted the legendarium to be imagined as England's own mythology (see p.47 panel, The Land of Lúthien), so it must somehow dovetail with England's *real* history and geography. But how? Each reboot was a new attempt to crack the problem.

Making precise geographical matches was not Tolkien's general habit. When he took inspiration from a place he knew or had read about, it did not usually matter much where it was on the map – he dipped and daubed at will.

But at the outset, the relationship between his legendarium and his real homeland was astonishingly direct. The *Lost Tales* devised in 1915–19 were meant to tell how elven Tol Eressëa, 'the Lonely Isle' itself, *becomes* Anglo-Saxon England. But Tolkien changed his mind. In a short-lived *Lost Tales* reboot around 1920, the Lonely Isle and Britain have always been completely separate places, though both are dear to

the Elves. In Tolkien's next reboot, which he worked on in the *Silmarillion* versions from 1926 to 1937, Beleriand gets broken at the end of the Elder Days and its fragments become the British Isles.

The Lord of the Rings was another reboot. From here on, Tolkien imagined only the most general geographical match between Middle-earth's north-west and Europe. Yet there are signs that he foresaw the British Isles ultimately emerging from the Shire and the area around it.

One sign is clear enough: the sheer, anachronistic Englishness of hobbits. Other signs are more subtle. There are glimpses of an elven presence in the Shire and to its west. Intricately tied in with this, there is the faint signature of Tolkien's personal life. The significance of all these points becomes clear only by tracing them from reboot to reboot, from world-picture to world-picture.

REJOICINGS AT DEATH OF DUN COW, WARWICK PAGEANT. II.

I. A LONE ISLAND: THE ORIGINAL *LOST TALES*

In Tolkien's earliest conceptions and in *The Book of Lost Tales*, the Lonely Isle and Britain are one and the same place. His 1915 lexicon of the Elvish language Quenya calls Tol Eressëa 'Faëry, England'.[3] With his Anglo-Saxon bias, and in keeping with wider habits of his time, Tolkien uses the name *England* for the whole geographical island of Britain, including Scotland and Wales. Likewise, Shakespeare's John of Gaunt speaking of 'this sceptred isle … this blessed plot … this England'. Tolkien's island derives its blessedness from its elven past and an elusively lingering elven presence. *The Lonely Isle*, a poem set in the present day, describes it as a land where still

> in the silence fairies with a wistful heart
> Dance to soft airs their harps and viols weave.

In all our mortal world, England is the heartland of enchantment.

Besides binding his homeland into his mythology, Tolkien also interwove his personal life. *The Lonely Isle*, written in France in 1916 after he crossed the English Channel for the trenches of the Somme, yearns most poignantly for one town in particular:

> *I long for thee and thy fair citadel,*
> *Where echoing through the lighted elms at eve*
> *In a high inland tower there peals a bell:*
> *O lonely, sparkling isle, farewell!*[4]

The 'citadel' town is Warwick, where Tolkien had spent happy hours with Edith Bratt over the past three years and where the two had married in March.

A MYTHOLOGY FOR ENGLAND

Pageant actors at Warwick Castle in 1906 celebrate the beheading of the monstrous Dun Cow by the town's legendary hero, Guy of Warwick.

'I was from early days grieved by the poverty of my own beloved country,' said Tolkien. 'It had no stories of its own … not of the quality that I sought, and found (as an ingredient) in legends of other lands.'[1]

He grew up in an era when mythologies were seen as vital to the identity of nations. But the 'Matter of Britain', the huge body of medieval stories of King Arthur and his knights, was Celtic at root and drenched in French influence. Even the great Anglo-Saxon epic *Beowulf* was essentially Scandinavian. Compared with the traditions of Greece, Finland, Wales and elsewhere, native English legends seemed to him 'impoverished chap-book' stuff.[2] Popularized anew during his youth, they were both a frustration and a creative spur to him.

The colossal Warwick Pageant of 1906 testifies to the common passion for a historical and legendary past. With 80,000 people flocking to see a five-day run, *The Times* enthused that nothing like it can have been staged since the days of Queen Elizabeth I.[3] It was a pioneering example of the 'pageant fever' or 'pageantitis' that swept England over the following decades.

Short dramatic tableaux were performed on Warwick Castle's lawn. One re-enacted the defeat of pagan Viking invaders a thousand years earlier by King Alfred's daughter, Æthelflæd, Lady of the Mercians. Other scenes had little or no historical basis, whether they showed druids attempting to sacrifice innocent children; or ancient British lords of Warwick such as Gwar the Mighty; or medieval townsfolk hauling the hewn-off head of the monstrous Dun Cow, its eyes still blinking and its nostrils aflame. Most of this came from a fifteenth-century history of Warwick by antiquary John Rous, who had concocted some of the legends and taken others from Geoffrey of Monmouth's entirely unreliable twelfth-century *History of the Kings of Britain*.

Perhaps it was partly with this pageant in mind that Tolkien wrote a poem about Warwick as a 'fading town' where 'old memory is waning' (see p.149, Watch and Ward).[4*] However that may be, he was frustrated by the incoherence and lack of mythic richness in such native legends. It was this, together with the shining examples of other nations' great mythologies, that spurred him to attempt to create 'a body of more or less connected legend … which I could dedicate simply to: to England; to my country'.[5]

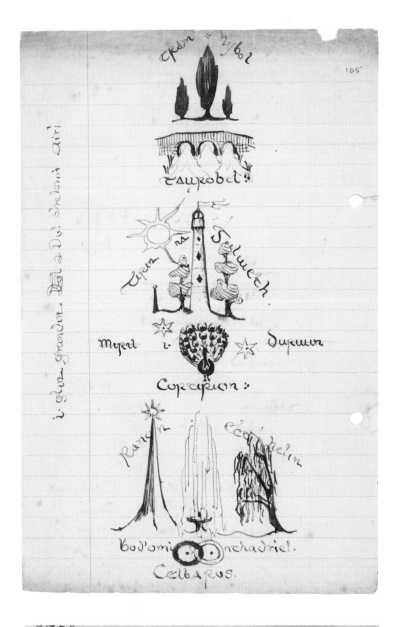

A personal place

Tolkien drew a set of three heraldic devices for places in the Lonely Isle that celebrate the milestones of his life with Edith – adding names and phrases in Gnomish, the second elven language he invented.

The device for Celbaros represents Cheltenham, where Edith had moved from Birmingham in 1910, seeking a fresh start after Tolkien's guardian banned all communication between them. It was here that Tolkien, on turning twenty-one in 1913, talked her out of her engagement to another man. The Elvish names *Ranon* and *Ecthelin* represent Ronald and Edith, and the pinnacle and laburnum probably do too. The phrase below probably means 'reunion' and the fountain symbolizes Cheltenham, which has several.

Ranon, Ecthelin and Celbaros never appear in any of Tolkien's stories. But the titular elven city in *The Fall of Gondolin*, the 'Lost Tale' that Tolkien began at the time of the drawing, features leaping fountains and a tree with 'blossom of gold' as landmarks. It also features Tolkien's first account of love and marriage between mortal man and elf-princess. His hero Tuor weds Idril, daughter of the elven king Turgon (see p.150, Watch and Ward).[5*]

The device for Cortirion or Kortirion stands for Warwick, where Edith had moved after their 1913 reunion. The trees are the ones that inspired Tolkien to call Warwickshire *Alalminórë*, 'Land of Elms', and which feature so prominently in a 1915 poem, *Kortirion among the Trees* (see pp.118–20, Tree-woven Lands). In the foreground is the peacock frequently seen on contemporary postcards of Warwick Castle. The tower perhaps

ABOVE Heraldic devices for towns of the Lonely Isle (from top, Great Haywood, Warwick and Cheltenham) inscribed in Gnomish *c.* 1917.

LEFT Peacocks like the one in Tolkien's drawing pace the grounds of Warwick Castle in a contemporary postcard.

recalls the one which, according to Warwick tradition, had once stood upon Ethelfleda's Mound, the conical earthwork beside the castle.

Tolkien names it the tower of Ingil, the elven lord who first settled the Lonely Isle, according to this earliest version of the mythology. In the earliest lexicon the island is *Ingilnórë*, 'Ingil's land' – an obvious pun on *England*. The lexicon gives Kortirion a resident goddess of 'love, music, beauty and purity', Erinti, who has a tower guarded by elves but lives in a circle or *korin* of elms. She seems to represent Edith, but is never seen again in the mythology.[6*] In the heraldic device and *The Book of Lost Tales*, the island has an elven queen instead – Meril-i-Turinqi, who also lives in a *korin*, on top of a hill probably inspired by Ethelfleda's Mound (see p.121, Tree-woven Lands).

The heraldic device for Taurobel or Tavrobel represents the Staffordshire village of Great Haywood (the Elvish names mean the same as the English one, 'enclosure in a wood'). Newlywed Edith had moved here from Warwick in 1916 to be near Tolkien's army training camp at Cannock Chase (see pp.*12*, England to the Shire; 167, Places of War). He was almost immediately despatched to the Western Front, but had rejoined her here as a convalescent soldier that December. This is where he drew the heraldic devices, perhaps for the January anniversary of their reunion. The Elvish phrase at the top may mean 'grey bridge', and the arched bridge represents Essex Bridge, which crosses the Trent at Great Haywood (see p.106, Rivers, Lakes and Waterlands).[7]

Tavrobel features in *The Book of Lost Tales*, which Tolkien began writing here. Standing beside the High Heath – recalling Cannock Chase – it has a 'House of the Hundred Chimneys', which must be a reimagining of Shugborough Hall, the family seat of the Earls of Lichfield at Great Haywood. The chimneys of this Georgian mansion are discreet, but local historian David Robbie points out that there are eighty, and in the cold winter of 1917–18 their smoke would have been something to behold.[8*]

2nd Lieutenant J. R. R. Tolkien and Edith in studio portraits at the time of their wedding, March 1916.

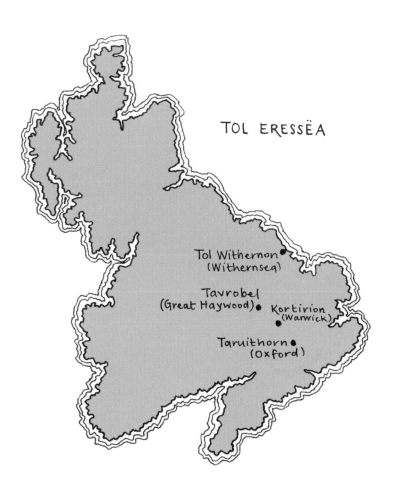

TOL ERESSËA

Tol Withernon
(Withernsea)

Tavrobel
(Great Haywood) · Kortirion
· (Warwick)

Taruithorn ·
(Oxford)

....

The Lonely Isle
before the calving
of Ireland, according
to Tolkien's earliest
conceptions (artist's
impression).

Isle of enchantment

The Book of Lost Tales opens with the arrival of
Eriol, 'a man of great curiosity', in the Lonely
Isle after a sea voyage.[9] Perhaps this began as
a conscious echo of Tolkien's recent return to
England by hospital ship (see p.62, The Shore and
the Sea). It is the beginning of a 'frame story' set
in Kortirion and Tavrobel, in which the Elves tell
their Lost Tales to Eriol – a kind of alter ego for
Tolkien, their actual author.

The Lost Tales recount a prehistory in which
the isle was mobile (like some enchanted islands
in European myth and legend; see p.66, The Shore
and the Sea). Before it was anchored alone in
mid-ocean, like a vast ship it had carried the Valar
to Valinor and many of the Elves to Elvenhome.
The tales continue with an exodus of one branch
of the Elves – the Gnomes or Noldor – back to
the mortal lands east of the Sea for war against the
great enemy called Morgoth in later versions of
the mythology. At the end of that war, survivors
would largely return to Elvenhome or to the
Lonely Isle. Here on 'the holy isle', Eriol sees the
Elves at Tavrobel in their days of glory, riding with
'the wind in their golden hair like to the glory of
bright flowers shaken at dawn'.[10]

Tolkien planned for Eriol to see the beginning
of the elven decline. Notes for the ending of the
unfinished *Book of Lost Tales* show that the Lonely
Isle would be hauled by divine power on a final
voyage so that the Elves could aid their kindred,

ESTIRIN, TOL WITHERNON AND FLADWETH AMROD

Tolkien's early lexicons give Elvish names to a few other places
important in Tolkien's life. *Estirin* is Exeter, the town that gives
its name to his Oxford college. *Tol Withernon* is Withernsea
in Yorkshire, near where Tolkien was posted in spring 1917
(see p.138, Ancient Imprints). *Fladweth Amrod* is Gipsy
Green, a house near Teddesley Hay in Staffordshire, which

was home for a while in 1918, when army duties brought
Tolkien back to Cannock Chase. Tolkien sketched vignettes of
High Life at Gipsy Green, including Edith at the piano and the
pram that held their newborn son John. Tol Withernon and
Fladweth Amrod never appear in Tolkien's narratives but his
lexicon links them with the mortal wanderer Eriol.

under attack on the mortal mainland – Europe. In a squabble of the gods off the shores of the continent, a chunk would break off the island, forming Íverin or Ireland. So the British Isles would reach the geographical situation we now know.

The elven mission would fail and Britain be invaded from Brittany (see pp.78–9, The Shore and the Sea) by a motley host of men and monsters. As mortals pour in, the Elves would begin to fade into the ethereal, filmy creatures of latter-day folklore and fiction. One day, they will be forgotten except as fable.

When that comes to pass, 'Tavrobel shall not know its name'.[11] Indeed, as we know, it will be called Great Haywood, and Kortirion will be Warwick. These ancient elven places under ancient names are not meant as 'allegorical' ciphers or codes for the modern locations. Tolkien, who said he disliked allegory and much preferred 'history, true or feigned', would probably have called it equally absurd to say Byzantium or Constantinople were 'allegories' for Istanbul in modern Turkey.[12]

In these stories the modern towns have a forgotten past and – for those who can catch it – a lingering enchantment or holiness. At Great Haywood, a few of the immortal folk linger, 'mystic half-transparencies' discernible in 'a sudden bending of the grass, and wistful voices murmuring on the bridge'.[13] Around Warwick, the Elves still 'undespairing … sing themselves / A wistful song of things that were, and could be yet'.[14] If Tolkien has a message, it is simple. Modern life tends to blind us to the true value of things – call it enchantment, if you will. Fantasy is a way 'to clean our windows' so we can see things as they are, he said, 'freed from the drab blur of triteness or familiarity – from possessiveness'.[15]

Enter the Anglo-Saxons

The transformation of elven Tol Eressëa into Anglo-Saxon England – the turning point from myth into history – involves a tidy genealogical connection between Eriol and the legendary leaders of the Anglo-Saxons.

Eriol's own era is the Dark Ages and he hails from Angeln, the real historical homeland of the Germanic people known as the Angles, on the north-east coast of what is now Germany. He has aptly been described as a kind of 'proto-Englishman'.[16] In its long-established mid-ocean location, Tol Eressëa is only a remote legend among his people. But after its final move to European waters and transformation into the British Isles, the place will be subjected to waves of invasions by the Guiðlin and Brithonin – the Celtic Gaels and Britons – and the Rúmhoth or Romans. Salvation of a sort will come from the Angles and their Germanic kin the Saxons and Jutes.

In English tradition, these Anglo-Saxon peoples arrived here in AD 449 led by Hengest and Horsa. Tolkien's notes

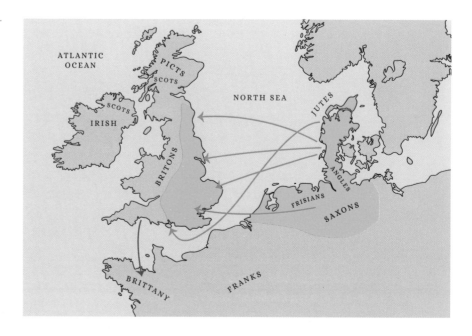

The Anglo-Saxon invasion of Celtic Britain in the wake of the Roman retreat. Tolkien visualized it as good news for the fading Elves of what had been the Lonely Isle.

make the two legendary war leaders the sons of Eriol himself – born to his mortal wife, a woman who died some time before he sailed for the Lonely Isle. By the time Hengest and Horsa reach Britain, they have a half-elven brother, Heorrenda, born to Eriol's second, elven wife. To each son, Tolkien assigned a 'capital' – Warwick, Oxford (Elvish *Taruithorn*) (see p.145, Ancient Imprints) and Great Haywood respectively.

The Book of Lost Tales, written down by Eriol and completed by Heorrenda, is passed on to their Anglo-Saxon descendants. So, while the Celtic Gaels and Britons have only 'garbled' accounts of the Elves, the English keep the 'true tradition'.[17] The Anglo-Saxons remain friendly to the Elves who linger in England.

The Book of Lost Tales is a hugely ambitious fusion of three literary genres that Tolkien admired. It is a lost-world story, like Henry Rider Haggard's *She*, with Eriol as the explorer stumbling on an ancient civilization still in its glorious prime. It is a collection of stories within a story, like Geoffrey Chaucer's fourteenth-century *Canterbury Tales*, with Eriol as the audience. It is also a foundational myth for England, like the one that Virgil's *Aeneid* had furnished for Rome – with Eriol taking the Aeneas role as foundational hero.

But there was a fundamental flaw in the timeline necessary for Eriol to be all these things. If he sailed to the Lonely Isle in its glory days some time before it became the Britain of the Celts, how could he have already fathered Hengest and Horsa, the mortal leaders of the Anglo-Saxon invasion in the fifth century?

It is this flaw, I suspect, that drove Tolkien to abandon the original *Book of Lost Tales* frame story – and to scrap the whole notion of the Lonely Isle turning into the British Isles.

RIGHT In Tolkien's second conception of faëry Britain, it is entirely distinct from the Lonely Isle of Tol Eressëa.

BELOW Tolkien was not alone in wanting to create a portmanteau world of Faërie. Birmingham artist Bernard Sleigh's 1918 *Anciente Mappe of Fairyland* celebrates numerous traditional tales.

II. ISLANDS APART: ÆLFWINE'S *LOST TALES*

In Tolkien's next world-picture, Britain and the Lonely Isle are separate places and have always been. But the two islands are deeply linked through the Elves, who inhabit both. They call Britain *Luthany* or *Lúthien* (a name that Tolkien would not give to his elf-heroine Tinúviel for another few years).

Tolkien seems to have developed the new world-picture around the end of 1920, as he began his first academic job, teaching at Leeds University.[18]* Now teaching Old English language and literature, he sensibly set the opening of his new frame story in the Anglo-Saxon era he knew so well. Yet despite its title, *Ælfwine of England*, this short text makes the legendarium a mythology not just for Anglo-Saxon England but for Britain as a whole – including its Celtic aspects. It is Tolkien's only prose narrative to describe Elves in the era of Christianity and real recorded history. It also uses the eleventh-century

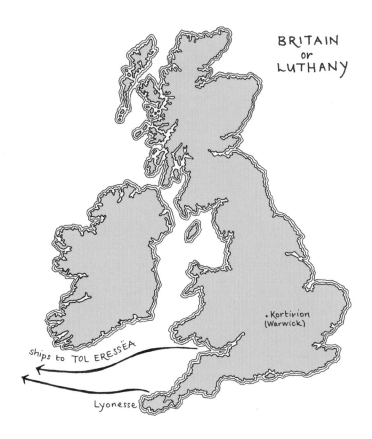

BRITAIN
or
LUTHANY

· Kortirion
(Warwick)

ships to TOL ERESSËA

Lyonesse

situation in Britain – Celts in the margin, Anglo-Saxons in the mainstream, marauding Vikings running amok – to outline the values that Tolkien thought vital.

By this era, the island is the Elves' very last foothold in mortal lands – 'even yet a holy land, and a magic that is not otherwise lingers still in many places of that isle'.[19] They are friendly with the Anglo-Saxon lord of Warwick, the town that stands on the site of their own ancient Kortirion. But successive mortal invasions have driven them either into hiding or into the west of the island. There, they are gradually sailing away from havens in Lyonesse, 'the lost land beyond Belerion'.[20] *Belerion* is the earliest known name for Land's End in Cornwall in classical histories, and Lyonesse is a drowned land that bordered it in Arthurian tradition (see p.77, The Shore and the Sea). So if the Elves are at home anywhere in Britain, it is not in the Anglo-Saxon heartland but on the edge where Celtic language and culture survive.

The mortal traveller who replaces Eriol as the hearer of the Lost Tales is Ælfwine of England – not a proto-Englishman but a proper one. But he is an in-betweener, a fusion of West and North. His mother is a Celt from Lyonesse, and is so friendly with 'the Foamriders, the Elves of the Sea-marge'

that they send congratulatory messengers to her in Warwick when Ælfwine is born.[21]* His father is an Anglo-Saxon who dies defending the town against the Vikings, while singing a 'song of ancient valour for the raising of men's hearts'.[22] This is the Old English poem *Déor*, with its refrain 'That passed, this can too' – lines that Tolkien cherished as an epitome of indomitable 'Northern courage' (see p.30 panel, Four Winds).[23]* The heroic tableau makes a clear distinction between Northern courage, compatible with Christian values, and the rapacious brutality of the heathen Vikings, 'Men of the North' (Elvish *Forodwaith*; see p.70, The Shore and the Sea). Ælfwine, who has inherited his Celtic mother's imaginative spirit and sea-longing, escapes the Vikings and sails from Britain to seek elven islands in the West.[24]

This reboot got no further than Ælfwine's first glimpse of the Lonely Isle. Perhaps the problem was just Tolkien's new teaching workload, or perhaps he saw problems with this revised world-picture. Eleventh-century Ælfwine himself could obviously not be a foundational hero for his long-established homeland. Having determined that Britain was not the elven Lonely Isle, Tolkien left no clues about how the rebooted *Book of Lost Tales* was going to be about Britain's origins at all.

TWIN TOWNS IN FAËRIE

In the *Ælfwine of England* world-picture, with its separate islands of Tol Eressëa and Britain/Luthany, Tolkien actually wanted *both* to have a Kortirion and a Tavrobel. In the Lonely Isle, these towns would be named by elves from Luthany out of nostalgia for the old country. We might think of them as remote, immortal faëry twin-towns to modern-day Warwick and Great Haywood. Kortirion was not to be the Lonely Isle capital, however. That would be *Rôs*, probably Tolkien's tribute to Roos in Yorkshire, where

Edith had inspired the 1917 *Tale of Tinúviel* (see pp.117–8, Tree-woven Lands).

In the next world-picture, for the early *Silmarillion*, the only Kortirion is on the Lonely Isle, which also has a Tavrobel – home of the elf-historian Pengolod, fictional author of the *Silmarillion*. Curiously, Tolkien also calls it *Tathrobel*, which certainly means 'willow-home'. So even though the Lonely Isle is certainly not Britain, this must be a playful private nod to willowy Oxford, home of *The Silmarillion*'s real author.[1]*

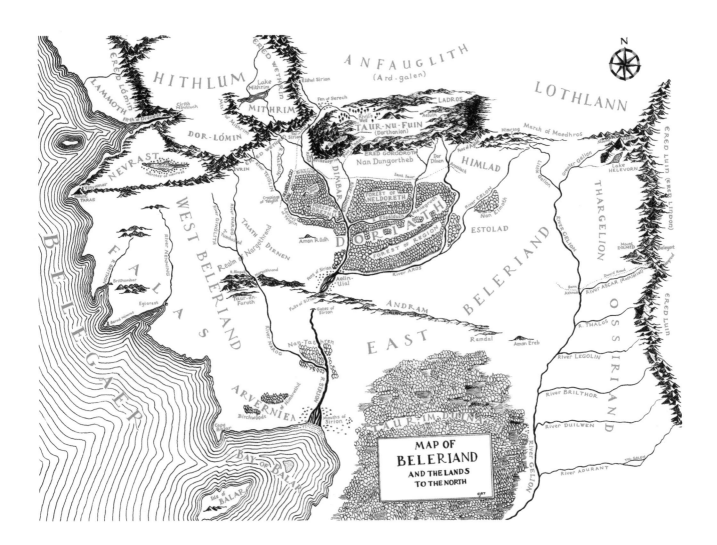

In a third conception, Britain would emerge in the break-up of Beleriand. The scale overlay supposes willowy Nan-tathren to be on the site of Oxford. Note that the *Silmarillion* map at top shows many details from later work.

III. FROM MAINLAND INTO ISLAND: EARLY *SILMARILLION*

The next reboot, set down in the 1926 *Sketch of the Mythology* soon after Tolkien's return to Oxford as Professor of Anglo-Saxon, is once again clearly a foundational myth for Britain or England. The violence of Morgoth's overthrow leaves the regions of war 'rent and broken' – their chief fragment forming the island of 'Lúthien (Britain or England)', from which the Elves sail west to the Lonely Isle.[25] The same idea underpins the longer 1930s *Silmarillion* versions. The land of war is called *Beleriand* (see p.78 panel, The Shore and the Sea), and also, punningly, *Ingolondë* or *Angolonn* ('Kingdom of the Noldor'). After its break-up, the British island remnant is called *Leithien*.

The direct geographical equivalences with specific English places, previously so important to Tolkien, are absent – either scrapped or just ignored by these elven histories, which do not trace Leithien's development into Britain. Ælfwine is now simply a translator of histories penned by elven hands. There is no single foundational hero. Britain is blessed now because its ancient Beleriandic soil was the setting of the long struggle for the recovery of the elf-crafted holy jewels, the Silmarils, stolen by Morgoth.

Standing out above all are the mortal warrior Beren and the elf-princess Lúthien Tinúviel, the characters whom Tolkien always closely associated with himself and Edith – so closely indeed that he ultimately had the lovers' names carved on their gravestone. The Silmaril they marvellously recover from Morgoth's iron crown in his fortress of Angband becomes the star of Eärendil (see pp.27–8, Four Winds; 64, The Shore and the Sea), the sign that heralds his final defeat.

When Beren is slain, by divine grace he and Lúthien are reborn to live out mortal lives together in the area that becomes known as the Land of the Dead that Live. If Tolkien wanted Britain infused with blessedness from Beleriand, this is surely the most blessed plot. For a long time he situated it in hills west of the River Sirion. It was a conveniently vacant tract, but putting reborn Beren and Lúthien there gave Beleriand its own enchanted west.

After much vacillation, Tolkien finally relocated the Land of the Dead that Live to Ossiriand, on the eastern fringe of Beleriand beneath the Blue Mountains. Narrative need probably decided it (so Beren could ambush the dwarves taking loot from ransacked Doriath to their mountain cities). But in due course, the new location of Beren and Lúthien's homeland – 'like a vision of the land of the Gods' – would take on an important symbolic value.[26]

WHAT'S IN A NAME? LÚTHIEN AND LEITHIEN

Tolkien attached deep significance to the names *Lúthien* and *Leithien*. The shape, perhaps, and certainly the variant *Luthany*, come from an enigmatic reference by Francis Thompson, his favourite latter-day poet, to 'the land of Luthany, and the tracts of Elenore'.[1] But what do the Tolkienian names say about Britain or England?

The Elves call Ælfwine *Lúthien* 'friend' and England *Luthany* or *Lúthien* 'friendship' because of the amity between elves and mortals there.[2*] Perhaps *Lúthien* still meant something like 'friend' a few years later when Tolkien made it the given name of his elf-heroine Tinúviel, lover of the mortal Beren.[3*]

Tolkien had once called England the 'Land of Release' or of 'Freedom'.[4] The long 1920s poem about Beren and Lúthien is called 'the Lay of Leithian, Release from Bondage' (recalling the *Oxford English Dictionary* definition of *free*, 'to release or deliver from bondage or constraint').[5] All this suggests that *Leithien* for ancient elven Britain or England also means 'Land of Release'.

Given all this, it is striking that the English words *friend* and *free* both come from an ancient verbal stem, meaning 'to love'.[6*] The philological Tolkien would know this, and perhaps it appealed to his sense that friendship and love can offer deliverance from oppression, suffering and heartache. Even if he did not intend the Elvish *Lúthien* and *Leithien* to be root-related in the same way as *friend* and *free*, they reflect a similar relationship of sound and sense. In Elvish, 'land of freedom' would sound so much like 'land of friendship' that one sense would always imply the other.

No doubt Tolkien's own given name *Reuel* (Hebrew 'friend of God') fuelled the fierce interest in friendship names that also inspired *Ælfwine* (Old English 'Elf-friend') for his fictional alter ego; *Elendil* (Quenya 'Elf-friend') later for the founder of Gondor and Arnor; and the use of 'Elf-friend' in *The Lord of the Rings* as an epithet of high praise.

The Tolkiens' headstone at Wolvercote Cemetery, Oxford, testifies to the importance of the Beren and Lúthien story for its author.

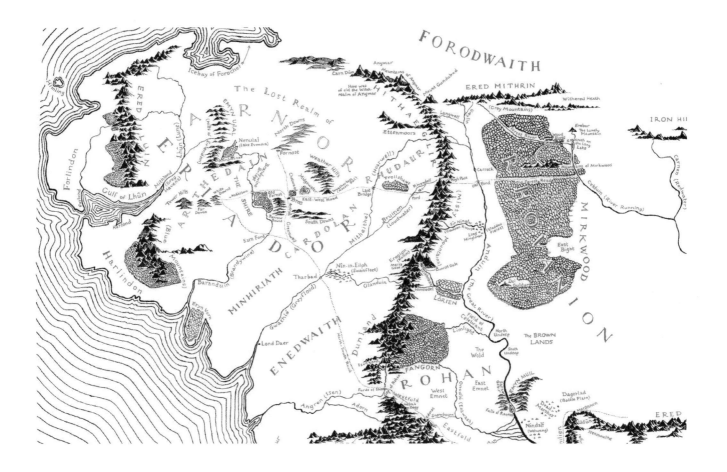

The wide lands of Eriador were invented to fill a gap between Wilderland of *The Hobbit*, east of the Misty Mountains, and the remnant of Beleriand of the *Silmarillion*, drowned long before the era of the hobbits. The scale overlay below, with the islands of Himling and Tol Fuin where Himring and Taur-nu-Fuin once stood, reveals old Beleriand as relatively small compared to the lands of *The Lord of the Rings*.

IV. ISLAND-IN-WAITING: *THE LORD OF THE RINGS*

The startling intrusion of Bilbo Baggins changed everything, though not until the success of *The Hobbit* in 1937 prompted Tolkien to undertake a sequel.

Hobbits are essentially English people of Tolkien's generation. They are absurd additions to the invented world, but when Tolkien began *The Hobbit* in the late 1920s that was the whole point. His sons were too young to enjoy serious epic, but they were thoroughly amused to see an unheroic almost-Englishman dragged into epic perils. Tolkien gave his children's story room to breathe by setting it sometime after the Elder Days and somewhere in the blank geography east of Beleriand, so there was no need to do any real work fitting it to the older legendarium.

But with *The Lord of the Rings*, that is exactly what Tolkien chose to do. One of his earliest decisions was to place elf-towers west of the Shire that gaze past elf-harbours to the sea (see p.157, Watch and Ward). But there is no island out there waiting to become England or Britain. At last, two decades after he had first dreamed up that idea, Tolkien dropped it. Hobbits, the full English, had short-circuited the connection between the legendarium and latter-day England. The Shire does not need to develop into latter-day England, because in effect that is what it already is.

Yet this is not the full picture. A careful look shows that Tolkien never truly let go of the original idea that England would be blessed by association with the Elves. Of all wide Beleriand, he wrote, only 'that land where Lúthien had dwelt remained, and was called Lindon'.[27]* So the westernmost shoreland of Middle-earth, which Sam Gamgee sings about as 'fair and free / between the Mountains and the Sea' is where the Land of the Dead that Live once stood.[28]

As Gandalf observes elsewhere, 'Much evil must befall a country before it wholly forgets the Elves, if once they dwelt there' – and this is especially so for any land still blessed by the memory of Lúthien.[29]*

Nor did Tolkien entirely give up on geographical parallels with Britain. Lindon is an enchanted west beside the Great Sea – the kind of region that Tolkien had previously imagined in *Ælfwine of England*, where Elves lingered in Cornwall and the 'lost land' of Lyonesse. And again this is an enchanted west between the sea and a largely unenchanted English territory – not eleventh-century Anglo-Saxon England this time, but the Shire, with its villages and farms, post offices and pocket handkerchiefs. It may not be coincidence that in Tolkien's Welsh-inspired language, Sindarin, *Lindon* means 'Land of Song', a phrase that is most famous in connection with Wales.

It seems doubtful whether he actively imagined an island Britain eventually emerging from Lindon and the Shire. Although he said that Hobbiton was about the latitude of Oxford, and implied that it was around that longitude too, he admitted it was tricky fitting his invented lands to past European geology, saying the story had got too far 'before the question ever occurred to me'.[30]* The scales are mismatched – Lindon is many times larger than Wales and the West Country.

If Hobbiton can be equated with Oxford, this is how a correctly scaled Britain would map onto Eriador. But Tolkien did not pay close attention to the idea.

Yet it is visually striking how the River Lhûn conforms to the shape of the Severn, each with mountains to the west; and how the gulf of Lhûn, dividing North Lindon from South, matches the Bristol Channel dividing Wales from Somerset, Devon and Cornwall (see p.110). If you superimpose Lhûn and Severn, you will find the Grey Havens around Clevedon, where Tolkien and his own Lúthien, Edith, took their honeymoon (see p.76, The Shore and the Sea).[31]* He cannot have expected readers to realize this kind of thing. But I suspect that he found private pleasure in it.

He wove into *The Lord of the Rings* a last autobiographical parallel. On the border between Lindon and the Shire is Westmarch, the home of Sam Gamgee's enlightened heirs. The western March-counties of England, on the border of Wales, were the home of the Suffields, maternal ancestors of Tolkien. What ties it all together is the Red Book of Westmarch, from which *The Hobbit* and *The Lord of the Rings* purport to be drawn.

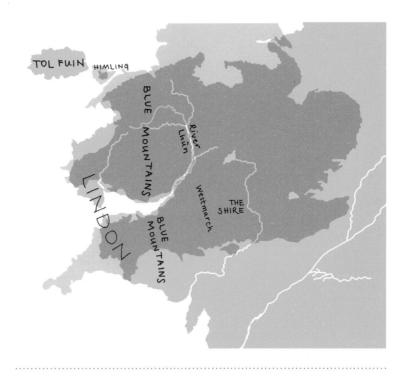

ABOVE A different mapping (with mismatched scales) reveals suggestive parallels between the rivers Lhûn and Severn, and between elven Lindon and Britain's Celtic West.

BELOW Philip Wilson Steer, *The Horseshoe Bend of the Severn*, 1909

THE SHORE
AND THE SEA

'Tollers is an inland animal,' C. S. Lewis's brother Warnie once observed.[1] But at this stage Warnie probably only knew *The Lord of the Rings*, still unfinished, and *The Hobbit* – stories that travel by river and lake, through forest, and over and under mountains, but in which the sea is scarcely more than a rumour. Yet the legendarium as a whole shows Tolkien not as an inlander but as an islander.

Neither mountains nor forests were as vital to Tolkien as the sea. Sea voyages brought extraordinary change in his childhood and the Great War. In academic and creative life, the sea was a timeless link with the ancient seafaring peoples of the north-west of Europe, whose stories inspired him. When he wrote that 'the thought of the Sea was ever-present in the background of hobbit imagination', he spoke for himself.[2] It was a mixed blessing, and he suffered a recurrent nightmare of the destroying sea.

In his stories and poems, the sea suggests an immeasurable spiritual dimension, and transforms those who hear or behold it. The music of the ocean plays a major part in the creation myth that opens *The Silmarillion*. The entire mythology sprang into life in 1914 with the image of a ship sailing into the sky, and *The Lord of the Rings* ends the same way.

Exploring this will involve four voyages of our own: through the awakening of Tolkien's sea-yearning; the formative reading that shaped his legendarium's Great Sea; the seaside inspirations behind his poems and stories for children; and finally, the nightmare cataclysm of his Atlantis-myth of Númenor.

·····················

'The sigh and murmur of the waves on the shores of Middle-earth … sank deep into his heart': for Tolkien it was as for Sam in *The Lord of the Rings*.

I. VOYAGES AND SEA CHANGES

On the evening of Friday, 29 March 1895, the SS *Guelph* carried Ronald Tolkien away from the land of his birth. Though only just three years old, he would always recall watching boys dive in the clear Atlantic waters of Cape Town harbour for coins thrown by passengers.[3]

The Union Company's latest twin-screw steamship was built for speed, but it took two weeks non-stop to chug along the west of Africa. Then came three stops in three days – Tenerife, Madeira, Lisbon. At 7 p.m. on Saturday, 20 April, the *Guelph* docked at Southampton, on England's south coast.[4*] With the death of his father the following February, this last island would turn out to be Ronald's permanent home.

His Channel crossing on 6 June 1916 was almost as momentous. He and Edith Bratt had married in March. Now he was embarking at Folkestone, Kent, to cross the U-boat-infested sea to France and war. 'One didn't expect to survive. Parting from my wife then was like a death,' he recalled.[5]

In camp at Étaples on the French coast, he wrote a poem that folds his sea-crossing into the legendarium on which he had been working for nearly two years. A farewell to a 'glimmering island set sea-girdled and alone', the poem looks back at England like a departing lover.[6] Gulls, skimming in the wake, call sadly above the varying voices of the sea. Green bays, silvery shingle, dark sea-caves and the white cliffs are seen through tears. But in the surf 'the shoreland spirits ride', because this is not only England – it is also the Lonely Isle of the Elves, Tol Eressëa (see p.47, The Land of Lúthien).[7]

His return voyage to Folkestone on 8 November has an obvious parallel in the story he wrote that winter to introduce *The Book of Lost Tales*, telling how the mortal wanderer Eriol arrives in the heart of the Lonely Isle to hear the Elves' Lost Tales (see p.50, The Land of Lúthien). But Tolkien does not describe Eriol's voyage or landing. His own – on the hospital ship *Asturias*

suffering trench fever – may have been a blur or blank.

Also that winter, however, Tolkien unleashed the sea in *The Fall of Gondolin*, the earliest Lost Tale to be written. It describes the journey of another mortal, Tuor, to the elven-city of Gondolin, via the seashores and an encounter with the divine Lord of Waters, Ulmo. It also introduces Tuor's son, born in Gondolin – Eärendel the star-mariner, whom Tolkien had actually invented before anything else in the mythology. It is plain that Tolkien's visit to Cornwall in 1914 helped inspire Tuor's experiences. But I think the night sky there also helped inspire the very idea of the star-mariner. So Tuor's story – seeing the sea, and later fathering Eärendel – is Tolkien's too.

On the Cornish coast

A poem about the sea pounding the shore had been brewing since a visit to St Andrews in Scotland sometime between 1910 and 1912. Further inspiration no doubt came from a fortnight near Folkestone in August 1912 with King Edward's Horse, the territorial cavalry unit his Oxford college had required him to join. Dibgate Camp, Shorncliffe, was perched on a hilltop above the sea, naked to the wind and rain that came daily. On the nights of 5 and 6 August 1912, a howling gale demolished almost every tent.[8*] Tremendous waves thundered onto the esplanade at the foot of the bluff. But the earliest surviving version of the sea poem, *The Tides*, was written down in December 1914 and subtitled *On the Cornish Coast*, reflecting his visit that summer to Cornwall's Lizard Peninsula.

Tolkien went there with a colleague of his guardian's from the Birmingham Oratory. In Lizard Town, perched at the southernmost point of mainland Britain, they stayed at a guesthouse called Bermejo. Father Vincent Reade was going to serve mass at a priestless chapel there with the extraordinary name of Our Lady of the Lizard.[9*] Father Vincent knew the area well from before his conversion to Catholicism, when he had been

Tolkien, *Cove near The Lizard*, painted on 12 August 1914 during a formative visit to Cornwall.

curate at Porthleven. The two walked to his old stomping ground and back via the Helford valley ('almost like a fjord', said Tolkien), the Goonhilly Downs and Ruan Minor.[10] On other days Tolkien sketched the rocky coastline – Lion Rock, Cadgwith and a cove near the Lizard with waves driving white surf against dark cliffs under a windswept moor. After a walk to similar cliff tops at Kynance Cove, he wrote to Edith:

> *Nothing I could say in a dull old letter would describe it to you. The sun beats down on you and a huge Atlantic swell smashes and spouts over the snags and reefs. The sea has carved weird wind-holes and spouts into the cliffs which blow with trumpety noises or spout foam like a whale, and everywhere you see black and red rock and white foam against violet and transparent seagreen.*[11]

No doubt Tolkien had been marvelling over the Devil's Bellows, described in a contemporary guidebook as 'an immense chasm' in the cliffs, into which the sea at high tide 'rushes with such impetuosity as to force the water out at an opening above', making the cavern boom like thunder.[12]

The sea poem from later that year launches its rolling waves of syllables so: 'I sat on the ruined margin of the deep-voiced echoing sea'.[13] Frenzied storm is followed by the restoration of deep calm; then the witness awakes and it all turns out to be a vision of ancient times. Another version in 1915, *Sea Chant of an Elder Day*, is accompanied by a painting, *Water, Wind & Sand*, showing the tiny figure of the witness inside a kind of visionary sphere. It seems to illustrate the lines describing how

> *a Dome of shouting waters smote a dripping black facade,*
> *And its catastrophic fountains smashed in deafening cascade.*[14]

In 1917 Tolkien locked the poem into his legendarium by making it Tuor's vision of a clash between two distinct sea gods. Profound Ulmo upholds the world and understands the hearts of Elves and Men. Capricious Ossë batters their coasts and wrecks their ships.

Even in this early poem, Tolkien was laying down material he would use decades later in *The Lord of the Rings*. Ossë's 'billowed cavalry' foreshadows the white horses of foam at the Ford of Bruinen near Rivendell (see p.105).[15] Ulmo's music is the same 'sigh and murmur of the waves on the shores of Middle-earth' that Sam Gamgee hears at the Grey Havens.[16]

The Fall of Gondolin, also written in 1917, turns Tolkien's seashore experiences into myth. Here Tuor is the first mortal ever to see the sea. He encounters its power before he even knows what it is, as a wall of water smashes its way up the river ravine from which he has just climbed.

The treeless, windswept upland – identified as Nevrast in the final *Silmarillion* version – is perfectly Cornish. Reaching the towering sea cliffs, Tuor stands with arms spread in embrace while the sun sets. Tuor marvels at seaweeds, rock pools, caves, spout holes and seabirds. Finally Ulmo rises awesomely from the waters and sends him to Gondolin, prophesying the birth of his son – the mariner who will become the Evening Star. Of course, this means the Evening Star is missing from the sunset sky seen by Tuor.

Yet it had been very visible on clear evenings at the Lizard in August 1914. Venus had sprung from the western horizon to vanish again due west after an hour and a half of brilliance.[17]* At this latitude, the planet only sets due west twice a year, for a few weeks each time – one of them around August. So Lizard Point had given a grandstand view only a few weeks before the September 1914 poem that launched Tolkien's mythology – *The Voyage of Éarendel the Evening Star*.

> *Éarendel sprang up from the Ocean's cup*
> *in the gloom of the mid-world's rim;*
> *From the door of Night as a ray of light*
> *Leapt over the twilight brim…*[18]

ABOVE *And His Heart Was Filled with Longing*, by Jenny Dolfen, was inspired by the Cornish landscape and depicts Tuor's first sight of the Great Sea.

OPPOSITE The Man in the Moon is fished from the sea in an illustration by Pauline Baynes for *The Adventures of Tom Bombadil*.

The star-mariner sails 'on sunlit breath of day's fiery death … from Westerland', just as Venus did as viewed from Cornwall a few weeks earlier. It is a myth made from observation.

Nonetheless, ancient myth and perhaps local legend also went into the brew. Cornwall has many tales of ships that sail miraculously out of the sea and over dry land. They are associated with the restless spirits of wicked seamen, rather like the more famous Flying Dutchman who is cursed to sail earthly seas forever. Nonetheless, if Tolkien heard such stories during his visit, they would have appealed to his new-found thirst for legends.

II. AN ODYSSEY FOR THE NORTH

A far older seafaring tale behind *Éarendel* had recently been much on Tolkien's mind. He had taken the name from Old English references to the Evening Star. Philologist Karl Müllenhof had argued that it went back to one of 'the oldest Germanic heroes', now forgotten – the central figure of 'a mariner myth corresponding in its main points with the Greek Odysseus myth'.[19]* This theory seems to have been Tolkien's guiding light. Not content just with the short September poem, he wanted to compose an Odyssey set in the cold northern seas. His hero must be a great mariner encountering wonders and adventures, like Homer's hero, but his seas would be Atlantic rather than Mediterranean.

A first, scribbled plot outline begins,

Earendel's boat goes through North. Iceland. Greenland, and the wild islands: a mighty wind and the crest of a great wave carry him to hotter climes, to back of West Wind. Land of strange men, land of magic… He … sees a great mountain island and a golden city…[20]

The mountain isle and city are probably the embryonic Lonely Isle and its haven, though Tolkien soon decided the city was a mainland one – Elvenhome's capital Kôr, much later renamed *Tirion* (see p.148–9, Watch and Ward).

The stark outline seems a stepping stone from the marvels that Tolkien saw through wondering three-year-old eyes in 1895. The mountain island suggests a deep memory of Tenerife or Madeira, islands with towering volcanic peaks. The golden city is reminiscent of a sight that Tolkien remembered vividly – 'pulling into a harbour at sunrise and seeing a great city on the hillside above' (he concluded it must have been Lisbon).[21]

FROM GREAT YARMOUTH TO BELFALAS

Introducing *The Adventures of Tom Bombadil*, his 1962 collection of verse, Tolkien says that the hobbit poem *The Man in the Moon Came Down Too Soon* 'is evidently based on the traditions of Men' because it mentions Dol Amroth and the Bay of Belfalas.[1] In reality it originated as a 1915 poem by Tolkien featuring the North Sea and Norfolk, which he seems to have visited twice in the previous two years.[2]* It gives an ingenious, playfully spurious explanation for the traditional nursery rhyme about the Man in the Moon asking his way to Norwich and burning his mouth on cold plum porridge.

Tolkien's Man in the Moon, tempted earthwards for good cheer and hot food, trips and plummets into the North Sea. Great Yarmouth fishermen catch him and send him to Norwich with the morning fish. There he exchanges his lunar riches for a bowl of cold porridge. A 1923 version adds references to Norwich's grand fifteenth-century Gothic church of St Peter Mancroft as well as the rivers Yare and Nen (see p.108 panel, Rivers, Lakes and Waterlands). In *The Adventures of Tom Bombadil*, Tolkien replaced the North Sea with the Bay of Belfalas and St Peter's with Dol Amroth's Seaward Tower. The English humour and mood survives, an easy fit with hobbit style.

When we voyage west in the early legendarium, however, we sail into the dim uncharted waters of the seafaring medieval imagination. After leaving ordinary waters, a mariner sailing Tolkien's Great Sea would encounter first the Magic or Enchanted Isles. Here, unwary visitors are plunged into endless sleep, like the Seven Sleepers whom medieval legend placed in Asia Minor, on the German coast, or on the shore of Greenland.[22]* Beyond the Magic Isles, the Shadowy Seas form a final barrier. They recall the region 'shrouded in darkness or mist' in the vicinity of Vinland, described by eleventh-century chronicler Adam of Bremen; or the obscuring fog through which St Brendan voyages to reach the Land of Happiness in the ninth-century Irish *Navigatio*.[23]

Tolkien probably imagined his Lonely Isle of Tol Eressëa as the true source of all later legendary 'fortunate isles' that are home to faëry folk, such as the Irish Hy Breasail, where the Tuatha Dé Danaan were said to have made their home (see p.34, Four Winds). Especially important was the Welsh Ynys Afallon ('Isle of Apples') – the Avalon of Arthurian legend. In Layamon's *Brut* (*c.* AD 1200), King Arthur ends up living with the *fairest alre aluen* – the fairest of all elves. In writings from the mid-1930s, Tolkien actually made *Avallon* a byname for the Lonely Isle.[24]* This means that in *The Lord of the Rings*, the wounded Frodo ends up sailing to Avallon – truly 'an Arthurian ending', as Tolkien once described it.[25] When Sam Gamgee eventually sails there in Frodo's wake, in effect he does something that Tolkien had meant Arthur's Lancelot to do in his unfinished poem *The Fall of Arthur*.

Tol Eressëa is not fixed but mobile (see p.50, The Land of Lúthien), like many islands in medieval legends. Ireland itself was said to have 'floated about in the sea at the time of the Great Flood'.[26] In the *Lost Tales*, the Lonely Isle is towed by a great whale. If medieval illuminated manuscripts do not feature whales towing islands full of elves, they really ought to. (They do show whales that sailors mistake for islands – the inspiration for Tolkien's poem *Fastitocalon*, about an 'island good to land upon' that turns out to be a gigantic whale or turtle and dives as soon as visitors have made themselves comfortable upon his back.)[27]

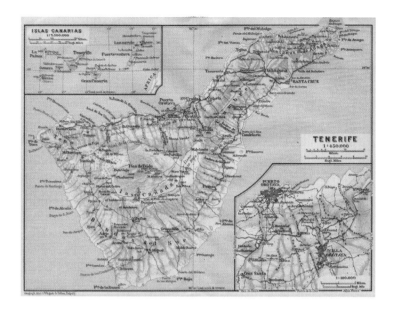

Blessed realms

In the Uttermost West stands the Blessed Realm, which Tolkien came to call Aman. It is hinted at in his first Éarendel outline by the words 'back of West Wind'.[28] George Macdonald, a favourite author of his childhood, had similarly described a country at the back of the North Wind where 'it is always the month of May' – 'a land of love and a land of light, / Withouten sun, or moon, or night…'.[29]

Tolkien followed Norse myth by placing Eldamar or Elvenhome directly beside Valinor, land of the Valar or 'gods'. The *Prose Edda* counts Alfheim ('Elfhome') as part of divine Asgard. The arrangement is crucial to the unfolding events of the legendarium. By bringing the Elves to live beside them, the Valar give them a paradise to lose – setting in motion the whole triumphant and tragic story. Once Tolkien had abandoned the idea of the Lonely Isle becoming Britain (see p.52, The Land of Lúthien), he settled it finally in the Bay of Elvenhome.

Further inspiration for a paradise in the West came from something that Tolkien found profoundly moving about the Old English poem *Beowulf*. A founding Danish hero, Scyld Scefing, first arrives in Denmark as an infant in a boat. It is not said who put him to sea in the first place,

Tolkien's first Middle-earth plot outline features a mountain island like Tenerife, a landmark on his own childhood sea voyage.

but when he dies, his Danish subjects send him back out into the waves in a ship. 'He came out of the Unknown beyond the Great Sea, and returned into It,' Tolkien commented.[30] He argued that such ship burials were not a purely symbolic ritual but also implied some 'actual belief in a magical land or otherworld located "over the sea"'.[31]

His argument may shed light on an enigmatic note for his 1930s novel *The Lost Road*, where he ponders including 'a Norse story of ship burial (Vinland)'.[32]* If this means he imagined the funeral ship being wafted west to Vinland, it would surely have been to a 'magical land or otherworld' rather than to North America.

Vinland brings us to what I suspect was a major and largely overlooked influence on Tolkien's world-building. In Icelandic sagas, it is a region of a westward landmass beyond the Atlantic. Even in Tolkien's youth, the landmass was understood to have been North America. By consensus, the Icelandic sagas were essentially accurate history.

However, in 1911 Fridtjof Nansen, the polar hero, diplomat and scientist, had broken ranks in a massive and scholarly book, *In Northern Mists*. His accompanying lecture to the Royal Geographical Society had been attended by statesmen, admirals and fellow explorer Ernest Shackleton, and had featured prominently in *The Times* and *Punch*. In Nansen's view, the Vinland saga of Thorfinn Karlsefni is partly fantasy and Vinland itself is a myth. He accepts that Icelanders did reach America, but argues that by the time the sagas were written down, generations later, the facts had become thoroughly mixed up with pre-existing legends of lands of bliss in the West.[33]* Vinland is a fairyland with magical or marvellous inhabitants.

At Oxford in autumn 1914, as Tolkien was brewing up his first mythological ideas, he was also studying *Thorfinn's Saga*. His tutor, W. A. Craigie, can hardly have failed to mention the Nansen controversy.[34]* Tolkien used Vinland as a yardstick for wonder in a talk to a student society that November, declaring that to read the Finnish *Kalevala* was to 'feel like Columbus on a new Continent or Thorfinn in Vinland the good'.[35] It may be noteworthy that this comment treats Columbus's continent and Vinland as two different places.

St Brendan celebrates mass on the back of a great whale in a seventeenth-century illustration. Traditions about the Atlantic voyage of the Irish saint informed Tolkien's ideas of the Great Sea, probably at an early stage.

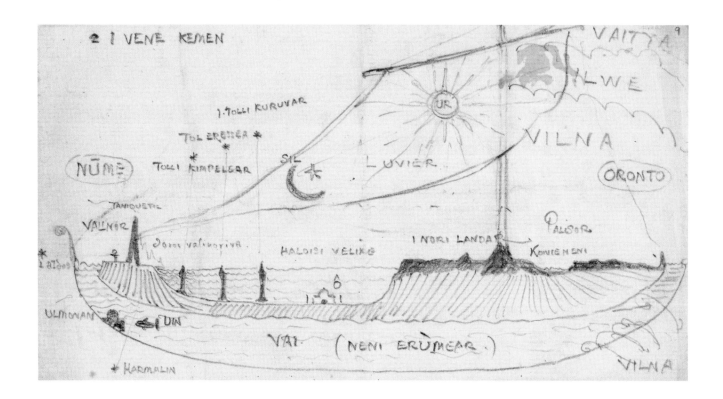

Tolkien bought himself a copy of Nansen's *In Northern Mists* in 1921, and around the same time he lamented: 'The unfortunate existence of America on the other side of a strictly limited Atlantic ocean is most constantly and vividly present in the imagination … there are no magic islands in our Western sea.'[36]* Much later, while writing *The Lord of the Rings*, he repeated the same lament in his now-famous paper *On Fairy-Stories*.[37]

Even from the beginnings with the first Éarendel outline, Tolkien's aim in his legendarium was to remove the 'unfortunate' fact of America and restore the means to imagine an earthly paradise in the West. The notion that Éarendel should visit Iceland, Greenland and a strange, magical land beyond certainly recalls Thorfinn's journey from Iceland to Greenland and then Vinland. The great wind that blows Éarendel into warmer climes is reminiscent of the one in the saga that blows Leif Eriksson off course and leads to the discovery of Vinland.[38]*

An early diagram for *The Book of Lost Tales* shows the flat earth in cross-section – but adds a vast

mast and sail so it looks like a Viking ship with prow pointing west.[39]* It suggests the westward voyages of the Icelanders were much on his mind in the early development of the legendarium. *In Northern Mists* itself is a veritable compendium of the kind of classical and medieval lore that Tolkien seems to have used in his imaginative explorations of the Great Sea and its islands.

Signs of Nansen's influence can be discerned as Tolkien developed the idea of Valinor. To Nansen, the Old Icelandic epithet *hit Góða*, 'the Good, the Fortunate', is key evidence that Vinland is a fabulous land of bliss, like the Fortunate Isles of widespread classical and medieval tradition. When Tolkien coined the name *Valinor* in 1915, it meant 'land of the Valar', as it always would; but it also initially implied 'the fortunate land', because the earliest Elvish lexicon defines *valin* as 'happy', in the archaic sense of 'fortunate, blessed'.[40]*

Nansen argues that Vinland's self-sowing wheat, along with the wild vines that give it its name

ABOVE *I Vene Kemen*, the World-ship, Tolkien's early diagram of his cosmology, implies that Viking voyages were on his mind at the time.

OPPOSITE Sami or Lapp hunters on skis, in a sixteenth-century illustration as adapted for Fridtjof Nansen's *In Northern Mists*. Tolkien acquired Nansen's book in 1921 but probably first encountered it several years earlier.

('Wineland' or 'Vineland'), both come from classical legends of 'the fortunate isles' that had reached Iceland via Ireland. A few telltale descriptions of Valinor include classic features of legendary fortunate lands – 'vine-clad valleys' and 'wild wheatfields' containing 'the tall wheat of the gods'.[41]

Northern ice

Exploring the far northern seas and shores, Tolkien seems to have tapped again into the medieval worldview, but mixed with contemporary accounts of polar exploration.

In his 1930s work *Ambarkanta* (Quenya, 'The Shape of the World'), the seas in the extreme north spill into the chasm at the edge of the world. It recalls the medieval view of the far north as summed up by Nansen: 'at the end of all gaped the immeasurable mouth of the abyss, the awful void of space'.[42]

The Arctic pack ice convinced Norse mariners that a land bridge joined Greenland to their west with Russia to their east. In Tolkien's North, western and eastern landmasses almost meet but for a narrow strait filled with clashing floes. Attempting to cross it, the Noldorin Elves of the *Lost Tales* lose a ship to a great whirling, shrieking eddy. It is reminiscent of a gyre in 'the stiffened ocean' beyond Iceland as described by eleventh-century chronicler Adam of Bremen.[43]

Yet Tolkien only had to open a newspaper to read true, modern-day stories of the terrors of the frozen wastes. He grew up in the era of polar exploration. Nansen himself wintered in the Arctic ice in his ship *Fram* in 1893–4; Roald Amundsen traversed the North-West Passage in 1905 and won the race to the South Pole in 1911; the defeated Robert Scott died heading back in 1912.

WHERE ON EARTH IS DORWINION?

The mysterious land of Dorwinion is best known from *The Hobbit*, where its 'heady vintage' puts the Elven-king's butler and chief guard to sleep, allowing Bilbo and the dwarves to escape.[1] In the 1960s, Tolkien instructed artist Pauline Baynes to mark it on her *Lord of the Rings* poster map, beside the Sea of Rhûn.

But this is not the only Dorwinion. Long before *The Hobbit*, Tolkien had referred to a wine-producing Dor-Winion in 'the burning South' of mortal lands.[2] And writing a version of *The Silmarillion* in the year that *The Hobbit* was published, he placed Dorwinion in the Undying Lands of the West.

So Dorwinion, like the Earthly Paradise that appears in many real traditions, can be found at almost every point of the compass.

Yet a clue to the origin of the idea can be found in its name. Tolkien's notes show that he intended the name *Dorwinion* to mean 'Land of Youth' in Elvish.[3*] On the other hand, the region's wine exports, put together with the common element *dor* 'land', inevitably suggest another meaning – 'Wineland'. That takes us directly to the Norse Vinland, which likewise means 'Wineland' – so named for the grape vines that reputedly grew wild there, alongside self-sowing wheat. The name *Vinland* must be a model for Tolkien's *Dorwinion*, as Roger Echo-Hawk has observed.[4*]

According to the 1937 *Silmarillion*, any mortal who chanced to land in Tol Eressëa would smell 'afar the undying flowers in the meads of Dorwinion'.[5] This must be the 'sweet fragrance on the air' that reaches Frodo at the end of *The Lord of the Rings*.[6] *The Lost Road* (also 1937) says Tol Eressëa's scent comes from *lavaralda* (see p.75, The Shore and the Sea), which is described as a tree rather than a vine. However, it would seem that for Tolkien vines were not needed for the characteristic wine scent that marks an earthly paradise. His King Arthur, returning home in *The Fall of Arthur* (mid-1930s), eagerly anticipates Britain's shoreland scent of

salt mingled
with wine-scented   waft of clover...[7]

In the *Lost Tales*, pack ice forces the Elves to abandon their ships and camp in the frozen wastes, until the ice at last provides a solid route to the eastern mainland ahead. This was absolutely topical. In 1915, Shackleton's ship *Endurance* was pulverized by Antarctic ice, yet he brought all his men miraculously home two years later.

The legendarium's only other ice narrative echoes a similar drama with a far darker outcome. Sir John Franklin's 1845 expedition to find the North-West Passage to the Pacific ended with the two ships, *Erebus* and *Terror*, likewise trapped in the ice. Their crews were last seen alive by Inuit in the Canadian Arctic. In the appendices to *The Lord of the Rings*, military disaster forces the last king of Arnor to flee to the shores of the Ice-bay of Forochel, which bites into Middle-earth to the North. King Arvedui's party survives only because of the aid of the wary Lossoth or 'Snowmen', last survivors of the ancient Forodwaith who adapted to the bitter colds that Morgoth produced in the North. The Lossoth 'run on the ice with bones on their feet, and have carts without wheels'.[44] Arvedui ignores their prophetic warning not to board the rescue ship that finally hoves into view, and so dies with his men in the crushing sea ice. The search for news of the lost Franklin expedition was being revisited in centenary newspaper articles around the time Tolkien probably wrote this.

III. THE MOON ON THE WATER

Writing for his children in the 1920s brought relief from the seriousness and growing complexity of the legendarium, with holiday-inspired stories or poems that often featured the shore and the sea.

Roverandom, the most ambitious tale prior to *The Hobbit*, is a classic example of Tolkien's knack for turning unhappiness into delight. In 1925 the family spent several weeks at Filey on the Yorkshire coast – their second holiday there. From the clifftop Edwardian cottage they rented, seven-year-old John watched in wonder as the full moon rose above the sea, laying a silver path from shore to horizon. One

day, four-year-old Michael lost a small toy dog on the long sand-and-shingle beach. His father and elder brother searched fruitlessly. Then a storm struck at night with such force that it shook the clifftop house and the Tolkiens feared the roof would come off. The next day revealed that high seas had swept in and churned up the shingle. There was no hope of recovering the dog.[45]*

To console Michael, Tolkien wove a fantasy around the facts. *Roverandom* briefly features the family itself (unnamed) 'in a white house that looked right out over the waves to nowhere'. The lost toy is actually a real dog, Rover, under a wizard's curse. When the spell partially wears off, he encounters

Shackleton's ship *Endurance* photographed by Frank Hurley in 1915 shortly before the surrounding pack ice crushed its hull.

a kindly sand-sorcerer, who sends him off on a fabulous adventure. The scenery beyond Filey's straight swathe of beach seems to come from a walk the Tolkiens took to Flamborough Head a few miles south. The sand-sorcerer's secluded cove is the kind of place they would have seen far below. The hills that Rover observes to his right as he is carried by the seagull messenger Mew must be the Yorkshire Wolds. The bird-thronged cliffs to which they fly must be weather-sculpted Flamborough Head itself, rising 400 feet (120m) from the sea. It is England's chief breeding ground for sea birds – skuas, shearwaters, gulls, guillemots and many more. Tolkien's sole creative touch was to make these chalk cliffs black, so that he could describe the marvellous sight of them 'covered with white things … hundreds of sea-birds'.

From here, Mew flies Rover over the 'Isle of Dogs' – not the Thames-side area of London, but a canine fortunate isle where bone-trees grow rather than wheat and vines. The idea was surely suggested by Dogger Bank, a huge submerged sandbank sixty miles (95km) east of the Yorkshire coast – the remnant of Doggerland (so named by archaeologists in the 1990s), a prehistoric landmass linking Britain and mainland Europe. The flight is the beginning of another wonder-voyage like Eärendel's, as Rover is borne along the moon's shining path to a fabulous, faëry version of the moon. In this tale, latter-day England coexists with the world of Tolkien's mythology. Rover sees the sea spill in waterfalls over the flat earth's rim, and even glimpses the Bay of Elvenhome.

South Coast and Cornwall again

After the Tolkiens moved back from Leeds to Oxford, the South Coast became their regular holiday destination. At Lyme Regis in Dorset in 1927 and 1928, Tolkien was back in childhood haunts. Father Francis Morgan had brought him and his brother Hilary here the three summers after their mother's death in 1904. In 1928, Father Francis joined the grown-up Tolkien and his family at Lyme.

Tolkien always drew or painted here. One 1928 pencil sketch, which Tolkien called *Tumble Hill*,

shows a Lyme hillside – perhaps Timber Hill above the shore east of the town, or possibly some other slope that is slowly tumbling to ruin. In childhood he had found a prehistoric jawbone in a huge, fresh landslide by the shore below and thought it a dragon's, or at least pretended he did.[46*] The trees in *Tumble Hill*, tall, straight and slender, look much like those in two Middle-earth sketches also made here in 1928. One shows the isle of Tol Sirion, where Beren is held captive in the *Lay of Leithian*. The other shows the forest of Taur-nu-Fuin, from the tale of Túrin Turambar – though Tolkien later adapted the scene for both Mirkwood and Fangorn (see pp.*124–5, Tree-woven Lands*).

The bird-haunted chalk cliffs of Flamborough Head, which Tolkien reimagined in black stone for his story *Roverandom*.

His spectacular picture of Valinor's holy mountain, Taniquetil, also from this holiday, has an unnoticed Lyme link. The swan-shaped ship in the foreground comes from Swanhaven, or *Kópas Alqalunten* as it is called in *The Book of Lost Tales*. The Noldorin form of Quenya *kópas* 'haven, harbour' also appears in *Cobas Haven*, an unused name for the bay north of Dol Amroth in *The Lord of the Rings*. When he coined these Elvish words, he was surely thinking of the Cobb, the wonderful old stone harbour that he must have marvelled at on his childhood visits to Lyme Regis. The etymology of *Cobb* is uncertain (the *Oxford English Dictionary* can only guess it comes from *cobble*-stones). It would be typical of Tolkien to want to imply an ancient, Elvish explanation.[47]*

Family seaside holidays also inspired their own body of writing, *Tales and Songs of Bimble Bay*, aimed at entertaining children familiar with Filey and Lyme Regis. Written around 1928, the Bimble Bay writings were just a short stepping stone from *The Hobbit*, begun within the next year.

The Hobbit has a Mr Baggins and a Green Dragon inn, while *The Dragon's Visit* has a Miss Biggins and a real green dragon. When the fire brigade is summoned to hose the dragon out of a cherry tree, it is a clash of cultures – medieval against modern. Townsfolk and town come to a sudden and nasty end. But the regretful dragon

Halls of Manwë on the Mountains of the World above Faërie, painted by Tolkien at Lyme Regis in 1928. The name of Lyme's harbour, the Cobb, echoes in the Elvish *Kópas Alqalunten*, Haven of the Swanships.

IN A CAVE BY THE SEA LIVED A...

The *Bimble Bay* poem *Glip* introduces a prototype Gollum, eyes shining pallidly at night when he emerges from his sea-cave

Under the floor, down a long hole
Where the sea gurgles and sighs...
He is a slimy little thing
Sneaking and crawling under fishy stones,
And slinking home to sing
A gurgling sound in his damp hole...[1]

The 'gurgling sound' looks ahead to the 'horrible swallowing noise' which, according to *The Hobbit*, earns Gollum his name.[2] *Glip*, onomatopoeic for the drip of water in a cave, points to another possible inspiration for *Gollum*. Tolkien had once briefly given the name *Gulum* to Ulmo, Lord of Waters, perhaps from the sound of waves glugging in sea-caves.[3]*

Though Glip scavenges the bones of sailors, there are 'darker and wickeder things' that prowl Bimble Bay at night – such as the local mermaid who lures the sailors onto the rocks.[4] Sharing an odd mixture of wicked and pathetic, Glip and Gollum seem less irredeemably malignant than their obvious inspirations in folklore or literature – the many-named goblins that lurk in Britain's caves, rivers or lakes, or Grendel and his mother in their underwater grotto in *Beowulf*. Perhaps they borrow their tinge of likeability from the kindly Hob-hole Hob, said to inhabit one Yorkshire sea-cave.

Hob-hole Hob is a contender for a far more important role – inspiring the idea of hobbits. Helen Armstrong suggests that Tolkien heard about him in his Leeds University years (1920–5) and the hob/hole association 'lodged in his subconscious'.[5]*

In fact, he could well have come across Hob-hole Hob a decade earlier, at Oxford, when he regularly visited his philology tutor, Joseph Wright, as both a student and family friend. In his great *English Dialect Dictionary*, Yorkshireman Wright cites this passage from William Henderson's 1879 *Folk-lore of the Northern Counties*:

In my own county we have a sprite of a more benign character. He bears the homely name of Hob, and resides in Hob-hole, a natural cavern in Runswick Bay, which is formed ... by the action of the tides. He was supposed to cure the whooping-cough, so parents would take children suffering from that complaint into the cave, and in a low voice invoke him thus:—

Hob-hole Hob!
Ma' bairn's gotten 't kink cough, [my child has the whooping cough]
Tak 't off! tak 't off![6]

Wright's wife, Elizabeth Mary, also recounts the Hob-hole Hob story in her *Rustic Speech and Folk-lore*, published in 1913 while Tolkien was at Oxford.

All the kindly Hob-hole Hob lacks is a more comfortable hole inland, a strong dose of rural Englishness (see pp.13–15, England to the Shire), and a diminutive suffix. (But as Edmund Weiner of the *Oxford English Dictionary* has pointed out, broad Yorkshire for 'hob in the hole' would be *hob i 't' hole*!)[7]

Could it really be that two of Tolkien's greatest creations emerged from a single sea-cave in Yorkshire? Perhaps Gandalf really was onto something:

'I can't believe that Gollum was connected with hobbits, however distantly,' said Frodo with some heat. 'What an abominable notion!'
'It is true all the same,' replied Gandalf.[8]

gives Miss Biggins and the other victims a decent, old-fashioned burial. Their grave is on a cliff overlooking the sea – like the barrow of Beowulf after his encounter with a far more serious firedrake in the Old English epic. *The Dragon's Visit* gives comic vent to Tolkien's serious sense of being out of place in the modern world. Another Bimble Bay piece, *Progress in Bimble Town*, is a tirade against the tourists of the motor era (see p.180, Craft and Industry).

To get away from the mob, from 1934 Tolkien used his own car to escape with the family to Sidmouth, which nestles between 500-foot (150m) rust-red cliffs on the fringe of beautiful East Devon countryside. On the final visit in 1938, he wrote the narrative from Bree to Rivendell at their favoured guesthouse, Aurora, in the town's genteel Regency area.

The 1932 family holiday to Lamorna Cove in Cornwall seems to have had a more direct, if subtle, impact on his writing. The Tolkiens had a month of splendid isolation with their Oxford friends,

the Wrenns, at this 'wild and fairly inaccessible' spot among the cliffs of Mount's Bay.[48] The Welsh poet W. H. Davies wrote of the cove, 'Who ever saw more beauty under the sun?'[49]* An artists' colony, it was the kind of place where people went to contemplate the Celtic past, both real and legendary, especially at this time of Cornish revivalism. That year, the recently formed Gorsedh Kernow, the Cornish community of bards, met at the Merry Maidens, a stone circle one mile (1.6km) from Lamorna. Tolkiens and Wrenns walked as far as Land's End across a country of knotwork stone crosses and holy wells, cromlechs and barrows. Wrenn (later of the Inklings) shared Tolkien's interest in the Celts and their contacts with the Anglo-Saxons.[50]*

For Tolkien, the return to Cornwall seems to have brought fresh inspiration, stored up until *The Lost Road*, his unfinished 1937 science-fiction novel. In the modern-day opening chapters, happy family memories of Lamorna seem to mingle

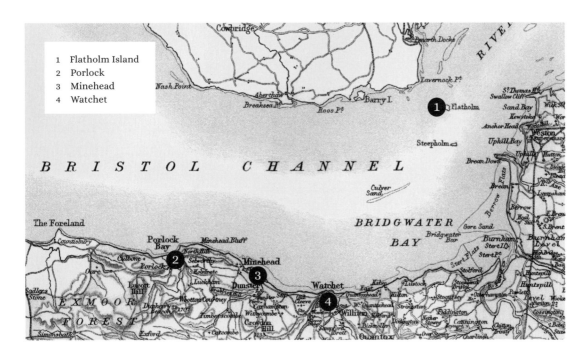

1 Flatholm Island
2 Porlock
3 Minehead
4 Watchet

with older and intensely solitary recollections of the Lizard. In Cornwall, young Alboin Errol first connects with the ancient past through dreams of Elvish. And again it is Cornwall where the adult Alboin meets Elendil of Númenor in a dream – the prelude to a journey back in time to Númenor, Tolkien's Atlantis.

The Errols' Cornish property, looking west over the open sea and apparently located on the Lizard Peninsula, is closely and deliberately mirrored by Elendil's house and garden in Númenor.[51]* The balmy Númenórean climate may have been suggested by Cornwall's, 5.5°C (10°F) warmer than similar latitudes. 'It bears in many ways a resemblance to the climate of Portugal,' says one Cornish guidebook; 'the camellia flourishes and displays its beautiful flowers to perfection, and the tea plant does so well that there seems no reason why it should not be grown for profit.'[52] With Elendil, Tolkien shares his own delight in gardens and flowers, writing lovingly of the Númenórean's hedge of *lavaralda* (Quenya, 'golden tree'), grown from seeds from the elven Lonely Isle. With its long leaves green above but golden beneath, and its pale-yellow flowers almost always in bloom, in many ways it

THE CURSE OF PORLOCK

What is it about Porlock in north Somerset? Samuel Taylor Coleridge, waking from a dream in which *Kubla Khan* came to him fully formed, was famously interrupted by a 'person on business from Porlock' so that he only managed to write down a fragment of the great visionary poem. And two Tolkien stories – about dream-visions too – stop dead at Porlock.

Tolkien wrote *The Lost Road* the year he walked in the area with C. S. Lewis and Owen Barfield of the Inklings, possibly all the way from Lyme Regis to Minehead.[1]* He began a time-slip chapter set in about AD 915 when a Viking fleet came up the Bristol Channel, attacked Anglo-Saxon Porlock and nearby Watchet, and occupied Flatholm Island. It is a spur for the ageing mariner Ælfwine and his son to sail off seeking the Paradise that St Brendan is rumoured to have glimpsed in the west. But the episode stops where it begins, in an Anglo-Saxon hall.

The scenario recurs in his 1945–6 novel *The Notion Club Papers*. Two members of an Inklings-like club sail circuitously to Porlock from Land's End via Wales, Scotland and Ireland, gathering rumours of vast ghost waves rolling across the land. At Porlock, they dream themselves into the minds of Anglo-Saxons at the time of the Danish attacks – with Lowdham (see p.27 panel, Four Winds) as the minstrel Ælfwine. They are about to sail to the rumoured western paradise – and the story breaks off.

anticipates the *mallorn* (Sindarin, 'golden tree') of Lothlórien (see pp.118–20, Tree-woven Lands).

IV. ANCIENT CATACLYSM

For as long as he could remember, Tolkien was troubled by a recurrent nightmare of a terrible wave rearing over green fields to engulf the land. He would jolt awake at the point of drowning. He called it his 'Atlantis haunting'.[53] In the 1930s he finally exorcized it in one fell swoop with the story of Númenor or Westernesse, from which come the kingdoms of Gondor and Arnor of *The Lord of the Rings*. But the violence the sea could do to the land had haunted his writings since his visits to the shores as a young man.

It is there in his poem *The Tides*, or *Sea Chant of an Elder Day*, suggesting the volcanic coastline at St Andrews in Scotland (see pp.95–7, Roots of the Mountains) as well as the granite shores of Cornwall. Even quiet Clevedon in Somerset, where the Tolkiens spent a honeymoon week in March 1916, can testify to the power of the sea. Here the tides of the Severn Estuary can rise forty-seven feet (14.5m) in four hours – second only to Canada's Bay of Fundy. (When he and Edith returned many years later, Tolkien wrote that his window at the Highcliffe Hotel dropped 'sheer into water at present as violent as the open Atlantic'.)[54]

In spring 1917, back from the Somme and convalescence, Tolkien was sent to do duty on a coast that is losing its battle with the sea – Holderness, East Yorkshire. It runs south between Flamborough Head's obdurate chalk mass and the long, narrow bank of silt called Spurn Head, which protrudes over the mouth of the Humber Estuary like a pendulous upper lip. Thirtle Bridge Camp stood in the midst of a low and flat land criss-crossed by drainage ditches and previously much wetter (see p.138, Ancient Imprints). (*Thirtle* is from Old Danish *Thyrkil*, equivalent of Old Norse *Thorketil* 'Thor's cauldron' and, shortened to *Tóki*, a source of the English surname *Took*.) Land in Holderness has been drowned many times through the centuries. Kilnsea, where Tolkien was posted

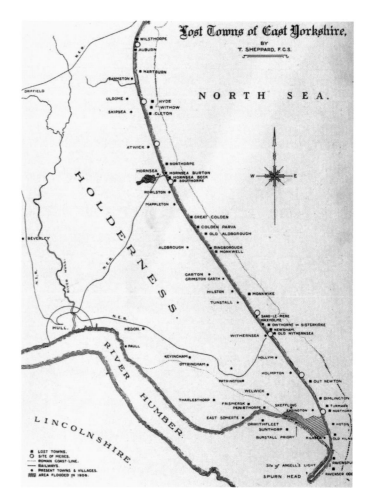

Stationed in Holderness, Yorkshire, in 1917–18, Tolkien was on the brink of a lost land. This map from *The Lost Towns of the Yorkshire Coast* (1912) shows the wide swathe of shore swallowed by the sea over the centuries.

The sea beside St
Michael's Mount in
Cornwall conceals
a drowned forest,
thought to be the
inspiration for
Arthurian tales
of lost Lyonesse.

through the winter, had been flooded every year
between 1906 and 1916. Here, guarding Britain
against German attack on this exposed coastline,
there was more to fear from the North Sea than
warships and U-boats.

Since Roman times, a strip of land three-and-a-
half miles (5.5km) wide had been washed away along
the entire 35-mile (56km) coastline. In Holderness,
the sole natural protection from the sea is a line of
clay cliffs rarely more than thirty feet (9m) high. *The
Lost Towns of the Yorkshire Coast*, an ambitious 1912
book by Hull Museum curator Thomas Sheppard,
recounts the history of drowned settlements including
Old Withernsea, Old Kilnsea and Ravenser Odd, a
seaport from the time of the Danelaw. Houses, farms,
piers, churches – all lay under the wave.

Drowned lands drew Tolkien's imagination. The
past itself was a kind of drowned land, and Celtic
tradition is as rich in lost lands as it is in fortunate
isles. It is thought that the real submerged forest
beside St Michael's Mount in Cornwall gave rise
to Lyonesse, the lost land of Arthurian tradition –
which briefly appears in Tolkien's legendarium (see
p.54, The Land of Lúthien). The offshore remnant
of another forest, in Cardigan Bay, seems to have
inspired the Welsh legend of rich Cantre'r Gwaelod,
drowned when its defensive dike was neglected.
Church bells can still be heard from the lost lands, it
is said. Breton tales say the same about glorious Ys, a
city overwhelmed by the sea because of its decadence.

Ys would seem to be an unspoken omen of
doom in the background of *The Lay of Aotrou and*

Itroun, Tolkien's 1930 adaptation of a traditional Breton *lai* or ballad. It tells of a mortal lord who strikes a reckless and fateful bargain with a witch in Broceliande, the enchanted forest of Arthurian legend in the heart of Brittany. Everywhere,

> *the breezes bear*
> *the sound of bells along the air*
> *to mingle with the sound of seas*
> *for ever moving in the trees.*[55]*

Such sounds belong in a Christian shoreland, of course; yet these are ominously reminiscent of Ys. And that last phrase conceals a phantom secondary

meaning – the seas are forever moving through a submerged forest.

The Great Wave

Tolkien speculated that his Great Wave nightmare was 'legend or myth or dim memory of some ancient history'. It is at least as feasible that the dream goes back to his first voyage to England, followed the next year by the death of his father far away.[56] Tolkien felt rather than knew, perhaps, a deep association between the green fields here, the power of the sea to take things away, and the incomprehensible personal loss that followed. He compared later bereavements to shipwrecks. At his mother's death in 1904, Father Francis Morgan's in 1935 and Edith's in 1971, he felt 'like a castaway left on a barren island under a heedless sky after the loss of a great ship', or 'like a lost survivor into a new alien world'.[57] Around the close of 1936 such grievous images of loss under the sea fused with the sudden idea of an Atlantis story.

Tolkien's version of Atlantis is Númenor, an island given as reward to the mortal Elf-friends who had fought Morgoth in the Elder Days. Eventually it becomes an imperial and naval power – ruling the waves like eighteenth- and nineteenth-century Britannia. Then its people become consumed with envy. Not content with their own 'fortunate isle' they crave the immortality enjoyed by the Elves of the Lonely Isle, so near yet so far to their west. The king of Númenor, convinced that endless life is there for the taking, finally sends an armada to land on the shores of Valinor. Ultimately, vain hope and colossal hubris bring ruin to Númenor.

December 1936 had opened with severe gales causing flood and devastation on the east coast of Britain. All the fear and awe that the sea had evoked for Tolkien goes into the story of the Númenórean cataclysm conceived at that time.[58] The Valar open up an undersea chasm into which the seas rush, swallowing the armada. The Great Wave overwhelms Númenor, turning it into a drowned land like Ys, Lyonesse and Cantre'r Gwaelod. One of its Elvish names, *Mar-nu-Falmar*, means virtually the same as the Irish *Tir fa Tonn*, 'Land

---

WHAT'S IN A NAME? *BROSELIAND* AND *BELERIAND*

A pattern of cataclysm emerges in Tolkien's names for the region of the Elves' wars against Morgoth. *Broseliand*, first used in 1925 in the *Lay of Leithian*, is a soundalike for *Broceliande* in Brittany and was perhaps chosen partly for its aura of legend. The pattern is clearer in 1931 with the replacement name *Beleriand*, a close echo of *Belerion* – a name applied to Land's End in Cornwall by the Sicilian historian Diodorus in the first century BC.[1]* In tradition, Brittany and Cornwall both stand next to drowned lands at Europe's extreme west. Tolkien's Broseliand or Beleriand, the most westerly mortal land, is drowned at the end of the Elder Days; but in the period when he conceived these names he imagined an island remnant surviving as Britain (see p.55, The Land of Lúthien). The implication must be that, just as Breton and Cornish traditions speak of drowned lands offshore, so the name of the drowned land of the legendarium leaves its echo in *Broceliande* or *Belerion*.

Boat spars hint
at loss and wreck
in one of Tolkien's
summer 1914
sketches from
Cornwall.

SHIPWRECKS

Tolkien's deepest feelings of loss were engaged by shipwreck, a potent symbol in the era of the *Titanic*, which struck its Atlantic iceberg in 1912. Many ships have foundered off the coast from St Andrews to Fife Ness, which he visited that year. The Yorkshire coast is a graveyard of ships through the ages, like the U-boat off Flamborough Head that the Tolkiens went to see in 1925. The Lizard Peninsula has seen more than two hundred wrecks. On his 1914 visit, Tolkien surely heard about the White Star liner *Suevic* that had run onto the rocks beneath Lizard Town in fog, gale and heavy seas seven years earlier. An all-night rescue by lifeboatmen and townsfolk saved all 523 passengers and crew, who were lodged overnight in houses for miles around. Cornish songs sing of sailors less fortunate, whose ships went down near a Lizard sea-cave (Cornish *ogo* or *oogo*):

> Drownèd men by Ruan Shore
> *Dolor Oogo, Dolor Oogo*
> *Lost aboard the Elsinore*
> *Down by Dolor Oogo*[1]

In Tolkien's 1914 Cornish landscape painting, *Caerthilian Cove and Lion Rock*, gulls swoop around the spars of a wreck. In his dreamlike early 1930s poem *Looney*, a traveller is borne over the sea to a dark, disturbing Faërie and stranded there like a castaway; then finally borne back, 'passing old hulls clustered with gulls'.[2]

In *The Last Ark*, another dream vision, a white ship lies on the rocks of the last shore, at the end of time, with

> *pale phantoms*
> *in her cold bosom*
> *like gulls wailing...*[3]

The Last Ark has no clear link to the legendarium, though Tolkien read an Elvish version in a talk on language invention in November 1931. However, a source may be found in *Barzaz Breiz*, Hersart de la Villemarqué's anthology of Breton *lais* (ballads), from which Tolkien adapted his *Lay of Aotrou and Itroun* in 1930.

Villemarqué cites a story told by sixth-century Greek historian Procopius about how the souls of the dead are ferried from Brittany to Britain. He also cites a description by fourth-century Latin poet Claudian of a place where one can hear 'the mournful weeping of the spirits of the dead as they flit by with faint sound of wings, and the inhabitants see the pale ghosts pass and the shades of the dead'.[4] *The Last Ark* appears to marry the two legends, which Villemarqué identifies with Brittany's westernmost peninsula, the Pointe du Raz.

The Procopius story may also lie behind the Black Ship Mornië, which carries the souls of dead mortals along Valinor's coast in *The Book of Lost Tales*. The Pointe du Raz must be what Tolkien means by 'the Promontory of Rôs', whence barbaric Men enter the Lonely Isle (Britain).[5]

under Wave'. From then on it has another Elvish name, *Atalantë*, 'The Downfallen', which Tolkien implies is the origin of the familiar *Atlantis*. In the fully developed version of the story, *Akallabêth* (in *The Silmarillion*) Númenor itself is like a vast shipwreck: 'overturned … it fell and went down into darkness'.[59] Yet Tolkien finds new hope in the same vision, because the few survivors of the disaster are swept to Middle-earth and wrecked upon its shores – there to found the kingdoms in exile, Gondor and Arnor.

The Round World and the Straight Way

The Númenor story also introduces a fundamental cosmological change. As Númenor drowns, the shape of the world itself is changed at a stroke. The flat earth is made round. Now any mortal mariner crossing the curving westward ocean can only reach the equally mortal Americas – literally part of a 'new world'.

But immortal Valinor, Eldamar and Tol Eressëa are removed from 'the circles of the world'.[60] This 'Ancient West' exists now like a mystic memory of the physical flat world of the Elder Days. Tolkien drew diagrams visualizing it as a flat line or plane co-existing with the reshaped round world – rather like a photographic double exposure.

Crucially, the Elves can still reach the Ancient West in specially hallowed ships. They sail the 'Straight Way' that follows the old line of the flat world while our curving seas gradually fall away below.

Tolkien's clearest description of the Straight Way comes in a later poem based on the *Navigatio* of St Brendan the Navigator, the most celebrated of all Irish wonder-voyage narratives or *imrama*. Tolkien's *Imram* ('Voyaging') makes St Brendan an eyewitness to the new cosmology as Eärendel had been for the old one. He sees the smoking mountain remnant of 'the foundered land' (see p.93,

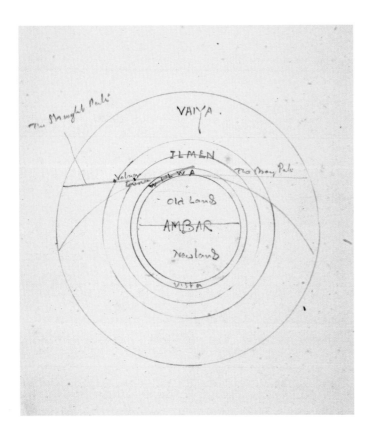

LEFT A Tolkien sketch shows his radical 1930s conception of how the old, flat world of his mythology became the globe we know. The Straight Path or Straight Way persists like a mystical memory of the old world.

BELOW The Straight Way is navigable only by specially hallowed elven ships, as visualized here by John Howe.

Roots of the Mountains), then a visionary fortunate isle, and then the place

> *where the round world plunges steeply down*
> *but on the old road goes,*
> *as an unseen bridge that on arches runs*
> *to coasts that no man knows.*[61]

As a route between Middle-earth and a distinct divine plane of existence, the Straight Way is a new incarnation of Tolkien's old abandoned ideas of a Path of Dreams and a rainbow bridge (see p.31, Four Winds). He meant it, no doubt, as the 'true' origin for the Norse Bifröst.

But the elegant and rather abstract idea also seems to go all the way back to inspirational moments on the coasts of Cornwall and Yorkshire. I have suggested that seeing Venus over the western sea from Lizard Point in 1914 helped to inspire Eärendel's voyage over the rim of the flat earth. In turn, Eärendel's trajectory, combined with the moon's reflection on the sea from Filey in 1925, went into the idea of Rover's flight to a faëry version of the moon. *Roverandom* was dusted off and revised in late 1936, at the invitation of George Allen & Unwin, the publishers who had just enthusiastically accepted *The Hobbit*. So Tolkien had engaged afresh with the idea of a mystical flight from mortal seas to Faërie

just weeks or days before the notion of Númenor struck him like a thunderbolt.

The Lord of the Rings, that virtually landlocked epic, reaches the western shore of Middle-earth in its final paragraphs. Here Tolkien merges the concept of the Straight Way with profound personal memories or half-memories.

The Silmarillion explains clearly how the ship carrying Frodo sails away 'until the seas of the Bent World fell away beneath it'.[62] This is why Sam Gamgee, watching from the Grey Havens in *The Lord of the Rings*, sees only 'a shadow on the waters'.[63] The elven ship sails from mortal waters onto 'the High Sea' – a deceptively familiar phrase Tolkien uses only here.[64] The matching passage in *The Silmarillion* calls it 'the high airs above the mists of the world'.[65]

Frodo's voyage via the High Sea to Tol Eressëa – the island initially conceived as a mythical version of England – inevitably brings to mind two of Tolkien's own sea-crossings. As a first sight of the 'far green country', it mirrors his passage to England at the age of three.[66] But Frodo is an adult back from the 'Great War of the Ring' with deep and obscure wounds to heal, so his voyage carries the imprint of Tolkien's return from the Battle of the Somme in 1916 by hospital ship (see p.62, The Shore and the Sea), ready to begin writing the stories of his legendarium.

ROOTS OF THE MOUNTAINS

'What has roots as nobody sees?' Bilbo guesses the answer to Gollum's first riddle immediately: 'Mountain, I suppose.' The fact that they are deep inside one at the time is a bit of a giveaway. But the question rightly directs us to the origins of the mountains of Middle-earth, together with their subterranean places, in Tolkien's intellectual and active life.

I. THE ALPS, 1911

A single visit to Switzerland laid the foundations for almost every mountain scene Tolkien wrote. His account of it, though neither comprehensive nor orderly, is his frankest statement of his debt to real places. He may have caught glimpses of mountains, barely comprehended, while leaving South Africa at three, and perhaps later in childhood he saw the Welsh mountains (see p.19, England to the Shire), which seem to be part of the imaginative foundations of the Blue Mountains west of the Shire (see p.59, The Land of Lúthien). But the Alps were a lasting revelation.

The valley of Lauterbrunnen, the first glory of Tolkien's 1911 Swiss walking holiday and the clear inspiration for Rivendell.

Tolkien was nineteen and on the verge of 'going up' to Oxford when he and his seventeen-year-old brother Hilary joined the 1911 Swiss walking tour with their aunt, Jane Neave, sister and intellectual equal to their late mother. Jane's friends and travelling companions, the Brookes-Smiths, were regular visitors to Switzerland and the Austrian Tyrol.

The party was twelve-strong, at some point swelled to fourteen – the size of Thorin's party in *The Hobbit* but roughly half women or girls. Carrying the long spiked staves called alpenstocks, they wore the waterproof woollen Loden cloaks of Austria and hobnailed boots. They looked the part – except for their tropical pith helmets, a wise addition in what Tolkien called 'the *annus mirabilis* of sunshine'.[1]

After their boat trip up the Rhine to Munich, Germany, the travellers took trains via Innsbruck in Austria and Zürich in Switzerland (see p.138, Ancient Imprints) to Interlaken. The Alpine trek began here, in the Bernese Oberland, and ended in the Valais region, at the railway station at

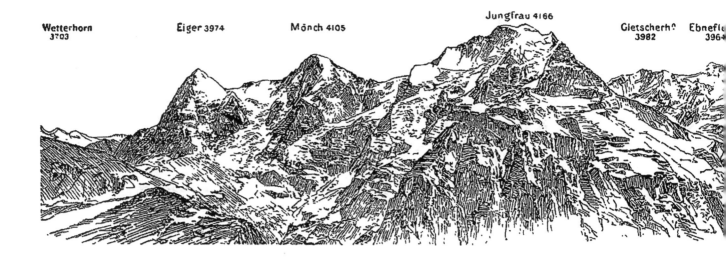

Sion. As the crow flies from point to point of their itinerary, they covered roughly 110 miles (177km); but the often-winding paths must have made it much further than that. Walking at sightseeing pace with heavy packs, mostly on mountainous terrain – including high passes and a glacier – it took more than three weeks.[2]*

Apart from the fact that they were in an orderly and well-populated country, this was close to the kind of travel that Tolkien describes in his books. No bookings were made for accommodation, and the men often slept in cowsheds or haylofts. Breakfasts were meagre and other meals were cooked in the open air on spirit stoves. They navigated by map and avoided roads wherever possible.

Over the edge of the Wild

Using his Alpine inspirations appears to have been one of Tolkien's earliest impulses when he began the legendarium. His outline of the voyages of Eärendel, no later than early 1915, included the unused idea that the star-mariner might lose his boat in the Mediterranean and travel 'afoot through wilds of Europe'.[3] The journey of Beren across the mountains to Doriath makes use of precipitous heights and hidden valleys for nightmare effect (see p.172, Places of War). But it is not until *The Hobbit* that Tolkien gave freer rein to his memories; it allowed his children to share in his own youthful wonder.

Bilbo voices Tolkien's own feelings in *The Lord of the Rings* when he tells Gandalf how he longs to see mountains again. Close to completing the book, Tolkien told his publisher, Stanley Unwin, 'How I long to see the snows and the great heights again!'[4] He expressed his feelings most fully to his own son, Christopher:

Much though I love and admire little lanes and hedges and rustling trees and the soft rolling contours of a rich champain, the thing that stirs me most and comes nearest to heart's satisfaction for me is space, and I would be willing to barter barrenness for it; indeed I think I like barrenness itself, whenever I have seen it. My heart still lingers among the high stony wastes among the morains and mountain-wreckage, silent in spite of the sound of thin chill water.[5]

Tolkien's life and mind were crowded. Anyone who has walked in mountains will recognize the sense of space they convey – both physical and mental. 'Mountain walking gives long, majestic sightlines and open sky,' geologist Sally Pehrsson points out.[6] Tolkien captures just such a receding mountain vista in the background of his painting *Bilbo Awoke with the Early Sun in His Eyes*. Mountains seen in the distance conveyed for him a 'sense of endless *untold* stories' – that same impression of potentially limitless exploration

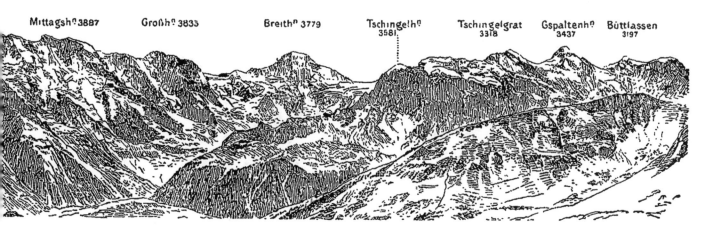

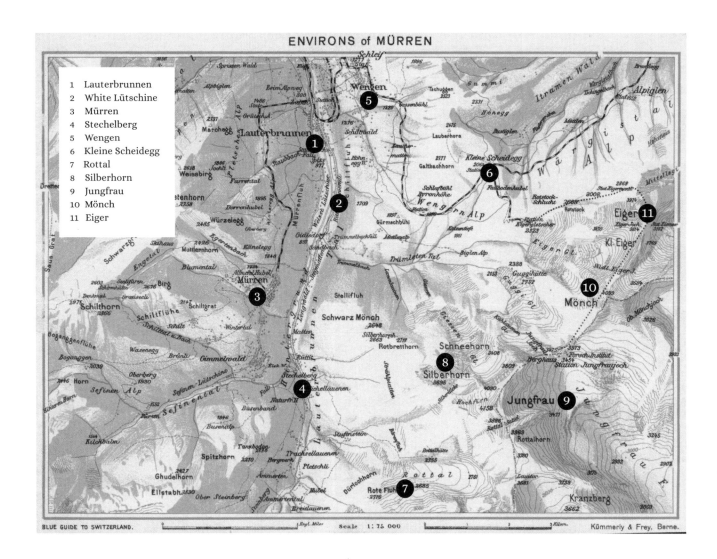

ENVIRONS of MÜRREN

1 Lauterbrunnen
2 White Lütschine
3 Mürren
4 Stechelberg
5 Wengen
6 Kleine Scheidegg
7 Rottal
8 Silberhorn
9 Jungfrau
10 Mönch
11 Eiger

BLUE GUIDE TO SWITZERLAND.   Scale 1: 75 000   Kümmerly & Frey, Berne.

which is vital to the success of his legendarium.[7]

Bilbo in *The Lord of the Rings* also tells Gandalf he craves rest, and it is especially telling that he finds this in the elven valley of Rivendell, on which Switzerland had the most particular impact. The inspiration came from the very first step in the trek – the valley of Lauterbrunnen. For Tolkien as for Bilbo, this was 'the very edge of the Wild'.[8] He recalled, 'We went on foot carrying great packs practically all the way from Interlaken, mainly by mountain paths, to Lauterbrunnen and so to Mürren and eventually to the head of the Lauterbrunnenthal in a wilderness of morains.'[9] In *The Hobbit*, the party travels through a stony upland until the valley

opens beneath their feet – perhaps a recollection of the view from Mürren to the west. From this hamlet on a terrace high above, the valley is reached by the kind of 'steep zig-zag path' that remains etched on Bilbo's memory.[10]

Lauterbrunnen is a half-mile (0.8km) span of woods and meadows between glacier-carved limestone cliffs rising up to 1,500 feet (457m). Many glacier-fed streams fill it with the sound of water, tumbling in seventy-two falls to join the White Lütschine in its rocky bed.

Tolkien stated his debt to Lauterbrunnen in the echoic names of the river of Rivendell, *Loudwater* and *Bruinen* (see p.105, Rivers, Lakes and Waterlands). Six pictures of Rivendell, perhaps

ABOVE Key points and sights during Tolkien's visit to Lauterbrunnen at the age of nineteen.

OPPOSITE *Rivendell Looking East*, one of several Tolkien illustrations in which features of Lauterbrunnen can be clearly discerned.

Rivendell.
looking East

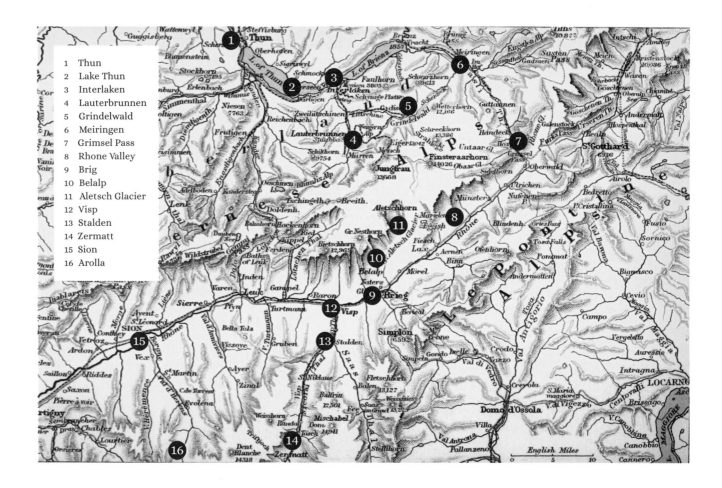

1 Thun
2 Lake Thun
3 Interlaken
4 Lauterbrunnen
5 Grindelwald
6 Meiringen
7 Grimsel Pass
8 Rhone Valley
9 Brig
10 Belalp
11 Aletsch Glacier
12 Visp
13 Stalden
14 Zermatt
15 Sion
16 Arolla

culminating in the exquisite painting for *The Hobbit*, capture an impression of the Swiss valley, reshaped and reshaped again.[11]

The skyless world

Indeed, the Lauterbrunnen area seems to have offered a superfluity of inspiration.

The name of the head of the Lauterbrunnen valley, *Stechelberg*, means 'Holly Mountain'. Despite an absence of hollies now, as Denis Bridoux points out, it may have been sufficient to suggest Eregion or Hollin, the land at the feet of the Mountains of Moria (see p.129 panel, Tree-woven Lands). Certainly there is a literary echo of one (at least) of the mountains, probably as seen from the high ridges of the Scheidegg as the party hiked from Lauterbrunnen east to Meiringen. Tolkien recalled seeing the Eiger and Monch on their right, and his pangs at leaving behind the Jungfrau, 'eternal snow, etched as it seemed against eternal sunshine' as

well as its northern outlier, the Silberhorn, 'sharp against dark blue: the *Silvertine (Celebdil)* of my dreams.'[12] The Silvertine, with the Redhorn (Caradhras) and Cloudyhead (Fanuidhol) comprise the Mountains of Moria.

Caradhras, with its sheer snowless precipices 'dull red as if stained with blood', appears a poetic rather than geological edifice. Red sandstone erodes too easily to create high mountains, and even the red-granite Red Cuillins on Skye off Scotland are low and gentle hills.[13]* There is an Alpine *Rottalhorn* beside the Jungfrau and a *Rothorn* near the Matterhorn – 'red horns' perhaps simply for the way they catch the light of dawn or sunset. As for Caradhras's cruelty, Denis Bridoux points to the 1936 tragedy that killed four climbers on the north face of the Eiger (often nicknamed 'the Ogre'). As *The Times* reported, in the morning guides found all four hanging from ropes – one killed in falling, a second dragged down with him and strangled by the rope, a third frozen to death. The fourth had lived only long enough

Staging posts on the
Swiss trek. The route
can be traced reliably
by number as far as
Belalp; beyond that
accounts differ.

to recount these terrible events, before dying of exposure just out of reach of rescue.[14]

Tolkien's memory may have returned to Lauterbrunnen again in *The Lord of the Rings* for Harrowdale and the River Snowbourn beneath the mountain retreat of Dunharrow in Rohan. With Merry at Harrowdale, Tolkien again contrives to bring a hobbit observer suddenly to the brink of a 'great valley in the gloaming below'.[15] His thoughts on the road are delivered in a breathtaking passage vivid with experience:

> *It was a skyless world, in which his eye, through dim gulfs of shadowy air, saw only ever-mounting slopes, great walls of stone behind great walls, and frowning precipices wreathed with mist. He sat for a moment half dreaming, listening to the noise of water, the whisper of dark trees, the crack of stone, and the vast waiting silence that brooded behind all sound.*[16]

Dunharrow has been compared by Christina Scull and Wayne Hammond with Mürren, on its high western terrace reached by a switchback bridle path. Marie Barnfield prefers Wengen on the opposite and eastern side of the Lauterbrunnen valley, which the party would have hiked en route to the Kleiner Scheidegg.

Harrowdale is dominated by three peaks again – the saw-edged Írensaga, the Starkhorn and the Dwimorberg, the Haunted Mountain that conceals the Paths of the Dead. But Tolkien's drawings of the Starkhorn – a pyramid with apex sheer-faced and skewed – are remarkably like the Matterhorn.[17] He only saw that mountain much later on the journey, a black horn beyond 'the dazzling whiteness of the tumbled snow-desert'.[18]*

It is very possible that Tolkien knew a famous account of supposed ghost encounters on the Matterhorn itself, by A. F. Mummery, first to scale it via the Zmutt ridge. Mummery recounts how, climbing by a different route, 'we were surrounded by the weird, unearthly flicker of innumerable will-o'-the-wisps' that appeared to shadow their every move. One of the terrified Swiss whispered,

'Look, sire, the dead people!' and all evidently felt that 'the fiends who haunt the crags of the Matterhorn were already gloating over their prey'. Local church authorities attested that anyone seeing such a ghost would certainly die within a day.[19]* Though this sounds more like the Dead Marshes (see pp.165–6, Places of War) than the Paths of the Dead, it attests to local superstitions of a haunted mountain.

The Alps surely outweigh a claim by Tolkien's friend George Sayer – perhaps based on a mishearing – that the White Mountains of Rohan were inspired by the Malvern Hills.[20] But the name *Dunharrow* is derived, like *Harrowdown* in Oxfordshire, from the Old English for 'heathen temple on a hill'.

Snow, storm and avalanche

The next leg of the Swiss journey carried the walkers from Meiringen over the Grimsel Pass to the Rhone valley. The party eschewed using the 'diligences' (stage coaches) and local railways, and the valley road to Brig was a memory of dusty fatigue for both Tolkien and Colin Brookes-Smith, at twelve the youngest traveller. From this point, aided by a map marked by a senior companion, he recorded the itinerary in a later memoir which hugely supplements and partly contradicts Tolkien's admittedly hazy recollections as to route.[21]* A notable memory is of Tolkien striking an attitude atop a high pass and declaiming, 'Hannibal crossing the Alps with one eye and a mackintosh.'[22]

Above Brig, they were photographed on the Aletsch glacier. At Belalp, a village beside the glacier, Tolkien and others dammed a stream, then broke the dam so a torrent rushed down to the inn below. It is tempting to see here the inspiration for the Ents' damming of the River Isen (see pp.170–1, Places of War), but Tolkien recollected that 'the beaver game … had always fascinated me' before this point.[23]

However, we have Tolkien's own word that two other incidents inspired the Misty Mountains

THE MOUNTAINS OF PARADISE

For the final stretch to Interlaken, the Swiss adventurers would have taken the train or boat from Thun. Denis Bridoux suggests that this ancient lakeside town was an inspiration for Tûn, Elvenhome's capital in *The Book of Lost Tales* – Tirion upon the hill of Túna in *The Silmarillion*. *Thun* is pronounced just like Elvish *Tûn*.

The Swiss town, with its white-walled medieval castle, stands in a valley between two Alpine ranges, on a hillside just above a lake. Tolkien's white-towered elven town, situated in the deep Calacirya (Quenya, 'Pass of Light') that cuts through the Pelóri or Mountains of Valinor, stands on a hill above the Bay of Elvenhome.[1]

Any similarity of name must be a late afterthought, however. In *The Book of Lost Tales*, Tolkien first called his town *Kôr* and intended the byname *Tûn* as Old English ('enclosed dwelling', origin of modern *town* and *-ton*).[2*] Philologists trace the Old English name to unrecorded Germanic *tŭno-* or *tŭna-*, and theorize a link with Celtic *dûnum* 'hill, fort'. So when Tolkien eventually decided *Tûn* or *Túna* was the Elvish for 'hill, mound', it looks as if he wanted to furnish a fictional origin for those Germanic and Celtic words.[3*] Celtic *dûnum* is the source for Swiss *Thun*.

Behind the barrier mountains of the Pelóri stand venerable sources. Classical Greek tradition speaks of a paradise, Hyperborea, at the back of the north wind behind a huge mountain range. John Mandeville places his eastern Earthly Paradise – the highest place on earth – beyond 'great crags and mountains' and a vast wall running from north to south.[4]

The similarity of Valinor's holy mountain Taniquetil to the Greek Olympus hardly needs stating, though it is the seat only of Manwë and Varda, not the full pantheon of Valar. Manwë, Lord of the Breath of Arda (the world), who sits atop Taniquetil attended by the eagle Thorondor, seems indebted to Mudjekeewis, 'ruler of the winds of Heaven' in Longfellow's *Song of Hiawatha*, in his high Rocky Mountains seat with his war-eagle Keneu.[5]

adventure in *The Hobbit*. One was a 'thunder-battle' while the party slept in a cowshed having lost the route.[24] The other was during a long tramp led by guides up a glacier – which Tolkien recalls as the Aletsch but which seems likelier to have been the Arolla, further south in the French-speaking Valais region. They were walking with a ravine at their left when the effects of the melting midday sun suddenly became apparent. Tolkien recalled, 'We were nearly annihilated, when strung out on a narrow path with a long snow slope to the right, down which boulders came thundering through our line: one of at least a ton missed me by a foot.'[25] On the same day, as it seems, Tolkien would have fallen into a crevasse in the snow if the party had not been roped together.

The Alps may or may not be the inspiration for a painting, *The Misty Mountains*, apparently made long before the Middle-earth mountain range was conceived.[26*] The evocative alliterating English phrase 'misty mountains' can be found in nineteenth-century descriptions of heights in Scotland, North America and Switzerland – though I wonder just how misty the high Alps actually where when Tolkien saw them in sunny 1911.

When first used at the start of *The Hobbit*, 'the misty mountains' is a description rather than a name. Indeed, given that Tolkien originally set this story in the lands of the *Silmarillion* (see pp.122–3, Tree-woven Lands; 169, Places of War), we might well wonder whether in the first typescript he meant the dwarven song line about 'the misty mountains' to refer to the Shadowy Mountains that fence Hithlum, Land of Mist.[27*]

Tom Shippey argues that *The Hobbit* adapts the name from lines in the Old Norse *Lay of Skirnir*,

> *úrig fiöll yfir*
> *þyrsa þióð yfir*

which he translates as 'over the misty mountains, over the tribes of orcs' (comparing Old English *orcþyrs* 'giant').[28*] However that may be, Tolkien's Misty Mountains are certainly a barrier befitting the hostile world of the Germanic imagination (see p.30 panel, Four Winds), rife with orcs and their demonic wolf companions whose Germanic name, *warg*, suggests not only 'wolf' but also 'felon' or 'monster'.

Another likely inspiration comes from the North American Rockies, as imagined in Longfellow's *Song of Hiawatha* – certainly an influence on other matters (see pp.35–36, Four Winds; 102–3, 109, Rivers, Lakes and Waterlands). The three-day mountain-top clash between Hiawatha and Mudjekeewis,

Gandalf duels with
the Balrog on the
peak of Celebdil in
a scene reminiscent
of *Hiawatha*.

while 'the Keneu, the great war-eagle' screams from
his eyrie, echoes in the Battle of the Peak between
Gandalf and the Balrog, on Celebdil's 'dizzy eyrie',
from which the Lord of Eagles rescues the spent
wizard.[29] Both fights seem like natural thunderstorm
and end in a vastness of rock tumbling to ruin.

II. FIERY MOUNTAINS

A 1961 interview provides a fascinating insight
into Tolkien's method:

> *'This is how I work:' And he throws binders on
> the floor in front of my feet; maps, sketches, a
> photograph of the latest eruption of volcano Hekla
> ('Such things interest me'), talented watercolours,
> tables that have helped him keep track of the
> multitudinous characters and events in his story,
> schemes showing the movements of armies on a
> battlefield.*[30]

Among drafts and workings that evidently relate
to *The Lord of the Rings*, the Hekla photograph
leaps out.

In a passage about his early taste in reading,
Tolkien refers to 'the tormented hills' as an object
of imaginative longing.[31] The earliest plot outline
for the legendarium features 'a great mountain
island' reminiscent of volcanic Tenerife or Madeira
(see pp.62, 65, The Shore and the Sea).

The interest extended into *The Lord of the Rings*,
where the Númenórean tower of Orthanc appears
to be 'riven from the bones of the earth in the
ancient torment of the hills'.[32] It sounds like a
volcanic plug, where hardened magma in a vent
has resisted the erosion that wears away the softer
stone of the surrounding cone. No doubt Tolkien
knew of various volcanic plugs, such as the one on
which Edinburgh Castle stands. One that might
have especially caught his attention is Borgarvirki,

which plays a part in an Icelandic 'lost tale'.
Heiðarvíga Saga (the Saga of the Heath-slayings)
tells of an eleventh-century blood feud that was
brought to an end by an unlikely hero, Bardi.
There is a gap in the text at the crucial point, so
that exactly how Bardi wins the feud is known
only by later tradition (confirmed by archaeology)
– he built and successfully defended a fortress,
Borgarvirki, on top of a forty-five-foot (14m) plug.
Archaeologist W. G. Collingwood called it 'a castle
almost ready made … with vertical walls of well-
marked basalt pillars … so that assault must have
been impossible even at the weakest points'.[33]* All
this is true of the much more impressive Orthanc
(see pp.142–3, Ancient Imprints).

The catastrophic island eruptions of Tambora
in 1815 and Krakatoa in 1883 were part of the
imaginative background when Tolkien was young.
The 1902 eruption of Pelée, on Martinique in the
Caribbean, must have caught his imagination, and
it also features in an influential book he owned from
the 1930s. This is J. W. Dunne's *An Experiment with
Time*, which contends that dreams can sometimes
offer visions of other times and places.

Dunne recalls an 'unusually vivid' 1902
dream in which he finds himself on 'the upper
slopes of some spur of a hill or mountain' from
which vapour was jetting through small fissures.
Realizing it was an island from previous dreams,
now in danger from a volcano, he gasps, 'Good
Lord, the whole thing is going to *blow up!*'
Recollecting Krakatoa, the dreaming Dunne
decides he must get the 4,000 inhabitants off the
island in ships, but his efforts are maddeningly
frustrated. The day after his dream, the *Daily
Telegraph* announced the eruption of Pelée,
estimating 40,000 dead and reporting that ships
were now removing survivors to nearby islands.[34]*

Verlyn Flieger argues persuasively that Dunne's
book offered Tolkien 'the ideal mechanism by
which to effect time-travel without magic or
machinery' when he was writing *The Lost Road*, the
unfinished 1937 time-slip novel about Númenor.[35]
More than that, I would say, the Pelée dream
offered Tolkien the scenario of a volcanic island
cataclysm witnessed by a modern observer who
is powerless to help. In *The Lost Road*, latter-day
teenager Audoin Errol dreams about 'the great
temple on the mountain, smoking like a volcano',
then 'a whole land slipping sideways, mountains
rolling over'.[36] Though he does not understand,
he is seeing Númenor's central mountain, the

Meneltarma, topped by Sauron's temple to Morgoth, before the destruction of the whole island (see p.78, The Shore and the Sea).

When Tolkien returned to his Númenor story in the mid-1940s, with *The Notion Club Papers*, similar dream visions afflict Oxford academics loosely based on Tolkien's own Inklings. In a trance, one of them proclaims, 'Behold, the mountain smokes and the earth trembles!'[37] Another writes a poem in which St Brendan the Navigator (see p.34, Four Winds) sees the sole remnant of Númenor, the Meneltarma – a volcano rising sheer from the sea:

> *then the smoking cloud asunder broke*
> *and we looked upon Mount Doom:*
> *tall as a column in high Heaven's hall,*
> *than all mortal mountains higher,*
> *the tower-top of a foundered power,*
> *with crown of redgold fire.*[38]

Tolkien removed the name *Mount Doom*, which already belonged to the volcano in Mordor in his larger work-in-progress, *The Lord of the Rings*. Yet there can be no doubt that now he wanted to suggest a series of parallels between ruined Númenor, Mordor and Morgoth himself. This is clear from a description – written when *The Lord of the Rings* was newly completed – of the rebel Vala on first entering the world, appearing 'as a mountain that wades in the sea and has its head above the clouds and is clad in ice and crowned with fire and smoke'.[39]

The back gate of hell

A claim that Tolkien identified the Italian island volcano Stromboli as the inspiration for Mount Doom appears to be hearsay.[40]* At most, Stromboli went into a large melting pot. Given his tastes, Tolkien can hardly have missed Jules Verne's 1864 science-fiction classic *Journey to the Centre of the Earth*, in which adventurers descend into a subterranean world through the cone of Mount Snæfellsjökull in the west of Iceland and are ejected by Stromboli in eruption.[41]

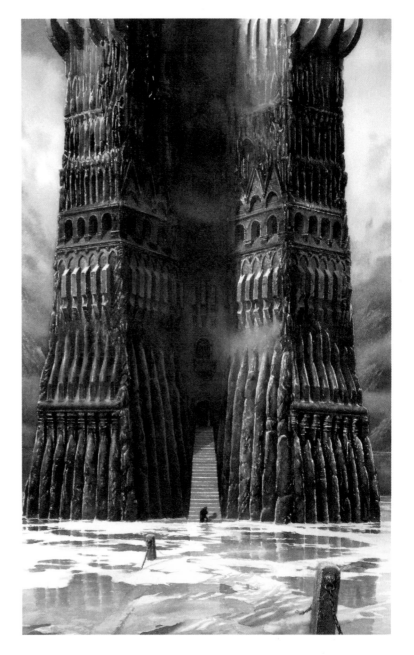

Volcanoes further afield may loom over the Middle-earth imagination, too. Tolkien's pictures of the Lonely Mountain in *The Hobbit* make it look as volcanic as Mount Doom, and Michael Organ has observed that both demonstrate his 'fondness for isolated mountain peaks in the Mount Fuji style'.[42] Tolkien admired and owned Japanese prints, which are so often dominated

Orthanc, seemingly the product of 'the ancient torment of the hills', as depicted by Alan Lee.

by Fuji. As a sufferer of recurrent dreams about a land-devouring wave (see pp.76, 78, The Shore and the Sea) he must have been struck especially by Hokusai's iconic *Great Wave off Kanagawa*, in which Fuji is central. Meanwhile it has also been suggested that the Lonely Mountain's Elvish name *Erebor* was 'subconsciously influenced' by Mount Erebus in the Antarctic, first climbed in 1908 with news fanfare.[43]* I cannot imagine the similarity escaping his notice.

But the volcanoes of Iceland were a particular interest. A 1927 letter to his children from 'Father Christmas' describes flying in his sleigh over Iceland – but quickly, because his reindeers 'always say they are frightened a volcano or a geyser will go off underneath them'.[44] By this time, Tolkien was an expert on Icelandic sagas and the family had an Icelandic au pair.

By this time, too, he had described how rivers of fire from Morgoth's Iron Mountains turn the green plain at their feet into ashes in the Battle of Sudden Flame (see p.169, Places of War); and he had devised their chief 'thunderous mountain' Thangorodrim.[45] In an outline a few years later for the *Lay of Leithian*, 'great fires and smokes burst from Thangorodrim' as Beren and Lúthien escape from Morgoth's stronghold beneath the mountain.[46] With Lúthien comforting the wounded Beren until eagles scoop them to safety, the scene strikingly anticipates Frodo and Sam on Mount Doom.

'Such things interest me.' Iceland's Hekla erupts in 1947. Tolkien kept such a photo in his writing files.

But Mount Doom itself brings us back to the photograph of 'the latest eruption of volcano Hekla', shown by Tolkien to the 1961 interviewer. The latest eruption had actually been several years earlier, running for thirteen months to April 1948 – the very year that Tolkien finally brought Frodo through Mordor to Mount Doom.

At the outset in March 1947, *The Times* reported that Hekla was 'belching smoke six or seven miles into the sky in what appears to be a major eruption – the first for 102 years'. Up to four inches (10cm) of ash fell in twelve hours, according to this and other *The Times* reports.[47] The lava travelled in slow, broad streams, but with some large gouts hurled much further and faster. But Hekla, with 'a character of desolation hardly paralleled anywhere else', had laid waste to its surrounding region centuries previously, covering the land with 'a thick layer of lava and pumice cinders'. In former centuries Icelanders had called Hekla 'the back gate of hell'.

Readying himself to describe both the desolation of Gorgoroth (see p.167, Places of War) and the climactic eruption of Mount Doom, Tolkien can hardly have missed such vivid contemporary witness. Even when a writer or artist knows in the abstract what needs to be created, a touchstone like this can make all the difference. An airline pilot's photograph of the Hekla eruption dominated a page of *The Times* three days after it began. Perhaps this is the very image that Tolkien had kept, squirrelled away ahead of the crucial Mordor chapters.[48]

Tolkien's unforgettable image of 'a huge shape of shadow, impenetrable, lightning-crowned, filling all the sky' as seen from the Black Gate of Mordor is not the ash plume of Mount Doom but the spirit of defeated Sauron.[49] It has been likened to the smoke from a Great War artillery shell (see p.165, Places of War). But in scale it is more like Hekla's 'enormous mushroom of smoke, fire, ash and cinders', visible across most of Iceland, and (*The Times* said) reminiscent of the 1946 Bikini Atoll atomic test explosions.

III. WORLD-BUILDING

'There are lands of the imagination that cannot exist, but seem real,' writes natural historian Richard Fortey, 'and there are lands that once existed that somehow seem remote and hard to credit. Perhaps their comparative solidity depends on the hand of a skilled writer.'[50] There is indeed a curious kinship between fantasy world-building and the scientific reconstruction of prehistoric supercontinents like Pangaea and Gondwanaland. The kinship is even closer in Tolkien's case because his fantasy world is supposed to be our own in a prior era (see p.43, The Land of Lúthien).

'Having geological interests, and a very little knowledge, I have not wholly neglected this aspect,' Tolkien said when he began to receive requests for geological maps of *The Lord of the Rings*.[51] In fact, Tolkien's mythological version of world-building had altered over the years as he began to bring it more into line with developments in geological science.

An interest in geology appears as early as 1914–15 in *The Tides*, or *Sea Chant of an Elder Day*, first inspired at St Andrews, Scotland (see p.62, The Shore and the Sea). In 1912, Tolkien had sketched the town from across the bay at Kinkell Braes, sitting – like the figure in the poem – 'on the ruined margin' of the sea. Just as in the poem, the land here has been

besieged for ever in an aeon of assaults
And torn in towers and pinnacles and caverned in
great vaults...[52]

The shore beneath the Braes is so twisted, slanted and fault-riven that decades earlier it was the focus of a special excursion by pioneering scientists including Sir Charles Lyell, so-called father of geology (and a predecessor of Tolkien's at Exeter College, Oxford).[53]* Kinkell Cave delves beneath, deep and roomy. Maiden Rock, a sandstone stack beside the stony beach, has endured the battery of ages. Past the headland of Kinkell Ness, the tidal rocks are the light, porous tuff of solidified volcanic ash. Here stands the Rock and Spindle, a thirty-foot (9m) tower of

For all his medieval and mythological tastes, Tolkien was fascinated by the geological discoveries first mapped by William Smith in 1815, above, and exemplified in his own lifetime by the emerging theory of continental drift.

solidified magma (the Rock) with what looks like a rugged stone wheel in its lap (the Spindle).[54]*

In one of his last touches to the sea poem (1917), Tolkien set it in primeval days,

*When the world reeled in the tumult as the
Great Gods tore the Earth
In the darkness, in the tempest of the cycles ere our
birth . . .*[55]

These are *geological* cycles – an idea from nineteenth-century science, not myth.[56]* The impression of vast ages is in line with the new understanding that the world is many orders of magnitude older than 4004 BC, the standard date of creation as calculated on biblical evidence (still being stated as fact as late as the 1870s).[57]*

Tolkien fuses myth and science, presenting geological processes as the actions of divine or supernatural powers. The world is crafted in beauty by the Valar, particularly Aulë the Smith. The satanic Melkor (Morgoth) violently disrupts their patterns and symmetries, as here in *The Book of Lost Tales*:

Beneath the very floors of [the sea god] Ossë he caused the Earth to quake and split and his lower fires to mingle with the sea. Vaporous storms and a great roaring of uncontrolled sea-motions burst upon the world… The sea leapt upon the land and tore it, and wide regions sank beneath its rage or were hewn into scattered islets, and the coast was dug into caverns.[58]

This early conception of a world remodelled in short, sudden episodes of violence matches one nineteenth-century theory of geological change, *catastrophism*.

Other geologists, notably Lyell, thought the world was shaped by uniformly slow processes still ongoing – a school of thought called *uniformitarianism*. While Tolkien always kept a major role for catastrophe, Gerard Hynes has noted how the alternative conception becomes visible in his writings from the 1930s onwards.[59] The *Ambarkanta* (Quenya, 'Shape of the World')

The Rock and Spindle, one of the volcanic features at Kinkell Braes in Scotland, visited by Tolkien at twenty.

says that the Earth 'has changed ever in the wearing and passing away of many ages'.[60]

At the same time, Tolkien made the Valar the agents of a geological process akin to continental drift, by which vast landmasses move across the Earth's surface. The *Ambarkanta* tells how 'the Valar thrust away Middle-earth and crowded it eastward... And the thrusting aside of the land caused also mountains to appear...'[61] This is very striking, because the theory of continental drift had only been proposed in 1915 by Alfred Wegener and remained hugely controversial until the 1960s.

But Tolkien was a newspaper reader and his interests were always (as he said) 'largely scientific'.[62] His abiding passion for lost worlds would surely have drawn him to a headline like 'Gondwanaland: A lost southern continent' in *The Times* of 1929, on an article with an early description of continental drift (Tolkien once called *Gondwana-land* 'that rare venture of geology into poetry').[63] Another report on continental drift, referring to the 'wandering of the pole', seems to have caught his eye in 1931.[64] A letter the following year to the Tolkien children from 'Father Christmas' says he has heard there was a 'time, long ago, when the North Pole was somewhere else', though he does not know whether it is 'nonsense or not'.[65]

Tolkien's supremely skilled hand gives Middle-earth such verisimilitude that quite a few geologists have been able to use current scientific theory to analyse its landforms. For example, similarities between the Great River Anduin and the Rhine (see p.111, Rivers, Lakes and Waterlands) extend deep into their geomorphology. The occurrence of highlands like the Emyn Muil beside lowlands like Nindalf, says geologist Mitch Liddell,

> is typical of 'horst and graben' structures created when the Earth's crust is locally stretched so that some portions drop, leaving other areas relatively high. Rhovanion has pulled away from Eriador, and the widening wound marking this is the impressively linear Anduin River. Germany and France, today, are undergoing a similar pulling apart, creating the Rhine river valley.[66]

Explorations like this can certainly be educational for non-scientists, and Tolkien would probably have been delighted to know that geology can indeed explain many of the features on his maps.[67]

IV. CAVES

Tolkien's stories are simply full of holes, caves, tunnels, hollow hills and underground cities and palaces. Inspirations seem to run from archaeology (see pp.134–6, Ancient Imprints) to folklore (see pp.34–5, Four Winds) to the troglodyte experience of the Great War trenches (see pp.163–4, Places of War).

Describing an underworld of the dead, Tolkien joins a venerable line of mythographers, from the Epic of Gilgamesh to Homer's *Odyssey*, from Virgil's *Aeneid* to Snorri Sturluson's *Prose Edda*. When Aragorn, the returning king, leads an army of the dead from underground to turn the tide in a battle for the nation's survival, Tolkien rewrites the tradition of the knights of King Arthur, the once and future king, sleeping beneath stone until their country calls them. In taking the drama so

often into goblin-infested mines, Tolkien followed a childhood favourite, George MacDonald's 1872 *The Princess and the Goblin*. He liked the idea so much that his letters from Father Christmas contrive to put goblin caves beneath the north polar ice.

But beneath Isengard, the machinery and the Uruk-hai – more human and terrible than mere goblins – probably owe more to the 'dark Morlocks tending their machines' in H. G. Wells's *The Time Machine*.[68] Tolkien first put a giant spider underground – in Shelob's Lair – after reading 'with some pleasure' another science-fiction thriller, Joseph O'Neill's 1935 *Land Under England*.[69] O'Neill's hero stumbles into an underland where his first encounter is with a giant spider 'with a pair of bulging bag-like bodies … supported by several stilt-like legs' which emanates a stench and produces entrapping silk with a noise of 'chuckling and slobbering'.[70]

One extraordinary piece of description comes directly from experience – Gimli's account of the Glittering Caves of Aglarond behind Helm's Deep. Tolkien told a reader, 'the passage was based on the caves in Cheddar Gorge and was written just after I had revisited these in 1940 but was still coloured by my memory of them much earlier before they became so commercialized.'[71]

The caves around Cheddar, tunnelled by rainwater and subterranean streams in the Carboniferous limestone of the Mendip Hills, were a wonder in Tolkien's childhood. One complex extending more than two miles (3km) was opened up by Richard Gough and his sons from 1892 to 1898. Half a mile (0.8km) of this became a show-cave lit by electricity, with areas dubbed the Swiss Village, St Paul's, Solomon's Temple and Aladdin's Cave. Visiting on their honeymoon in 1916, Tolkien and Edith probably saw this and the neighbouring Cox's Cave, described in one book as 'a gem of fantastic architecture, embellished with the most lawless and fairy-like designs of the subterranean artificer'.[72]

A recurrent note in writing on Cheddar's caves is that they are indescribable. But through

Cox's Cave, part of
the Cheddar Gorge
underworld that
inspired the Glittering
Caves of Aglarond.

Tolkien, they may have inspired the description of Thingol and Melian's palace, the Thousand Caves of Menegroth (see p.131 panel, Tree-woven Lands), created by elven craft but with lantern-lit pillars 'hewn in the likeness of the beeches of Oromë, stock, bough, and leaf', and 'fountains of silver, and basins of marble, and floors of many-coloured stones'.[73] By proxy through Aglarond, the caves of Cheddar awake the poet in the taciturn Gimli as he evokes the colours, the crystals, the columns; the fluted forms and endless avenues; the mirrored images of many pinnacles… 'And plink! a silver drop falls, and the round wrinkles in the glass make all the towers bend and waver like weeds and corals in a grotto of the sea.'[74]

Both of these descriptions postdate the Tolkiens' second, 1940, visit. In the 1930s, Gough's Cave was being advertised in newspapers in New York and Paris. The Marquess of Bath, already owner of Cox's Cave, had acquired Gough's Cave and installed new visitor buildings in 1934. Two years later, visitors had soared by more than one-third, to 273,000. The Gough families' industrious excavations, and the later commercialization of which Tolkien complained in his letter, seem to colour Legolas's rather knee-jerk response to Gimli's effusions. With a typically elven perception of dwarves as greedy materialists, he warns his friend not to tell his dwarven kinsfolk because 'one family of busy dwarves with hammer and chisel might mar more than they made'.[75]

RIVERS, LAKES AND WATERLANDS

The inland waters of Middle-earth are nature's sanctuaries and sacred places, the sites of towns and towers, and way stations, obstacles or conduits for travel. They run with the thought of the Vala Ulmo, Lord of Waters; and the tiniest rill can refresh the spirit, even in the desert of Mordor. When Beleriand is destroyed, perhaps the saddest line is that 'Sirion was no more'.[1]

Some rivers literally have personality – a resident spirit. Others get their individuality from a breath of description, a line on the map, a mysteriously evocative name. A few are carolled more fully. At Lake Ivrin,

> newborn Narog,   nineteen fathoms
> o'er a flickering force   falls in wonder,
> and a glimmering goblet   with glass-lucent
> fountains fills he   by his freshets carven
> in the cool bosom of the crystal stones.[2]

The verse flows on to describe Narog's course and confluence with the great Sirion until their conjoint waters reach the Sea.

For the inspirations behind Tolkien's writings, rivers are a rich but cautionary symbol. Our word *influence* comes from the Latin for 'flowing in', and one influence is likely to mingle with others to make something both new and protean.

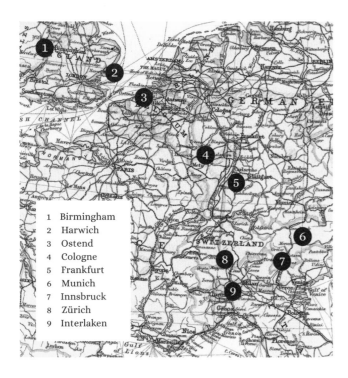

1	Birmingham
2	Harwich
3	Ostend
4	Cologne
5	Frankfurt
6	Munich
7	Innsbruck
8	Zürich
9	Interlaken

ABOVE Tolkien's route to Switzerland.

Spring, spate and gorge

When Ivrin emerged as above in the *Lay of the Children of Húrin*, Tolkien was living in Leeds, and it is tempting to think that he took inspiration from Yorkshire rivers and waterfalls. But as far as we know, Ivrin has the purest of origins, as a celebration of natural beauty and its healing powers. It is here that Túrin Turambar, stricken dumb by a mortal guilt, is restored to sense and speech (see p.172, Places of War). In later versions of the saga, Túrin returns to Ivrin after much further grief has befallen him; but he finds no healing. The lake has been defiled by the dragon Glaurung.

Sources can be confidently identified for other rivers or falls in Túrin's saga. The 'merry stream that came singing out of the hills' of Hithlum past his childhood home is Nen Lalaith, 'Laughing Water' in Sindarin Elvish. People name his younger sister *Lalaith* after it, because of the sound of her laughter. This motif is familiar from Longfellow's *The Song of Hiawatha*, in which the hero's wife Minnehaha, 'Laughing Water', is named after the waterfall beside her home. Tolkien attended a performance of Samuel Coleridge-Taylor's haunting cantata adaptation *The Death of Minnehaha*

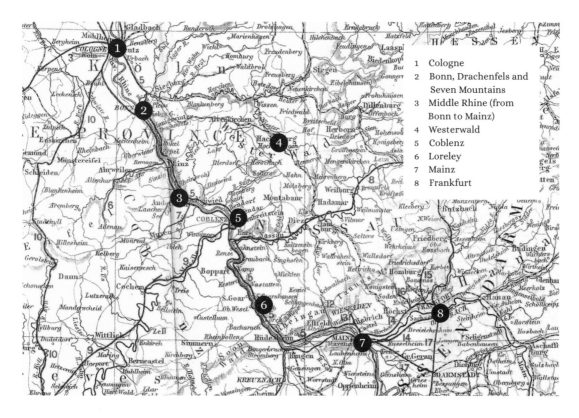

1	Cologne
2	Bonn, Drachenfels and Seven Mountains
3	Middle Rhine (from Bonn to Mainz)
4	Westerwald
5	Coblenz
6	Loreley
7	Mainz
8	Frankfurt

LEFT The 1911 steamboat voyage along the Rhine Gorge, a land of legend.

in 1912. Lalaith dies in a mysterious pestilence, and so does Minnehaha, crying out that her waterfall is calling her.

Túrin has another sister, Nienor or 'Mourning', whose eventual fate is bound up with a waterfall. This one harks back to the 'furious foaming cataract' into which Kullervo's sister plunges in the Finnish *Kalevala*, Tolkien's primary inspiration.[3] In the Túrin saga, Nienor has previously been overcome by an inexplicable shivering at the waterfall, whence its name, *Nen Girith* or 'Shuddering Water'. Clearly, Tolkien named the *Kalevala*-inspired Nen Girith and the Longfellow-inspired Nen Lalaith as an ironic and tragic mirror images.

But Túrin's climactic battle with the dragon was inspired by the Germanic Sigurd or Siegfried (see pp.24–6, Four Winds), linked in German tradition with the Rhine. Tolkien and his brother Hilary travelled there in 1911 on the way to Switzerland (see p.84, Roots of the Mountains). Having taken the ferry to Ostend, Belgium, and the train to Cologne, Germany, the English party steamed up the Rhine by boat from Mainz to Frankfurt – a two-day voyage unless they alighted at any of the thirty halts. From level plain, the riverboat entered a land where (as a contemporary book put it) 'every crag and valley on either bank, and every island from Bonn to Mainz has its two or three deep layers of romance'.[4]

The ruin-topped Drachenfels, one of the Seven Mountains at the gateway to this landscape, is reputedly the lair of the dragon slain by Siegfried. South and upstream at Coblenz, the Rhine enters its famous gorge, halfway through which it loops around a precipitous mass of stone, the Loreley. Here, the modern legend runs, a maiden spurned in love leapt to her death – becoming the Lorelei, a siren who fatally tempts unwary sailors onto her rock.[5*] There is no gorge in either the Sigurd-Siegfried story or the *Kalevala*, so Tolkien's impressions of the Rhine probably helped shape the Taiglin or Teiglin river gorge, setting for Túrin's dragon-slaying and Nienor's suicide.

The story of the Rhinegold also has its parallels in Middle-earth. Crude comparisons between *The Lord of the Rings* and Wagner's *Der Ring des Nibelungen* irritated Tolkien, but he knew it and had no qualms about borrowing its motif of the treasure that brings misfortune until it is sunk deep in water. Glaurung's hoard is ultimately cast into the River Ascar, renamed *Rathlóriel*, 'Goldenbed'. In *The Hobbit*, the gems studding Smaug's underside end up beneath the Long Lake.

Switzerland, Tolkien's 1911 destination, left a profound impact on Tolkien's mountains and valleys (see pp.83–90,

CASTLE AND CARROCK

Much like the Rhine, as Denis Bridoux has pointed out, is the course of the Sirion into Beleriand through 'a narrow vale, whose sheer walls were clad with pines' and which is guarded by fortresses at the source and upon Tol Sirion.[1] In a passage written for the *Lay of Leithian* in 1928, this island stands

> *like a stone*
> *rolled from the distant mountains vast*
> *when giants in tumult hurtled past.*
> *Around its feet the river looped*
> *a stream divided, that had scooped*
> *the hanging edges into caves.*[2]

The Carrock devised for *The Hobbit* in the early 1930s also has a riverside cave, stands 'right in the path of the stream which looped itself about it', and is compared to 'a huge piece cast miles into the plain by some giant among giants'.[3] Geologists would call this an erratic, a stray rock that nature has transported from far away. So physically it matches what its name is linguistically – a Celtic word (related to Welsh *carreg* 'stone') that has strayed into northern English dialect to mean (among other things) a stone boundary marker.

Tolkien also considered calling it the *Lamrock*, perhaps an Elvish-English hybrid for 'echo-rock'. That may indicate the inspiration of the Loreley, which the 1911 Baedeker interprets as 'rock ("Lei") of the "Luren", or mountain-imps who raise the teasing echo.'[4*] By the time he drew the Wilderland map, Tolkien certainly visualized the Carrock as an island; but the text, written earlier, does not specify whether the river 'looped itself about it' on both sides or just one.

The Lord of the Rings has its own 'Great Carrock', as drafts call it – Tol Brandir, in Nen Hithoel, above the falls of Rauros.[5]

Bilbo comes to the Huts of the Raft-elves

Bilbo Comes to the Huts of the Raft-elves,
from *The Hobbit*, is Tolkien's most
evocative river-picture.

Roots of the Mountains) and on the river of Rivendell. Together the river's English and Elvish names, *Loudwater* and *Bruinen*, clearly echo *Lauterbrunnen*, the name of the valley that inspired Rivendell – as David Masson first pointed out.[6] Marie Barnfield notes how the Bruinen flows through the elven dale in the same course that the White Lütschine takes through the Alpine valley; and joins another stream just below, as the White unites with the Black Lütschine.[7]*

But the sudden spate that unhorses the Black Riders at the Ford of Bruinen may sweep us right back into Tolkien's Sarehole childhood. In rain, the swollen headwaters of the usually quiet little River Cole (see p.13, England to the Shire) can run rapidly off the clay soil. Men and horses were swept away in several tragedies below Greet weir until a bridge was built in the eighteenth century. A little upstream, the tiny ford nearest Sarehole is also prone to flash floods. Bob Blackham, who also grew up in the area, believes it would have permanently impressed Tolkien as a small boy.[8]

Imagine Tolkien's delight at being able to raise his own children near another quiet river. The Cherwell is not liable to flash floods (although it can certainly flood slowly); rather, it winds lazily among reeds and willows a stroll away from Northmoor Road, where they lived from 1925 until the boys had all grown and left home. In those days, before the nearby Marston Ferry Road and the bypass beyond were built to ease traffic in central Oxford, the river was a green strip of tranquillity to Wood Eaton (see p.127, Tree-woven Lands) and beyond. During walks, Michael would hide in the crack of an old riverside willow. During a picnic, he tripped over a willow root and his father had to leap into the river in his best tennis flannels to haul him out.

By 1931, the Cherwell (and an echo of Michael's escapades) had filtered into a poem, *The Adventures of Tom Bombadil*. The mysterious but comical hero is sung to sleep and shut in a crack by Old Man Willow, and later yanked into a river by 'the Riverwoman's daughter', Goldberry. But all ends happily as Bombadil subdues Willow-man and other perils (see pp.139–41, Ancient Imprints) and marries Goldberry.

The roots of Old Man Willow reach deeper than the 1920s. As a student, Tolkien had suffered from what he called the 'Oxford "sleepies"' – a drowsiness often associated with its river-valley atmosphere – until 1914, when morning military drill drummed it out of him (see p.148, Watch and Ward).[9] In his 1916 poem *The City of Present Sorrow*, Oxford's

The River Cherwell, inspiration for the willow-meads of Nan-tathren in *The Silmarillion* and the Withywindle in *The Lord of the Rings*.

wartime alertness and sacrifice (see pp.148–9, Watch and Ward) seem all the more praiseworthy for the willows that droop about the sluggish Cherwell and the old Thames under its 'coverlet' of leaves.[10] After the Battle of the Somme, 1917's *The Fall of Gondolin* embodies this drowsy ambience in the Land of Willows on the Sirion, visited by the hero Tuor (see p.62, The Shore and the Sea):

> *willows of untold age were about its borders, and its wide bosom was strewn with waterlily leaves… Now there dwelt in these dark places a spirit of whispers, and it whispered to Tuor at dusk and he was loth to depart…*[11]

Yet there are concealed signs of war, for 'beneath the willows the green swords of the flaglilies were drawn, and sedges stood, and reeds in embattled array'.[12] This is philological wordplay. Sedge is a grassy, sharp-edged plant, and the word comes from Old English *secg*, which also meant 'sword' or 'warrior'. But perhaps Tolkien's ability to visualize in double exposure came into effect here, for the Ancre, where he had fought the previous year, was also a sluggish, willow-lined river. The divine Ulmo personally has to summon Tuor out of his apathy into duty. For all its sublimity, this scene foreshadows how, on the banks of the somnolent Withywindle, Bombadil frees the hobbits from Old Man Willow's power so they can resume their quest.

If Bombadil is meant to be the spirit of the Oxfordshire-Berkshire countryside as Tolkien said (see p.17, England to the Shire), Goldberry and her mother must be the spirits of its rivers. British folklore has several river-women, including the spirit of the Tees in Yorkshire, Peg Powler, described by an early folklorist as 'a sort of Lorelei, with green tresses, and an insatiable desire for human life', who likes to drag people underwater and drown them.[13] Tolkien's friend Elizabeth Wright (see p.73, The Shore and the Sea) names several Northern and Midland variants – Jenny Green-teeth, Grindylow and Nelly Long-arms. Goldberry seems a laughing cousin to these, dunking Bombadil for mischief, not malice.

John Bowers has compared her with Sabrina, thought to be an ancient embodiment of the River Severn, whom Milton pictures sitting underwater 'in twisted braids of lilies'.[14]* In *The Lord of the Rings*, where Goldberry sits enthroned among waterlilies and sings a 'rain-song' as it pours outside, she might indeed be a local water deity – though the hobbits are too commonsensical to see it that way.[15]

Similarly halfway to divinity is Nimrodel, the Silvan elf who once lived beside the stream of the same name. Near the Nimrodel waterfall, 'almost Frodo fancied that he could hear a voice singing, mingled with the sound of the water.'[16] Tolkien briefly called this river the Taiglin, like the one into which Nienor vanishes – an association that perhaps seeded the idea of the very different tragedy of Nimrodel (she disappears in the mountains en route to a tryst with her lover).[17]

The confluence of the Trent with (upper right) the Sow at Great Haywood. In *The Book of Lost Tales*, Tolkien reimagined the two rivers as the Gruir and Afros.

RIVERS OF WAR

Tolkien wrote *The Fall of Gondolin* in Great Haywood, at the confluence of the Sow and Trent. The two rivers appear in his contemporary writings as thresholds between safety and danger. In his 1917 poem *The Grey Bridge at Tavrobel*, evidently about his reunion with Edith after battle, a 'damozelle' laments that her man has been away beyond these 'two rivers running fleetly'.[1] Tavrobel is Great Haywood itself (see p.49, The Land of Lúthien), with its grey Essex Bridge, a narrow seventeenth-century packhorse bridge just below the confluence. In notes for the ending of *The Book of Lost Tales*, the rivers are called Afros and Gruir (Gnomish *grui*, 'ferocity, horror'). The fading Elves and their mortal friend Eriol flee across the bridge from the Battle of the High Heath (see p.167, Places of War). The 'Brook of Glass' winding down from the heath – surely the pretty Sher Brook (Old English *scír* 'bright') – is 'fouled with the war of men'.[2]

Before locating the Battle of Unnumbered Tears on Anfauglith (see p.168, Places of War), Tolkien originally envisaged it being fought in 'the Valley of Weeping Waters' near or on the River Sirion.[3] This might be equated with the Land of Willows or the neighbouring 'Pools of Twilight' (Nan-tathren and Aelin-uial in *The Silmarillion*). Either way, memories of the Ancre and the Battle of the Somme may be discerned, pointing ahead to the Dead Marshes (see pp.165–6, Places of War).

RIVER-NAMES

River-names in Britain can be very ancient and appealingly enigmatic to philologists. The Elvish word *nen*, seen in *Nen Girith*, *Nen Hithoel*, *Núrnen* and many other Middle-earth names, seems to have been invented to fill a gap in English place-name history. A lost Celtic word of that shape lies behind the Nene (sometimes pronounced and spelt *Nen*), which runs from Northamptonshire to the Wash. Tolkien mentions 'the winding Yare and Nen' in a 1920s version of his poem *The Man in the Moon Came Down Too Soon* – among the many references to the English region that he removed for his 1962 Middle-earth verse collection *The Adventures of Tom Bombadil*.[1] It looks as though Tolkien invented his Elvish *nen* as a fictional source for England's river-name *Nen* or *Nene*, just as his poem was meant to 'explain' a nursery rhyme.

Tolkien made sure that Middle-earth place-names also contained obscure elements, such as *lim-* in *Limlight*, name of an Anduin tributary. Yet here again he was perhaps thinking of a real river-name – the Lim that gives its name to Lyme Regis, where he holidayed (see pp.71–2, The Shore and the Sea). This *Lim* is thought to be from the same ancient British word as Welsh *llif* 'flood, stream'.

In many cases the meaning of a river-name (often generic) may be little guide to influence. Warwick's Avon, which gets its name simply from the Celtic word for 'river' (Welsh *afon*), is renamed 'the River Gliding' in Tolkien's poem *Kortirion among the Trees*. But Tom Shippey explains the name *Withywindle* as dialectal *withy* 'willow' plus Old English *windol* 'winding brook', which (he suggests) Tolkien also believed to be the original meaning of Oxford's *Cherwell*.[2*]

Jason Fisher notes that the River Poros (Sindarin, 'boundary'), scene of historic battle on the border of Gondor and Harad, is a soundalike for Greek πόρος, which is both 'a means of passing a river; a ford or a ferry' and 'a narrow sea, strait'. He argues that Tolkien was influenced by the Bosphorus, dividing Europe from Asia.[3*] But the medieval legends of Alexander the Great, which fascinated Tolkien (see pp.40–1, Four Winds), also had a Poros or Porus with associations befitting the Haradrim. This Indian king resisted invasion so bravely at the River Hydaspes in 326 BC that Alexander made him a satrap (local ruler). Alexander's forces 'captured four hundred elephants, on whom were there stood armed archers, and the elephants carried towers and platforms, on which the mail-clad warriors stood'.[4]

Her stream is a threshold to elven Lothlórien, paired with the Silverlode, and so recalls other rivers on the brink of Faërie – the Narog, Esgalduin and Forest River, on the doorsteps respectively of Nargothrond, Menegroth, and the hall of the elven-king of Mirkwood. But the two rivers of Lórien, encountered soon after the loss of Gandalf in Moria, have been compared with the stream in the medieval poem *Pearl*, which Tolkien translated. Beyond this lies a vision of heaven and the healing of grief.

The name *Silverlode* was perhaps suggested by the lovely-sounding Evenlode, which runs into the Thames in Oxfordshire.[18*] In place-names, *lode* usually means 'watercourse' or 'path', and Tolkien translates *Silverlode* into Elvish *Celebrant* 'silver-course'. But in modern English, *lode* more familiarly means 'a vein of mineral ore'. So the name of this river, born in the Mountains of Moria, inevitably brings to mind the 'lodes' of *mithril* or truesilver that Gandalf describes in his potted history of the mines there.[19]

Pool, marsh and flood

At Titterford millpond (now Trittiford), one mile (1.6km) up the River Cole from Sarehole, young Ronald and Hilary Tolkien would make whistles from the reeds that stood in ranks on one shore. Hilary once fell in the reed pond but 'wasn't even scolded', so relieved was their mother by his survival.[20] We are close to the world in which the hobbit-like Sméagol grew up with his friend Déagol, making little reed boats in the Gladden Fields (English *gladden* 'iris') beside the Great River Anduin. It seems that to depict Sméagol's fall into evil as Gollum, Tolkien reached back to his own paradise lost.

In the Shire, the fertile lowland of the Marish (archaic English 'marsh') is a region of managed bogs with dikes and a causeway to carry the one main road. During his army duties in 1917–18, Tolkien lived in the midst of such a region, Holderness in Yorkshire. Marishes Road Station, serving the hamlets of High and Low Marishes, is on the railway network that Tolkien would have used travelling to Holderness and also to Whitby in 1910 and Filey in the 1920s (see pp.70–1, The Shore and the Sea). Meanwhile, lowland Holderness itself (see pp.76–7, The Shore and the Sea; 138, Ancient Imprints) is home to Hornsea Mere, near where Edith lived for a while in 1917. With a heronry, and island nests for mallard, water rail, coot, pochard and great crested grebe, it is a small-scale version of reed-forested, bird-thronged Linaewen in *The Silmarillion*.

The busiest station on another branch of the Yorkshire rail network towards Holderness was Wetwang. Its name is all that connects this village with the 'wide region of sluggish fen' where the Entwash flows into Anduin.[21] If he ever visited, Tolkien would have been struck by the distinct lack of wet in this *wang* (Old Norse *vangr*, 'field') atop a chalk ridge fifty feet (15m) above the streamless chalk valleys. It is a comfortable walk from the highest views over the Yorkshire Wolds. The dry-as-dust origin for *Wetwang* seems to be a Norse legal term for a 'field of summons for the trial of an action'.[22] As the great etymologist W. W. Skeat once obstinately declared in the face of

such evidence, 'Wet's wet, and Wang's a field, and there you are.'[23] The colossal Middle-earth marsh, elvished unambiguously as *Nindalf* 'wet field', is a Wetwang that Skeat would have appreciated.[24]

With the Midgewater Marshes east of Bree – home of the maddeningly noisy Neekerbreekers – Tolkien again adapted a place-name freely from its real-world use. The name, as he told a correspondent, is a straight translation of Mývatn, a place mentioned in the Icelandic sagas. Tolkien added that he was familiar with Iceland's landscapes through photographs, so presumably he knew that Mývatn is not a marshland but a volcanic lake.[25]

It can hardly be doubted that the Somme-haunted Dead Marshes east of this (see pp.165–6, Places of War) take a literary colouring from Longfellow's description of Hiawatha's night voyage towards battle, through a nightmarish waterland ruled by the evil spirit Megissogwon:

that sluggish water,
Covered with its mould of ages,
Black with rotting water-rushes,
Rank with flags and leaves of lilies,
Stagnant, lifeless, dreary, dismal,
Lighted by the shimmering moonlight,
And by will-o'-the-wisps illumined,
Fires by ghosts of dead men kindled,
In their weary night-encampments.[26]

The reeds of the 'dreary and wearisome' Dead Marshes rot perpetually.[27] When the will-o'-the-wisp 'candles of corpses' shine, the spectral images appear in the Mere of Dead Faces.[28] The lights have also been compared with the 'wonder grim, fire on the flood', visible at Grendel's mere in *Beowulf*.[29]

The pool at the West-gate of Moria certainly bears comparison with Grendel's mere, a gloomy place among 'highlands wolfhaunted … where the mountain-stream goes down beneath the shadows of the cliffs'.[30] The setting in the Old English poem inspired two line-drawings by Tolkien titled *Wudu Wyrtum Fæst* (Old English 'a wood clinging by its roots').[31] It is home to a 'monstrous upheaver of the waves' and other 'strange dragons of the sea' –

reshaped by Tolkien as the Watcher in the Water, a quasi-alien tentacled intelligence like the giant cephalopod that attacks the *Nautilus* in Jules Verne's *Twenty Thousand Leagues under the Sea*.[32]

Further west of Moria lies 'a network of swamps, pools, and eyots, where the only inhabitants were hosts of swans, and many other water-birds'.[33] The Swanfleet is strictly landlocked, where the River Glanduin meets the Greyflood. Yet its name is suggestive of a unique shoreland site that Tolkien doubtless knew and perhaps visited on his holidays to Lyme Regis (see pp.71–2, The Shore and the Sea). Abbotsbury swannery stands on the Fleet, an arm of the sea sheltered behind the long spit of Chesil Beach. 'Considerably more than a thousand swans may be seen in this oozy region of creeks and pools, and the spot is haunted by wild-fowl,' says a contemporary guidebook.[34] The swannery was established by medieval monks as early as the eleventh century.

We do not know where Tolkien travelled in Wales or whether he ever went to the Lake District, famously 'romantic' and relatively easy to reach by train. Who knows what small mountain lakes may shimmer faintly behind Mirrormere in *The Lord of the Rings*, or laughing Ivrin and blessed Tarn Aeluin in *The Silmarillion*. In Switzerland, Tolkien would have seen some memorable sights – Denis Bridoux notes the Wallensee, the Thunsee and finally, and 'mightiest of all', Lake Geneva or Leman as the train journey home would have run along it as far as Lausanne.[35] Swiss lake discoveries certainly inspired the prehistoric structure of Lake-town (see p.138, Ancient Imprints).

Great rivers

Tolkien's descriptions of the Swanfleet and Greyflood appear in his account of the often destructive incursions by the Númenóreans into the coastlands of Middle-earth in the Second Age. In the circumstances, his description of the seafarers' first expedition up the Greyflood is redolent of Joseph Conrad's description of the Congo in *Heart of Darkness* (1899). 'The forest drew down to the river-banks, and wide though the waters were the huge trees cast great shadows on the river, under which the boats of the adventurers crept silently up into the unknown land.'[36] But Tolkien's impressions of vast forest rivers probably derive from his readings about early European trade and exploration in the New World (see p.36, Four Winds). In her *Atlas of Middle-earth*, Karen Wynn Fonstad measures the Greyflood at 689 miles (1,109km) long, more than three times the length of Britain's longest, the Severn, and approaching Rhine size. As one guide says, 'on a European and global scale Britain's rivers are mere tiddlers', so the scale of continental rivers would have impressed the islander in Tolkien.[37]

The sheer Englishness of the Shire probably means Tolkien imagined its rivers no broader than English ones. Fonstad maps the Brandywine at roughly half a mile (0.8km) wide at Buckland, guessing it is 'possibly comparable to the upper Mississippi'.[38] This is like turning the Hill in Hobbiton into a small Alp. From source to Buckland, the Brandywine is about 175 miles (280km) long – like the Thames at Westminster, not the 1,200-mile (2,000km) upper Mississippi. I suspect even the Westminster width, 820 feet (250m), is more than Tolkien visualized. The Thames at Oxford or the Severn near Malvern in Worcestershire, less than 200 feet (60m) across, might seem quite wide enough to hobbit eyes. Intriguingly, a rejected *c.* 1950 passage says the Brandywine's older name was *Malvern*, supposedly a hobbit adaptation from Elvish *Malevarn* 'golden-brown' but transparently a nod to the English spa town or its hills, where Tolkien had walked with C. S. Lewis and his brother Warnie in August 1947.[39]*

Despite some mismatch in scale, it looks as if Tolkien wanted to trace the shape of the Severn (220 miles/350km) in the Lhûn (307 miles/494km). Each runs from western highlands (the Welsh Cambrians and Lindon's Blue Mountains) in a rough, sweeping semicircle east, south and then west to open into a wide gulf (the Bristol Channel and the Gulf of Lhûn). It supports the notion that elven Lindon, west of the Shire, somehow reflects the Celtic west of Britain (see pp.57–9, The Land of Lúthien).

The Severn was certainly featured, however briefly, in Tolkien's earliest concepts for the Lonely Isle of the Elves, when the island was actually meant

A foggy Thames at Oxford. Such rivers, rather than continental giants like the Mississippi, doubtless shaped Tolkien's view of the Shire's streams.

to be Britain. An early note applies *Sirion* to the Severn, altered from the Trent.[40] Britain's third-longest river, the Trent flows from Staffordshire moorlands through the English Midlands to join the Humber Estuary, via Great Haywood and Gedling – where Middle-earth began (see p.27 panel, Four Winds). But Tolkien emended this early note again to make *Sirion* the Rhine – evidently now visualizing it on the continental mainland.

At 1,388 miles (2,234km), the Great River Anduin is much longer than any Tolkien had seen. Shippey sees shades of *The Last of the Mohicans* in the boat journey from Lothlórien to Rauros-falls, on canoes that must be manhandled along on an old portage-way past rapids. For the same features and the great delta, Christina Scull prefers the Nile, in keeping with

the ancient Egyptian elements in Tolkien's Gondor (see p.143, Ancient Imprints). Geologists, meanwhile, have suggested the Rhine as a geophysical model for the Anduin – apparently without knowing Tolkien had travelled on it in Germany (see p.84, Roots of the Mountains). His memories of the 1911 Rhine voyage surely played their part, especially where the river enters the ravine at the Emyn Muil.

Yet by the time Anduin has reached the Great Sea, its mighty waters have gathered strength from all the tributary lands that Tolkien created, with their vast and various histories of migrations, settlements, wars, uprootings and resettlements. This is how the many wellsprings of inspiration intermingle to create something new and irreducibly itself – the Great River of Middle-earth.

TREE-WOVEN LANDS

A deep feeling for trees is Tolkien's most distinctive response to the natural world. As a child, he drew them and he liked to be among, beside or up them. Forests are places of wonder, or of wandering, even in his very earliest writings.

One of his very first poems, *Wood-sunshine*, is a 1910 vision of 'sprites of the wood'.[1] *The Story of Kullervo*, adapted from the Finnish *Kalevala* in 1914, takes us into the boreal 'blue woods' of Karelia, Finland.[2] A faëry 'shadow-folk' move unseen in the highland beechwoods of *A Song of Aryador* (the legendarium's first description of mortal lands), a mystery to the men gathered around campfires down in the valley.[3] The imagery of this 1915 poem, written at an army camp in Staffordshire, seems likely to have come from Tolkien's immediate environment – the whispering bracken of Whittington Heath and the nearby hilltop beeches of ancient Hopwas Hays Wood.

The 'tree-woven lands' of Tolkien's own imagination are places of liberty and entrapment, refuge and terror.[4] They can renew the spirit or weigh it with autumnal cares. Increasingly, they stand for nature itself, and against the axe and furnace. Tolkien seeded them from the forests of adventure yarn, fairy-story and philology, the woods of childhood play and adult rambles, and the potent myth of a world once blanketed in green.

Childhood woods

Tolkien's first, childhood taste of forest atmosphere was in a 'wonderful dell' with orchids, mushrooms and gigantic blackberries, outside Birmingham. He and his brother Hilary named it *Bumble Dell* after a local dialect word for blackberry, but it may have been Moseley Bog, which still survives. This had once been an artificial pool feeding the nearby mill, but had been drained and allowed to run back to wilderness.[5] It was a place to contemplate nature, to make a world without grown-ups and to play. Moseley Bog, next to the village of Sarehole that inspired the Shire (see pp.12–13, England to the Shire), is often said to have inspired the Old Forest in *The Lord of the Rings*. But such a primal place as Bumble Dell probably had a deeper and more

pervasive influence on Middle-earth's forests. Other inspirations will be uncovered, too, for the Old Forest.

At Sarehole, the Tolkien brothers would climb a sycamore and hoist up a basket of treats. The wooded Lickey Hills near Rednal had made tree-climbing a highlight for the boys during their mother's final convalescence in 1904 – the swansong of their rural childhood outside Birmingham, brought to a sudden end by her death (see p.15, England to the Shire). In Tolkien's later stories, climbing a tree brings relief from danger or oppression. Thorin and company scramble up pines to escape goblins and wargs. The Fellowship take refuge for the night in Lothlórien's mallorn-trees. Even Gollum, imprisoned by the Wood-elves of Mirkwood, is allowed to climb a high tree to feel 'the free wind'.[6]

It is tempting to see a genuine memory behind one highly specific, sensuously delightful moment in *The Hobbit*. The dwarves, desperate to know how far Mirkwood extends, send Bilbo up a huge oak to peer above the forest canopy. Bilbo sees the green treetops all around him 'ruffled here and there by the breeze; and ... everywhere hundreds of butterflies'.[7] Bilbo pauses until recalled to the 'real business' by the impatient dwarves, and the plot resumes. *Hobbit* historian John Rateliff suggests this may be a memory from Oxford, though childhood is perhaps likelier.[8]*

THE KING'S OAK

In such an English and tree-ish book as *The Lord of the Rings*, it pays to pay attention to oaks, England's most iconic trees. The oak has been held sacred in many cultures. An oak can live a thousand years as long as its branches are pollarded, cut back to promote a dense regrowth of lighter and more useful timber. It makes the tree a natural symbol of royalty and continuity. Bilbo's rhyme about Aragorn applies equally to the oak:

> *The old that is strong does not wither,*
> *Deep roots are not reached by the frost.*[1]

When Frodo and company creep inside a huge hollow Shire oak, it recalls the traditional English saying, 'fairy folks are in old oaks'. But the hobbits have been spooked by their first encounter with a Black Rider, and this points to another English tradition, known to Tolkien since childhood.

Near their home stood a huge oak tree where Charles II reputedly hid from the Roundheads, Hilary Tolkien recalled. The same has been said of many trees along the young king's escape route after defeat at the Battle of Worcester in 1651. All these legends are inspired by the fact that Charles did take refuge up an ancient oak at Boscobel in Shropshire, while Parliamentarian patrols searched beneath all afternoon.[2]*

The Royal Oak became part of the landscape of the English imagination; it is still Britain's third-commonest pub name. The 29 May anniversary of King Charles's 1660 return to his capital was kept for two centuries as a public holiday. Even when Tolkien was writing, people still remembered wearing oak sprigs to celebrate.

The king's secret journey had special resonance for Catholics like Tolkien. Viciously persecuted under Oliver Cromwell's Puritan regime, Catholics provided several of the hiding places on Charles's escape route, including Boscobel's oak. His only hope – like Frodo's – was to travel in secrecy with few companions. *The Lord of the Rings* is not about Charles II, of course. But Tolkien listed 'the hidden King' among 'several deeply-rooted "archetypal" motifs' used in the story.[3]

Frodo and Sam later take refuge in a holm oak, when they come to the end of the woodlands of Ithilien. A Mediterranean species, it is suited to

the warmer climate there, but holm oaks are now naturalized in southern England, and several grew in Oxford's University Parks, a fifteen-minute stroll from Tolkien's front door in Northmoor Road. The holm oak in Ithilien seems another descendant of the Royal Oak. This chapter ends memorably at the Cross-roads below Morgul Vale when Frodo sees flowers growing around the fallen stone head of a royal Gondorian statue (see pp.143, Ancient Imprints; 162 Places of War). 'Look! The king has got his crown again!' he exclaims.[4]

The wodewoses of medieval
English pageantry and heraldry
may be a folk memory of
outsider peoples living
reclusively in the wilds.

Woses, the name used among the Riders of Rohan for the Wild Men of Drúadan Forest, recalls an English tradition of mysterious woodland denizens that probably long predates Robin Hood.

Tom Shippey believes that Tolkien would have pondered it when sitting in his Leeds University office in Woodhouse Lane, named after a former village nearby (swallowed up, like Sarehole, by urban sprawl). In heraldry and in medieval pageantry, *woodwoses* or *woodhouses* are wild men of the woods: reclusive and dangerous outsiders clad in little more than their own shaggy hair. So the Leeds place-name *Woodhouse* may preserve 'old belief in "the wild men of the woods" lurking in the hills above', says Shippey.[1]*

The hero of the Middle English poem *Sir Gawain and the Green Knight* goes through the wildernesses of north Wales or north-east England fighting *wodwos*, which Tolkien's 1925 edition with Leeds colleague E. V. Gordon translates as 'wood-trolls'.[2] Further back, in Anglo-Saxon literature, they are *wudewásan*. Tolkien suspected that Old English *wása*, 'a forlorn or abandoned person', pointed towards 'the actual existence of wild folk, remnants of former peoples driven out by invaders, or outlaws, living a debased and savage life in forests and mountains'.[3]

The intriguing scenario is brought to life when the Anglo-Saxonesque Riders of Rohan meet a representative of the Woses or Wild Men, most archaic human society in Tolkien's legendarium writings. They are archers who move unseen, 'remnants of an older time ... woodcrafty beyond compare' – but comparable indeed to Longfellow's Hiawatha, or Uncas in James Fenimore Cooper's *The Last of the Mohicans*.[4]

But Drúadan's culture draws from truly far-flung forest societies. The long-distance talking drums recall West Africa or New Guinea. The grass skirt worn by chieftain Ghân-buri-Ghân perhaps suggests Pacific island cultures. Poisoned arrows, like those the Wild Men reputedly use, are fairly universal. Tolkien would have seen similar items whenever he stepped inside Oxford's astonishing showcase of anthropology, the Pitt Rivers Museum.

Greenwood liberty

As an adult, Tolkien found heart's ease in the beauty and tranquillity of woodlands. When academic work weighed heavily, he sometimes wished he were in the woods rather than poring over the printed page. In a long essay reviewing many hundreds of pages of philological essays and books, he began with a quotation: 'It is merry in summer "when shaws be sheen and shrads full fair and leaves both large and long". Walking in that wood is full of solace. Its leaves require no reading.'[9] *Shaw* means 'wood', *sheen* here is 'bright' and *shrad* is 'glade'.

The lines, from the medieval ballad of *Robin Hood and Guy of Gisborne*, point to the idea of the greenwood as a realm of liberty. In English culture, the epitome of greenwood liberty is Nottinghamshire's Sherwood Forest, where the noble outlaw Robin and his 'merry men' resist the tyranny of King John. But the true origins of the Robin Hood legend may be far older than the reign of this thirteenth-century monarch.

Tolkien planted Middle-earth with several Robin-style Sherwoods. Barahir in *The Silmarillion* leads Beren his son and eleven other men as outlaws under the greenwood tree in

Dents Garth, the wood at Roos, Yorkshire, where Edith Tolkien inspired the story of lovers Beren and Lúthien in 1917.

Morgoth's forces in the *Lay of Leithian* before escaping to Doriath.

Doriath

The heartwood of Middle-earth is a glade in Roos, Yorkshire. Here, as if in a vision, Edith Tolkien danced for her husband among a froth of white flowers in summer 1917. He had just been declared fit after a bitterly cold winter recovering from trench fever caught in the Battle of the Somme. Now, put in charge of a garrison outpost, he had been able to bring Edith there to live with him, and they had a few brief weeks of happiness amid the sorrows and burdens of war. Trench fever returned and Edith, by then six months pregnant, left for Cheltenham, her old home town in Gloucestershire, to have the baby among friends. But Tolkien, left behind at Brooklands Officers Hospital in Cottingham Road, Hull, turned that moment at Roos into a fairy-story that has outlived them: the story of Beren and Lúthien.

As *The Silmarillion* puts it, Beren flees enemy-occupied Dorthonion by paths of nightmarish horror (see p.172, Places of War). Then, 'grey and bowed as with many years of woe', he reaches Neldoreth, Doriath's northward forest of beeches. There he glimpses the elf-princess Lúthien dancing among 'hemlocks'; her song releases nature from 'the bonds of winter' and frees Beren from his 'spell of silence'.[12] Tolkien left no clearer example of life transformed into myth. The names *Beren* and *Lúthien* are on the headstone he and Edith share in Wolvercote Cemetery, Oxford.

Hemlock here has nothing to do with either the poison or the North American hemlock pine. As Tolkien's favourite book from youth observes, 'Country people are in the habit of calling by the name of *Hemlock* many species of umbelliferous flowers.'[13] One species, also called cow parsley or Queen Anne's lace, riots every summer in a small

Dorthonion, ambushing and undermining a superior enemy. So does Faramir in Ithilien, the 'garden of Gondor' on the very border of Mordor.[10]* Barahir and Faramir also love the woodland in its own right, fighting to protect it from being swallowed up and ruined by the enemy.

No doubt Dorthonion, Ithilien, Doriath and Lothlórien – indeed all Tolkienian haunts of stealthy woodsmen and lethal archers – owe at least as much to a childhood enthusiasm for tales of 'Red Indians'. Tolkien loved these stories for their forests, among other things (see pp.35–6, Four Winds); he said they gave him 'a wholly unsatisfied desire to shoot well with a bow'.[11] He exercised that desire vicariously through Legolas of Mirkwood, and through lone bowmen like Beleg of Doriath in *The Silmarillion* or Beren, harrying wood beside Roos church called Dents Garth, as I learned while reconnoitring the area for *Tolkien and the Great War*. Michael Flowers has since suggested Tolkien was splicing other aspects from Dents Garth into his Beren and Lúthien story. Notably, a tall and venerable tree has three trunks like Hírilorn, the beech in which Lúthien is imprisoned by her father King Thingol; and a stone escutcheon displays a disembodied hand, like the heraldic device of Beren, whose hand is shorn off by a gigantic ravening wolf.[14]

However, Doriath's literary roots extend far further than personal memory, through Arthurian and other medieval romance into the deep subsoil of Celtic legend. In his elven forest-kingdom, outsiders lose themselves while supernatural hunting horns sound in the green distance, like they do in the Middle English *Sir Gawain and the Green Knight* and *Sir Orfeo* (which Tolkien translated) and in the tale of Pwyll son of Pryderi, part of the Welsh *Mabinogion*.

Lothlórien

Springing to life apparently without prior planning in 1941, Tolkien's most famous faëry treescape had actually been rehearsed in his earliest.

Scholars have long pointed out Lothlórien's debt to medieval visions of paradise – notably to the silver-leaved, heavenly land in *Pearl*, a Middle English poem that Tolkien revered and exquisitely translated.[15] There are overall resonances with the lost realm in the Henry Rider Haggard romance *She* (see pp.136, Ancient Imprints; 154, Watch and Ward). Meanwhile, the *flet* or tree-house of Galadriel and Celeborn, with its tree trunk through its midst, recalls the more earthbound hall of the Germanic Volsungs, built around a living tree, the Barnstock. Tolkien had described it in his own retelling of the story of Sigurd the Volsung:

> *tall and branching,*
> *that house upholding,*
> *the hall's wonder;*
> *its leaves their hangings,*
> *its limbs rafters…*[16]

However, Lothlórien's most formative influence was surely the 1915 poem *Kortirion among the Trees*, a celebration of Warwickshire as 'the Land of Elms, Alalminórë in the Faery Realms' (see pp.48–9, The Land of Lúthien).[17]* The English elm, *Ulmus procera*, dubbed by one writer 'the quintessence of the English landscape', was a dominant feature of the county's fertile marl terrain.[18]

Lothlórien is a land of mallorn-trees, a species of Tolkien's own invention. He compared the mallorn to the beech – upright grey bole and perpendicular branches upswept at the tips – but he gave it the same massive majesty that he praised in the elm. In a punning piece of early language-invention, he had made *elm!* the Elvish exclamation for 'marvellous!'[19]*

But the mallorn stands for longevity, the very opposite of the elm. The mallorn does not suffer winter as other trees do: in autumn, its leaves turn gold, but they do not fall until spring, when its branches fill with golden flowers. English tradition associates the elm with transience and death. Its timber was used for coffins and ships' keels. It had a

Lothlórien with its mallorn-trees, depicted here by Tolkien, owes much to his early imaginings of Warwickshire, 'land of elms'.

The Forest of Lothlorien in Spring

Ethelfleda's Mound, at the western end of Warwick Castle, finds its way into *The Book of Lost Tales* and even *The Lord of the Rings*.

reputation for dropping branches without warning, and it was notoriously prone to disease, long before Dutch elm disease killed up to thirty million British trees in the 1970s. Mortality hangs heavily over *Kortirion among the Trees*, as might be expected from a poem written when Tolkien's generation was being cut down on the battlefields of France and Belgium (see p.160, Places of War).

In both Lothlórien and Kortirion, Tolkien visualizes the trees as ship masts. Lothlórien is 'a bright ship masted with enchanted trees'.[20] In summer, Kortirion's elms are like 'masts of verdurous ships' under full sail; but in naked winter they are 'like vessels floating vague' in the distance.[21] Perhaps in 1915 the long narrow island in the Avon below Warwick Castle, planted with trees by eighteenth-century landscape gardener Capability Brown, had brought the image of a masted ship to Tolkien's mind.

Lothlórien and Kortirion have a yet more striking arrangement of trees in common. In *The Book of Lost Tales*, Kortirion's elf-queen Meril-i-Turinqi lives on a hill among glorious elms in a circle of 'three lessening storeys of bright foliage'.[22] The inspiration for that hill, Ethelfleda's Mound in Warwick (see p.49, The Land of Lúthien), has no such ring, but across the Avon in Castle Park stood Lord Brooke's Clump, one of the many hilltop tree landmarks that enrich the British skyline.[23]*

Clumps or clusters of trees like this look timeless, though typically planted by eighteenth-century landowners for scenic reasons. Some actually stand on ancient sites, like the Seven Sisters beeches in the Quantock Hills, where Tolkien walked at least once, with fellow Inklings C. S. Lewis and Owen Barfield in 1937.[24]* The mysterious wizard-like figure in Tolkien's 1914 painting *Eeriness* walks below three prominent hilltop trees. In *The Silmarillion*, the Two Trees of Valinor stand on the green mound Ezellohar. Other people, too, have linked such clumps with unseen power. Alfred Watkins, in his 1925 book *The Old Straight Track*, argued that they marked Stone

Wittenham Clumps, by Paul Nash, typifies the British fascination with landmark tree clusters.

Age 'ley lines'. To artist Paul Nash (1889–1946), the beeches of twin Wittenham Clumps, on a Bronze Age site near Wallingford in Oxfordshire, seemed in his youth to be as significant as the Pyramids.

As a circle, Meril's hilltop clump in Kortirion resembles English tree formations like Chanctonbury Ring on the Sussex Downs. In *The Book of Lost Tales*, the shape is given a Quenya name: *korin*, 'a great circular hedge, be it of stone or of thorn or even of trees, that encloses a green sward' – a definition that links it with sacred Celtic and Germanic groves and even Neolithic henges (see p.142 panel, Ancient Imprints).

Meril and the *korin* of Kortirion are forerunners of Galadriel and her tree-city of Caras Galadhon. But the landmark at the very heart of Lothlórien is even more reminiscent of Meril's *korin* – Cerin Amroth (Sindarin *cerin* 'round enclosure'), a mound topped by a lawn within a 'double crown' of tree-circles.[25] Here, in a moment of vision, Frodo sees Aragorn as if made young again, speaking words of love to his betrothed, Arwen. In his memory as he wrote this, perhaps, Tolkien was with Edith in Warwick again, in the springtime of their younger days.

Mirkwood

Over the years, Tolkien's own writings became a trove of material to reshape for new uses, as with Kortirion and Lothlórien. But one of the most startling acts of reshaping was in the creation of Mirkwood for *The Hobbit*. It grew directly out of a different forest in *The Silmarillion*.

This Forest of Night first sprang into brooding life in *The Book of Lost Tales*, perhaps partly out of Tolkien's war experiences (see p.171, Places of War). But Tolkien gave the forest a fresh injection of Gothic horror in the *Lay of Leithian* in 1928, when he developed the Necromancer, a servant of Morgoth with extraordinary shapeshifting powers. After Beren and Lúthien drive him from his island fortress, formerly Tol Sirion (see p.103 panel, Rivers, Lakes and Waterlands), the Necromancer flees in 'a vampire shape with pinions vast … to Taur-na-Fuin, a new throne / and darker stronghold there to build'.[26]

The later *Silmarillion* calls it *Taur-nu-Fuin* ('Forest under Night') and describes its metamorphosis from greenwood Dorthonion. The Necromancer, of course, is the figure we know best as Sauron.

When Tolkien was working on the *Lay of Leithian* in 1928, vampires were back in vogue. Bram Stoker's late nineteenth-century novel *Dracula* had just gone viral thanks to a four-year run for its first real dramatization, by Hamilton Deane. But the stage action was confined to London, and this was a distinctly drawing-room Dracula, with no Transylvania, no 'mighty slopes of forest' carpeting the forbidding Carpathian Mountains. In the Necromancer, Tolkien created a villain with all the Gothic powers and attributes of Stoker's character – vampirism, necromancy, shapeshifting, wolf companions, a dark castle. The Necromancer's flight to build 'a darker stronghold' also gives him a vast, wild-forest domain.

Soon after, and no later than 1929, Tolkien began writing *The Hobbit*. Strange as it seems in retrospect, he initially set this story for his boys in the same region as the *Lay of Leithian*, not more than a century after its events (see p.44 panel, The Land of Lúthien). In the *Hobbit* manuscript, Bilbo learns that the Necromancer's 'castle stands no more and he is flown to another darker place'. As John Rateliff has pointed out in his *History of The Hobbit*, this is a clear echo of the lines from the lay quoted above. The 'darker place' can only have meant Taur-na-Fuin.

Before too long, Tolkien realized his children's story must be set in a region and later era of its own. Somehow the Necromancer must have moved in the long interim out of Taur-na-Fuin and into a different forest at least as vast and daunting. During a long pause for thought at the Eagles' eyrie in the Misty Mountains, Tolkien scribbled down 'Mirkwood'.[27]*

The name *Mirkwood* was no invention, and it belonged to a real place of mythic stature – a forest that had haunted the European imagination two thousand years ago.

Tolkien had read about the real Mirkwood at school in Julius Caesar's *Gallic Wars*, which uses its classical name, the Hercynian Forest. Caesar had heard that it would take sixty days to cross the forest from the Rhine eastward. The place was said to be home to bizarre creatures including various gigantic quadrupeds and (according to the naturalist Pliny) flaming birds.

To the Germanic peoples who lived north of the forest, it was *Myrkviðr*, forming a barrier to southward expansion as well as a contested borderland between the Germanic Goths and the Huns. Tolkien judged the Old Norse word *myrk* to be primordially 'weighted with the sense of "gloom"'.[28]

The old name was Englished as *Mirkwood* by nineteenth-century writers, notably William Morris, whose romance *The House of the Wolfings* – a favourite of Tolkien's after he bought it in 1914 – tells of a confederated Gothic tribe fighting the incursions of Rome into their homeland within the Germanic forest.

Tolkien had actually seen first-hand the western remnants of this same enormous central European forest. It was in 1911, in Germany and Austria, en route to Switzerland. From Cologne, the riverboat had steamed upriver with the tree-clothed Siebengebirge (Seven Mountains) and Westerwald on the left, and then onward through the Rhine Gorge to the fabled and equally green-clad Loreley rock (see p.103, Rivers, Lakes and Waterlands). By train from Frankfurt via Munich and then Innsbruck to Zürich, he would have seen further stretches. Oxford archivist Robin Darwall-Smith, who has made the same journey, tells me, 'German forests feel so much larger and thicker than English ones. It is quite something to see hills completely covered in trees – which I don't think we really see in England. For someone who clearly loved trees like the young JRRT, seeing all this from the Rhine must have made a very deep impression on him.'

FOREST OF THUNDER

In a 1933 lecture, Tolkien explores the etymology of the name *Hercynia*. He favours a derivation from the Indo-European *perqu* 'oak' (also the source of the Latin *Quercus* used for the tree genus). He observes links with the names of Perkúnas, the Baltic thunder god, and Fjörgyn, Thor's mother. Tolkien suggests that these etymological connections support the oak's symbolic connection with thunder, widely noted by scholars of comparative religion.[1]*

The same thunder association seems to underlie his description of the great forest in an unfinished poem from this period, *The Fall of Arthur*. King Arthur of Britain is leading an expedition against the pagan Germanic tribes:

> *Thus at last came they*
> *to Mirkwood's margin   under mountain-shadows:*
> *waste was behind them,   walls before them;*
> *on the houseless hills   ever higher mounting*
> *vast, unvanquished,   lay the veiled forest.*
> *Dark and dreary   were the deep valleys,*
> *where limbs gigantic   of lowering trees*
> *in endless aisles   were arched o'er rivers*
> *flowing down afar   from fells of ice....*
> *Cold blew the wind,   keen and wintry,*
> *in rising wrath   from the rolling forest*
> *among roaring leaves.   Rain came darkly,*
> *and the sun was swallowed   in sudden tempest.*
> *The endless East   in anger woke,*
> *and black thunder...*[2]

Over Arthur's head, implicitly, hangs a stark warning from history that reads: do not mess with Mirkwood. In AD 9, Germanic tribes in the Teutoberg Forest slaughtered three entire Roman legions and their auxiliaries. Rome's most notorious military defeat is also in the background in *The Hobbit* when Wilderland's Mirkwood engulfs the goblin escapees from the Battle of Five Armies.

Even after Tolkien had propagated his fictional Mirkwood like a vast cutting from the original Taur-na-Fuin, he deliberately entangled the two forests. So readers would not miss the connection, Taur-na-Fuin is given the byname *Mirkwood* in the version of the *Silmarillion* that he hoped to publish in the immediate wake of *The Hobbit*. A very late essay on *The Disaster of the Gladden Fields* does the opposite, giving Mirkwood in Wilderland the Elvish name *Taur-nu-Fuin*. The point is that both places are types of the primal forest made nightmarish by the malign influence of Sauron the Necromancer.

Yet Mirkwood, which virtually swallows Wilderland on the map, is vastly larger and more varied than the *Silmarillion* forest. Thrice the size of Taur-nu-Fuin and elven Doriath put together, it has room not only for the Necromancer's nightmare forest in the south and Thranduil's elf-kingdom in the north, but also for a greenwood margin of settled human habitation. Mirkwood is a portmanteau forest of forests.

With the elf-kingdom of Northern Mirkwood, *The Hobbit* explores a faëry forest much like Doriath, a pleasure ground for elves with a subterranean capital. But it is seen entirely from the perspective of outsiders – mortal intruders for whom it is alluring, alarming and perilous. Many debts to faëry lore are catalogued by Rateliff, or by Douglas A. Anderson in his *Annotated Hobbit*: the enchanted stream, fay folk

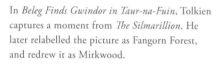

In *Beleg Finds Gwindor in Taur-na-Fuin*, Tolkien captures a moment from *The Silmarillion*. He later relabelled the picture as Fangorn Forest, and redrew it as Mirkwood.

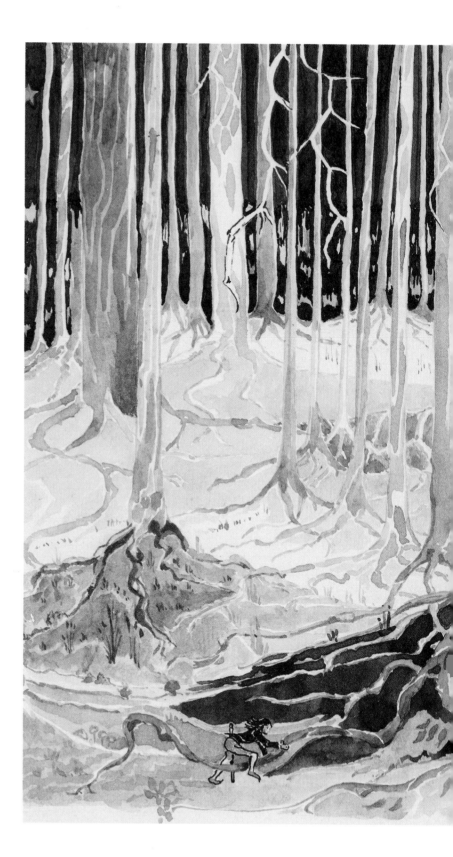

who vanish in the blink of an eye; elf-lights like misleading will-o'-the-wisps; fairy-rings to ward off evil; enchanted sleeps and delusive dreams; abductions into the hollow hills; fairy cavalcades hunting otherworldy white deer.

Spiders are another matter. They often spin their webs in Tolkien's nightmarish borderlands (see p.172, Places of War), but he put them in Mirkwood especially to 'thoroughly frighten' his son Michael.[29] In the north, where Bilbo encounters them, they are an invasive species from the Necromancer's region to the south.

Before the Necromancer's arrival and after his downfall, Mirkwood is Greenwood the Great – a name that marks it as a vast region of liberty. Even during his tenure, there is freedom and hospitality among the rolling lands of oak and elm at its fringes, home to the Woodmen and the people of Beorn. Tolkien only gives one of these settlements a name – *Rhosgobel*, Elvish for 'brown village' yet oakily echoic of Shropshire's *Boscobel* (Italian, 'beautiful wood'), where Charles II took refuge in his famous oak tree.

RADAGAST AND MEDWED

A small but nagging question in discussions of Tolkien's inspirations is why he would name Radagast, Gandalf's wizard cousin at Rhosgobel in Mirkwood, after an obscure Slavic deity, Radegast. It dates back to the manuscript version of *The Hobbit*, which also uses a Slavic name, *Medwed* ('bear'), for the hospitable shapeshifter whom Tolkien eventually renamed *Beorn*.

All this seems less mystifying if we consider the initial inspirational roles of *Dracula* and the ancient European forest. Slavic names would have pointed readers towards the forested Carpathian Mountains, home to Stoker's vampire and considered by some classical authors to be the eastward reach of the Hercynian Forest. Had Tolkien taken the scheme further, he might have unlocked a story for Radagast befitting his name, as he did for Beorn (Old English 'warrior' but originally 'bear') by making him half-man, half-bear. The naive dupe in *The Lord of the Rings* is almost certainly not what Tolkien originally had in mind for Radagast.

When he came to write the history of Mirkwood's greenwood fringes, Tolkien turned back to the European Mirkwood of medieval history and legend. He created the kingdom of the Northmen, ancestors to the Riders of Rohan, the Beornings and the Men of Dale alike. Their names are Gothic, and some of them – Vidumavi, Vidugavia – are attested in real histories of the Goths, a Germanic people who ruled a vast area in the fourth century. Their long-extinct language was one of Tolkien's first linguistic loves.

The dealings of the Northmen with Gondor recall the relations between the Goths and Rome. But their struggle with the Wainriders from the East echoes the bitter fourth- and fifth-century struggle of the Goths against the Huns.[30] Around the time he was writing *The Hobbit*, Tolkien had depicted the historical European clashes directly in a poem retelling the saga of the Volsungs:

> *By mighty Mirkwood*
> *on the marches of the East*
> *the great Goth-kings*
> *in glory ruled.*
> *By Danpar-banks*   [*Danpar*: the River Dnieper]
> *was dread warfare*
> *with the hosts of Hunland,*
> *horsemen countless.*[31]

The Old Forest

In December 1937, when *The Hobbit* had sold 1,500 copies, an article on current children's book trends in *The Times* newspaper declared that goblins, giants and scariness in general were out of fashion. 'All the rage' instead were cosy animal tales, like the New Forest pony story that had sold 18,000. If Tolkien saw the piece, he was undeterred. He was eager to scare his characters.

He adopted remarkably uniform scare tactics in the sequel just begun – *The Lord of the Rings* – and in *Farmer Giles of Ham*, which he was rewriting in the same weeks. In the revisions Tolkien now made to this short story, Giles faces 'dubious marches' rife with peril, 'dubious lands where legendary creatures were reputed to dwell'.[32] Writing the opening chapter of *The Lord of the Rings*, Tolkien placed the Brandybuck family home, Buckland, right next to 'the Old Forest – a dubious region'.[33*] He made it an invasive forest in conflict with its pioneer hobbit neighbours.

RIGHT Goths battle Romans in a third-century frieze. Tolkien recast the relationship in a more positive way with his Northmen (or Rohirrim) and Gondorians.

BELOW The Old Forest seems to have emerged partly from wordplay on two local Oxford names, Buckland and Wood Eaton.

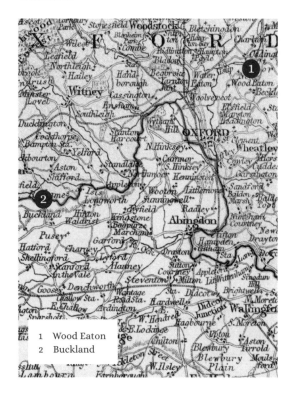

1 Wood Eaton
2 Buckland

Tolkien seems to have teased that idea out of topographical English names and words. He first named the hobbit settlement *Wood Eaton*, like the village just three miles (5km) from his Oxford home (see p.105), before switching to *Bury Underwood*, a name he concocted. Both are simply sinister puns on the idea of a village endangered by voracious woodland. *Buckland*, his ultimate choice for the area, is a common English place-name originating in a phrase from Anglo-Saxon property law. Tolkien adopted the Anglo-Saxon term *folkland* (land held in common and inalienable) for the old family areas of the Shire, such as Tookland. Anglo-Saxon *book-land* (land held by charter and therefore transferrable) was an innovation and the source of the many English *Buckland* place-names. Tolkien's Buckland is a new addition to the Shire; its name fits the Brandybuck surname, but also proclaims their land as a property claim, staked on a piece of the Wide World beyond the Shire's old borders.

The name of the Old Forest looks plain enough, but it is equally pregnant. *Forest* is from medieval Latin *forestem silvam*, 'the outside wood' (*forīs*, 'out of doors', *silva* 'wood'), referring to woodland that is not fenced in. The Old Forest is very emphatically fenced *out* by a strip of scorched earth and a high hedge, to deter the seemingly mobile trees from invading Buckland.

Meanwhile, the *Old* Forest parodies the *New* Forest – and Tolkien's fearsome woodland inverts everything represented by its near namesake. This Hampshire tract of woods and heathland was the first of several huge swathes of England to be seized exclusively for the hunting pleasure of William the Conqueror or his Norman heirs (reputedly, thirty-six villages were destroyed to create it). The new Norman forest laws defined a *forest* as a place for the royal hunt, not as a place with trees; indeed, some so-called forests were mostly open heathland, like Cannock Chase. But Tolkien's Old Forest is a *forest* in the romantic, everyday sense: wildwood. It is so wild, indeed, that (as in a Grimm fairy-tale forest) anyone straying in might never come back out.

Its leaves rustle with hatred of hobbits; branches quiver angrily for the rewilding of the rural Shire. As Frodo and company pick their nervous way through it, shaggy and crooked trees seem to crowd in, like overbearing guards. The route becomes scrambled, and the hobbits' wits nearly do so as well. The green power and the ground itself seem to conspire. Ever-thickening undergrowth and mysterious folds in the earth (see p.139, Ancient Imprints) hustle the travellers constantly towards the perilous Withywindle (see p.106, Rivers, Lakes and Waterlands).

When Tolkien dreamed up the Old Forest in early 1938, the New Forest had long ceased to be a royal hunting preserve and had become a pleasant Arcadia for tourists. Biographical evidence suggests that at this very time he may have been contemplating an Easter walking tour there with C. S. Lewis and Owen Barfield.[34*] So by sending his hobbits into the far more 'dubious' Old Forest, Tolkien could expect to raise a few appreciative chuckles from Lewis, who was reading or listening to each chapter of the new story as it was written. Similarly the science-fiction novel begun in 1937 for Lewis to hear, *The Lost Road*, had referred to Somerset, where the three Inklings had walked that year (see p.75 panel, The Shore and the Sea).

Small wonder that the Old Forest is on the defensive. Something rivalling Mirkwood has shrunk to a rump – no bigger, indeed, than the New Forest. Elrond says that 'all that now remains is but an outlier of its northern march', recalling his journeys there 'when a squirrel could go from tree to tree from what is now the Shire to Dunland west of Isengard'.[35] He echoes a saying about the Forest of Arden, which once extended over half of Warwickshire and covered what is now Birmingham.[36*] He also taps into a foundational myth that England's landscape was once all wildwood. Jacquetta Hawkes, in her 1950s classic *A Land*, speaks of 'the deciduous forests of oak and elm which would still form the natural covering of this country had we not stripped it off'.[37]

The culprit in the destruction of Eriador's vast primal wild wood is Númenor, its naval ambition modelled on England's own. From the reign of Henry VIII the demand from shipyards for native oak, mostly from the south-east, was so high that today only scattered woods are left from the Weald (Old English *weald* 'forest') that once covered a large tract of Kent and Sussex. When supplies fell to a critical level in the final two centuries of sail, the shipyards turned to the Baltic and the New

HOLLIN AND THE DOORS OF DURIN

One arm of the great forest of Eriador is old Eregion
or Hollin, the Second Age elven realm at the feet of
the Mountains of Moria – perhaps an offshoot from
Tolkien's 1911 visit to Stechelberg, 'Holly Mountain',
in the Swiss Alps (see pp.*86, 88, Roots of the Mountains*).
The Middle English word *hollin* 'holly' is a common
element in minor place-names in West Yorkshire near
Leeds, where Tolkien lived in the early 1920s – a reflection
of its medieval use as winter fodder. Charles Kingsley uses
it in *Hereward the Wake* as a motif for greenwood liberty –
'beneath the hollins green'.[1]

There is much speculation that the Doors of Durin,
with their sentinel holly trees, were inspired by the yew-
flanked church door (*right*) at Stow-on-the-Wold in the
Cotswolds. This is indeed on one of the main roads across
the Cotswolds from Oxford to Evesham. On the other hand,
Tolkien's visual interest in portentous doorways and pathways
between trees is evident from before Hilary lived there, in
pictures like *Eeriness*. In *The Fall of Gondolin*, the doors of
Gondolin's palace are flanked by trees of silver and gold,
shoots of the Two Trees of Valinor.

World for their oak. Likewise, it is in Númenor's
abundantly forested south-east that vast plantations
supply its shipyards. Dissension over the destruction
of native trees spurs the shipbuilding king Aldarion
to look to the virgin forests of Eriador, so that
'shiploads innumerable passed west over the sea'.
Rather than forest, the River Gwathló ends up
flowing through 'a land that was far and wide on
either bank a desert, treeless but untilled'.[38*]

Fangorn and the lost forests of Beleriand

Middle-earth is a world of lost forests that only
survive in the long memories of elves and a few
others. Tom Bombadil recalls 'the first acorn'.[39] But
the ancient forests are held in remembrance most
poignantly by Treebeard, eldest of the Ents, the
tree-like tree-shepherds that may be Tolkien's most
profound creation (see p.143, Ancient Imprints).

Fangorn itself is the very epitome of the
primordial forest. Its name means 'tree-beard', like
the tangled lichen called old man's beard, native
to Britain, Europe and elsewhere. Pippin can only
describe Fangorn as 'frightfully tree-ish'.[40] We do
eventually see this forest act forcefully on the fury
that the Old Forest can only mutter about (see
pp.169–70, Places of War); but Fangorn does not
terrify the hobbits. Instead, it seems to make them
part of its own primeval world, 'like elf-children in
the deeps of time peering out of the Wild Wood in
wonder at their first Dawn'.[41]

The pillars and the branching ribs of a medieval cathedral suggest a forest in stone, like Tolkien's descriptions of the subterranean elven halls of Menegroth.

FORESTS AND CATHEDRALS

French Romantic author Chateaubriand saw medieval cathedral architecture as a distant memory of the forests of Celtic Gaul, 'the first temples of the Divinity'.[1] Cathedrals' pillars rise like tree trunks; the ribs of their vaulted ceilings spread and meet like branches; their stonework is often carven with the imagery of tree and leaf. Menegroth, the subterranean palace of Doriath, is just such a forest in stone, its pillars carved like beech trees, with birds and beasts peering through their leaves (see p.99, Roots of the Mountains). Tolkien may well have visited Wells Cathedral near Cheddar Gorge, Ely near Cambridge, or England's most celebrated exemplar, Southwell Minster with its thirteenth-century vault of carven foliage (*left*), near his Aunt Jane Neave's Nottinghamshire farm (see p.27 panel, Four Winds).

Seeing that Tolkien initially called this ent-house *Fonthill*, Mathew Lyons visited Wiltshire's Fonthill, site of William Beckford's famous nineteenth-century mansion (a monstrosity that ended up crushed by its own outsized cathedral-like spire). But surely he was right to conclude at length that the visit was 'a futile chase'.[2]

With Wellinghall, Tolkien takes cathedral architecture and turns it back into forest. It has its own font with blessed water – a stone basin filled by the new-sprung River Entwash, supplying the ent-draughts that make Merry and Pippin grow taller. Wellinghall's 'great hall' pillared with trees and roofed with their interlacing branches equates to the nave (lacking only the transept that would make its floorplan cross-shaped); the bay at its inward end is the apse.[3]

When Treebeard thinks back to the forests of Beleriand, drowned long ago in the cataclysm at the end of the First Age, he does not remember them the way an elf or mortal might, as faëry forests, gothic forests or greenwood liberties. He remembers them simply as forests. He finds words of rising rapture for the willow-meads of Nan-tathren (good), the elm-woods of Ossiriand (better) and the beech-groves of Neldoreth ('more than my desire'); but when he recalls high Dorthonion and its northern pines he goes off the scale: 'My voice went up and sang in the sky.'[42]

In old age, Tolkien could no longer access the visionary feelings of his youth when (as Christopher Tolkien writes) 'for him Elvish magic "lingered yet mightily in the woods and hills"'.[43]

But exploring the forests of *The Lord of the Rings* at his zenith as a writer, he still could recapture them. His memory was shorter than Treebeard's, but no less heartfelt.

In fact, through the old Ent, he seems to recall the very woodlands that mattered to him personally in his formative years. Nan-tathren clearly originated as a mythic Oxford, and Neldoreth recalls Roos. So might Ossiriand's elm-woods be a memory of Warwickshire, land of elms? Tolkien's favourite tree was a black pine in the Botanic Garden at Oxford, but do Dorthonion's pines hark back to the coniferous forests of the European heights seen on his 1911 trip to Switzerland

ANCIENT
IMPRINTS

*Surveying the last thirty years, he felt he could say that his most permanent
mood … had been since childhood the desire to go back. To walk in Time,
perhaps, as men walk on long roads; or to survey it, as men may see the world
from a mountain, or the earth as a living map beneath an airship.*[1]*

Tolkien is writing about Alboin, a boy who becomes a historian in his
unfinished 1936 time-slip story *The Lost Road*, but he is also writing
about himself. His own road into the past was language (see pp.25–7,
Four Winds), but here he gives a nod to archaeology, which by now was
revealing ancient earthworks across Britain using aerial photography
techniques first developed for trench warfare.

He especially enjoyed the occasional fruits of 'the alliance of
Philologia and Archaeologia'.[2] One discovery that delighted him was of a
Roman mosaic pavement in Fawler, Oxfordshire, which finally explained
the name – from Old English *fág flór*. Coincidentally but pleasingly, that
phrase also appears in *Beowulf*, where monstrous Grendel treads *on fágne
flór* 'on the bright-patterned floor' of the hall Heorot.[3] Tolkien took care
to give the Heorot-inspired hall of Rohan, Meduseld, a floor 'paved with
stones of many hues' (see pp.152–4, Watch and Ward).[4]

Hollow hills

Three stones stand at the centre of the foreboding image – one lying across the top of the other two, forming a doorway. Tolkien's drawing *Before* is highly enigmatic, like others that he drew in 1911–12 soon after his arrival at Oxford. Much later, a disturbing dream of the megalithic 'Great Door, shaped like a Greek π with sloping sides' troubles one of the characters in his unfinished novel *The Notion Club Papers* (see p.75 panel, The Shore and the Sea).[5] Whatever it means in these visions, this arrangement of three stones is a trilithon – so named by eighteenth-century antiquarian William Stukeley, whose fieldwork at Stonehenge and elsewhere had first truly opened up Britain's prehistory.

Trilithons were an often-used image for the ancient past when Tolkien drew *Before*. One appears in the opening pages of *Ayesha, the Return of She*, Henry Rider Haggard's 1905 sequel to *She* (one of Tolkien's favourite stories, see pp.38–9, Four Winds); the stones preside over a death and a vision of reincarnation at a megalithic circle set 'by some primeval people' upon an English hilltop. The trilithic doorway in Tolkien's *Before*, at the end of a narrowing passageway, recalls illustrations in Bertram Windle's 1904 *Remains of the Prehistoric Age in England*, where such entrances are shown recessed into the sides of barrows at Uley in Gloucestershire and West Kennet, near Avebury in Wiltshire.[6*]

So the trilithon doorway in *Before* looks back to the archaeological remains of the forgotten peoples of Europe. It looks ahead to the Barrow-downs and the Paths of the Dead in *The Lord of the Rings*, but first of all to the entrances of subterranean elf-palaces in *The Silmarillion* and *The Hobbit*.

Fairies of the British Isles were believed to live inside the many tumuli or barrows that dot the landscape. The Tuatha Dé Danann of Ireland are also called *Áes Sídhe*, 'People of the Mounds'. The entrances to these fairy mounds were said to open onto enchanted palaces of grandeur, wealth and beauty.

In Tolkien's formative years, it was hotly debated whether Europe's ancient mounds and

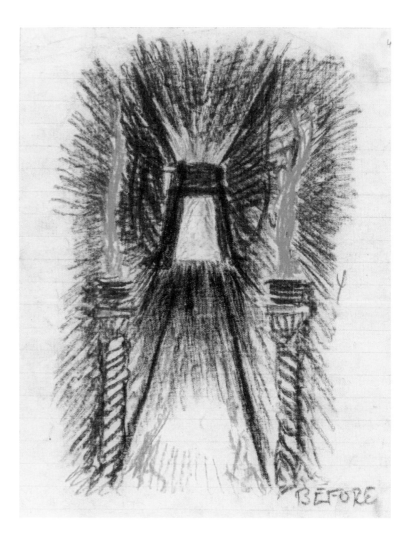

fairy traditions pointed to the existence of a real prehistoric race of diminutive humans. Driven into hiding by Indo-European invaders, they would have been forgotten except in distorted form as supernatural beings. The idea is an example of euhemerism, the school of thought that explains mythological traditions as the distorted remnant of some plainer actuality. It gained credibility from new European contacts with true pygmy peoples in the African Congo basin and New Guinea.

Chief proponent was David MacRitchie in his 1890 *The Testimony of Tradition*, but Celticist Sir John Rhys, a prominent supporter, summed up part of the case in 1901. In lowland Scotland, Orkney and Shetland, the prehistoric Picts or

ABOVE *Before*, one of Tolkien's early symbolist drawings, features a trilithon entrance that recurs in his later images of elven doorways.

'Pechts' had a faëry-like reputation, and had left archaeological remains of homes 'either wholly underground or else so covered over with stones and earth and grass as to look like natural hillocks and to avoid attracting the attention of strangers'. Inside, the rooms were often so small that they can only have been used by 'a small people like our own fairies' but true.[7]

On the other side of the debate, Bertram Windle, an anatomist by profession, pointed out that there was no evidence of any truly 'pygmy' race in Scotland; and that the mounds of the 'little people' were really either natural features or tombs. As he saw it, 'the half-forgotten memory of skulking aborigines' could only be 'one strand in the twisted cord of fairy mythology'.[8] Folklorist and anthropologist Andrew Lang agreed and said that any memory of an aboriginal pygmy people was probably less important than the idea of ancestral spirits of the dead, who were 'naturally earth-dwellers'.[9]

Years later, Tolkien explicitly rejected the notion that fairies were 'a branch of the human race'.[10]

Very early on, he appears to have been open to the euhemerist argument. His Oxford undergraduate notes refer to a legend on the Frisian island of Sylt regarding Finn, 'the dwarf-king (of the aborigines) whom the giants (*éotenas* or Frisians) conquered in settling the island'.[11]* But the legendarium is the opposite of euhemerism. Rather than suggesting that the mound-dwelling fairies were originally just like us but smaller, it takes them as a supernatural reality.

It is no coincidence that Tolkien named one of his elven kings *Finn* (or *Finwë* in *The Silmarillion*) and often housed the Elves in subterranean citadels – Nargothrond and Menegroth in Beleriand, and later the halls of the Elven-king in Mirkwood. The connection with British and Irish faëry tradition is signalled by a description of Nargothrond's doors 'with posts and lintels of ponderous stone' and a watercolour also from 1928 showing three trilithic entrances.[12] Later he redrew the scene and then remodelled it for *The Hobbit* to depict the entry to the Mirkwood halls instead – a single trilithon.[13]*

Inventing hobbits at the end of the 1920s, Tolkien cannot have forgotten the old euhemerist claim that a non-supernatural 'little people' had once lived in the tumuli of Britain. But at the outset his motives in this children's story were entirely light-hearted. If anything, by making hobbits effectively Edwardian rustics and squires (see pp.13–15, England to the Shire), Tolkien was parodying the idea that MacRitchie and Rhys had so seriously proposed.[14]*

Lost and found

The legendarium texts themselves, from the Book of Lost Tales to the Red Book of Westmarch, purport to be records from our own forgotten past. They are meant to be relics comparable to the tablets of Nineveh (see p.40, Four Winds),

like Haggard's fictional Sherd of Amenartas, the inscribed pottery fragment that launches the quest for the lost city in *She*.

But the *Book of Lost Tales* and *Silmarillion* depict the world when Elves and mortals first walked in it, so they are notably lacking in remnants of older civilizations. With *The Fall of Gondolin* in 1917, Tolkien was loosely working in the new 'lost world' genre pioneered by Haggard in *King Solomon's Mines*, with the hero overcoming almost impassable obstacles to find a hidden city. Tolkien may have taken some inspiration from the 1911 discovery of the remote Incan cities of Vilcabamba and Machu Picchu, as Christina Scull has observed.[15] But Gondolin is portrayed at its height, in a story supposedly written down long ago, rather than encountered by explorers today in its venerable age or decrepitude.

BELOW Whitby Abbey, which Tolkien visited in his youth, is one of many English ruins left by the dissolution of the monasteries under Henry VIII.

Certainly, Haggard, Tolkien and others absorbed the excitement of contemporary archaeological discovery. Ancient Egypt had been opened up during the Napoleonic Wars, ancient Mesopotamia from the 1840s onwards. Troy had been proven not myth but reality in excavations from the 1870s. Minoan Knossos was excavated in 1900–5, and in 1922 Howard Carter dug his way into Tutankhamun's tomb. In *The Hobbit* we breathe some of this atmosphere, with an expedition to a long-inaccessible realm seeking subterranean treasures.

Back, and back again

Setting out with Bilbo, we are almost immediately in 'the Lone-lands', where wooded hills are crowned by 'old castles with an evil look', evidently abandoned.[16] This is essentially sheer atmosphere – *Gothic* atmosphere.

The English landscape was dotted with old ruins too. The seventeenth-century English Civil War had laid waste to castles and other strongpoints. A century earlier, the Protestant revolution under Henry VIII had seen Roman Catholic abbeys ransacked. To the classically minded commentators of the Renaissance, they typified an older architectural style that seemed as barbaric as the Goths who had once sacked Rome (see p.38, Four Winds). In the eighteenth century, however, such 'Gothic' architecture came back into favour, and with it a taste for the ruins themselves. 'In the venerable state of ruin, there is an awful romantic wildness in the Gothic remains, that moves the mind very powerfully,' wrote one essayist.[17] The new taste gave rise to new-built antiquities or *follies* right up to Tolkien's day (see p.156, Watch and Ward); and also to the use of medieval edifices as backdrops in Romantic verse like Lord Byron's and in 'Gothic' novels, beginning with Horace Walpole's 1764 *The Castle of Otranto*. In *The Hobbit*, we never learn more about those 'old castles'. They have done the job of generating atmosphere.

Further on Bilbo's journey, however, real-world antiquity begins to make its presence felt. Tolkien

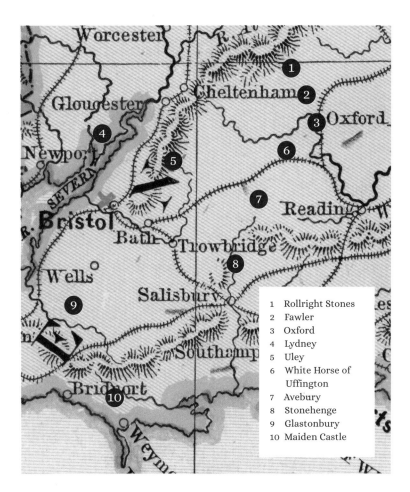

depicted Beorn's hall by adapting a drawing from a 1927 book by his friend and former Leeds colleague E. V. Gordon. This illustration in *An Introduction to Old Norse* was not original, and goes back to a three-dimensional model of a medieval Norse hall reconstructed for an 1892 exhibition in Copenhagen.[18*]

Lake-town, on the other side of Mirkwood, is yet more closely drawn from one of the archaeological icons of Tolkien's era. From the shore, 'A great bridge made of wood ran out to where on huge piles made of forest trees was built a busy wooden town…'[19] Tolkien drew it exactly as the Greek historian Herodotus had described such a town in the Balkans in the fifth century BC, 'on platforms supported on long piles and approached from the land by a single

ABOVE Oxfordshire and counties to west and south are rich in archaeological sites.

1 Rollright Stones
2 Fawler
3 Oxford
4 Lydney
5 Uley
6 White Horse of Uffington
7 Avebury
8 Stonehenge
9 Glastonbury
10 Maiden Castle

narrow bridge'.[20] But in the decades up to the writing of *The Hobbit*, lake settlements had been at the forefront of archaeological inquiry.

A 'lake-town fever' (*fièvre lacustre*) had been sparked in the dry winter of 1853–4, after Lake Zürich drew back its waters to reveal rows of ancient wooden piles driven into the lakebed. Just so in *The Hobbit*, 'The rotting piles of another greater town could be seen along the shores when there was a drought.'[21] Tolkien's illustrations of thriving Lake-town have been justifiably likened to pictures from *The Lake Dwellings of Switzerland and Other Parts of Europe* (1866) by Ferdinand Keller, who discovered the site at Obermeilen on Lake Zürich, and *Les Stations Lacustres de l'Europe* (1908) by Robert Munro.[22]

But Tolkien could easily have seen an impressive model of a lake village during his Swiss holiday in 1911 (see p.84, Roots of the Mountains), as Denis Bridoux has pointed out. Zürich Station, where the party changed trains, was opposite Switzerland's National Museum. A gallery devoted to lake villages displayed a huge hand-built diorama, measuring ten feet

by seven feet (3m by 2m). Because of the discovery that several such settlements had been destroyed by fire, there was also a memorable painting by Léon Berthoud of a lake village ablaze.[23] This, of course, anticipates the terrible fate of Lake-town.

Lake-villages had been discovered in Britain, too, most famously in 1892 at Glastonbury, Somerset. Papers from *The Book of Lost Tales* hint that Tolkien was already thinking about them in 1917, when he was with the army near Withernsea in Holderness, Yorkshire (see pp.76–7, The Shore and the Sea). The cover of the 'Gnomish' dictionary begun that year says it was compiled at *Tol Withernon*, a transparent local reference. Elvish *tol* means 'island', but modern Withernsea is no island. It gets its name from a shallow mere (Old English *sǽ*), long since dried up after centuries of drainage works begun under Edward I. Remains of lake dwellings had been found in similar dried-up meres at neighbouring Sand-le-Mere and at a scattering of sites from Skipsea northwards.[24]*

While *The Hobbit* was being written, headlines regularly reported Iron Age finds at Meare, another lake-village near Glastonbury.[25]* A three-dimensional model may have been on display by then at Oxford's Ashmolean Museum, as Deborah Sabo has found.[26]*

John Rateliff has expressed surprise that Lake-town's culture is 'right out of the High Middle Ages' rather than the Iron Age. But the tools, ornaments, carpentry and woven stuffs recovered from real lake-villages had virtually upturned the whole notion of a primitive Iron Age. The barbarians had turned out to be civilized. Tolkien's anachronism 'is actually in line with the general perception of lake-dwellings and their inhabitants at that time,' says Sabo.[27]*

His evident interest in these discoveries help explain why Lake-town marks a crucial point in the development of Middle-earth. It is neither a mythological settlement like Gondolin or Rivendell, nor even a parodic latter-day England like the Shire. Instead it is an historical reconstruction of a working town broadly based on what was then understood about lake-villages. That makes it a significant step towards the rich cultural backdrops that Tolkien developed from *The Lord of the Rings* onwards.

Forgotten wars

Frodo's journey into the past begins far nearer home than Bilbo's did. That is partly because Tolkien, with no idea where the plot of this *Hobbit* sequel was going, had decided early in 1938 that he would recycle some ready-made material. Tom Bombadil, 'spirit of the (vanishing) Oxford and Berkshire countryside' (see p.17, England to the Shire), was to be recruited from an old poem, *The Adventures of Tom Bombadil*, along with

> *Barrow-wight dwelling in the old mound*
> *up there a-top the hill with the ring of stones round.*[28]

It meant the hobbits were going to enter an ancient landscape like the one around Oxford.

Putting ancient archaeology so close to the hobbits' home made artistic sense too. It was another way to equate the Shire with rural England, where the visible past is never more than a few miles away.

In the 1930s this was more apparent than it had ever been, and in the words of Alexandra

Harris, 'country walks were now journeys into ancient history'.[29] The Tolkiens, taking the new family car to ancient sites on the Cotswold Hills and Berkshire Downs, were part of a very modern, partly motorized pilgrimage into the past. Since 1931, a famous Shell advertising campaign had been using Britain's earthworks and old buildings to lure drivers out of the towns. In the 1938 *Shell Guide* to Oxfordshire, artist John Piper had given pride of place to the Rollright Stones in the Cotswold Hills. It all seeped into wider culture, with other artists such as the sculptors Henry Moore and Barbara Hepworth depicting Neolithic sites as symbolic abstractions.

Meanwhile, Britain's archaeological past was big news. Alexander Keiller had re-erected fallen stones at the circle in Avebury, Wiltshire, the focus of a three-year dig. Mortimer Wheeler, the leading British archaeologist of the day, had just completed four years of excavations at Maiden Castle, the vast Iron Age hill-fort in Dorset, amid unprecedented media excitement and a steady stream of revelations. The dig drew visitors including T. E. Lawrence (Lawrence of Arabia) and inspired *Maiden Castle*, the last of four Wessex novels by John Cowper Powys in which modern characters reconnect with the mythic and ancient past.

Frodo and company literally stumble into archaeological remains in the Old Forest (see pp.126–8, Tree-woven Lands), 'deep folds in the ground … like the ruts of great giant-wheels or wide moats and sunken roads long disused and choked with brambles'.[30]* They feel like part of the forest's delusionary attempt to mislead the intruders, but Tolkien was thinking of old forgotten wars.

It looks as if his immediate spur was Wheeler's Maiden Castle reports in *The Times*, small literary masterpieces filling two long columns annually from 1935 to 1938. No one interested in British antiquity would have missed them – least of all Tolkien, who had provided a learned appendix to Wheeler's report on a previous dig (see pp.188–9, Appendix).

Maiden Castle might not be Greek Mycenae, wrote Wheeler, but 'to wanderers on the Wessex

Downs there is something strangely moving and dramatic in the tumultuous and gigantic earthwork of whose builders it can only be written that "not a page, not a stone has preserved their fame"' – a quote from Thomas Hardy, who had lived nearby.[31] The dig had uncovered a short-lived Stone Age settlement, followed by fifteen centuries when 'the downland was as desolate as it is to-day, used only by the wayfarer, by occasional flocks and herds, or by tomb-builders who from time to time wrought their burial mounds upon the open sky-lines'. But the fourth century BC saw a 'prehistoric armaments race that has crowned so many of the Wessex hills with massive ramparts and entrenchments'.[32]

Bombadil paints the same nameless past for the Barrow-downs using the same brushstrokes:

Green walls and white walls rose. There were fortresses on the heights. Kings of little kingdoms fought together, and the young Sun shone like fire on the red metal of their new and greedy swords. There was victory and defeat; and towers fell, fortresses were burned, and flames went up into the sky. Gold was piled on the biers of dead kings and queens; and mounds covered them, and the stone doors were shut; and the grass grew over all. Sheep walked for a while biting the grass, but soon the hills were empty again.[33]

In 1938, Tolkien knew scarcely more than this about the old wars of Eriador. A clear picture of doomed Arnor, the North-kingdom that splintered into oblivion, would be a matter for later imaginative excavations.

Wheeler's memorable final despatch was an all-action account of the taking of Maiden Castle by the Roman general Vespasian, when 'men and women, young and old, were cut down by the legionaries with the short keen-edged swords'. *The Times* carried a photograph of a ballista arrowhead embedded in the vertebrae of one defender's skeleton: 'it had passed into the body from the front, below the heart'.[34] The defenders had crept back in to bury their dead, almost all accompanied by grave goods – weapons, armlets, toe rings. Finally, Wheeler revealed another Neolithic discovery – a mound containing a body so butchered as to suggest cannibalism.

Tolkien surely read this in early 1938 while he was mulling what to write about the barrow-wight.[35]* A mere bogey in the Bombadil poem, in *The Lord of the Rings* it is the centre of one of Tolkien's most chilling scenes. Barrow-wights come from the mounds and tombs of Iceland, not Britain. Citing Glám in *Grettir's Saga* as the prime example, Tolkien would tell students: 'They are

not living: they have left humanity, but they are "undead". With superhuman strength and malice they can strangle men and rend them.'[36]* But the scene at the barrow carries telltale echoes of Wheeler's discoveries.

The hobbits, picnicking like tourists beside an old megalith, are plunged into sleep and entombed alive in the regalia of ancient burial – circlets, chains, rings and swords. Merry Brandybuck's strange outburst upon waking – 'Ah! the spear in my heart' – shows they have been dragged into atavistic dream visions of antique battle.[37] Part of the peculiar horror of all this is the sense of meaningless grievance. Time has made a mockery and mystery of the causes for which the old wars were fought.

The same sense could not be achieved later in *The Lord of the Rings*, when ancient history has come into sharp focus. When the hobbits see those same hilltop castles that Bilbo saw before them, Aragorn is on hand to explain who made them and why. While still furnishing an ominous Gothic atmosphere, the ruins take their place along with many other relics in what amounts to a vast archaeological exhibition explaining the origins and course of the current War of the Ring. But by revealing the historical facts about some ancient sites while leaving others hazy, Tolkien creates a tremendous sense of perspective. This is vital in making us feel that Middle-earth was not invented for the story, but existed before it.

DOOM-RINGS

Tolkien also drew on other traditions about stone circles, making them places of judgement or (to use a Germanic-rooted word) doom. In the heart of Valinor stands the Ring of Doom or Máhanaxar, where the Valar hold council and judgements are made. It is composed of thrones rather than stones, and it encircles the mound on which the Two Trees grow. But it is a reworking of the doom-rings mentioned in several Icelandic sagas.

Eyrbyggja Saga, as translated by William Morris, describes a ring surrounding a 'stone of Thor over which those men were broken who were sacrificed, and the colour of the blood on that stone is yet to be seen'. Upright stones like Stonehenge feature in some descriptions. Such 'doom-rings' particularly interested English antiquarians. Morris makes them the scenes of judgement and council in several of his works, including *The House of the Wolfings* and *The Roots of the Mountains*.

Tolkien describes a rather different 'Moot-ring' in his saga-like story *The Wanderings of Húrin*, where it is the setting for the 'Folk-moot' of the people of Brethil. It has a semicircular bank cut into seven tiers for seating, and is fenced, with only one entrance. Instead of a stone of sacrifice, it has the 'Doom-rock' on which the chieftain sits.[1]

The old work of giants

Ancient earthworks on the Barrow-downs also include a dike marking an old boundary, like Offa's Dyke on the border of Anglo-Saxon Mercia, or Wansdyke, which runs from the Severn to Hampshire, its purpose and origin now a matter for conjecture. Later, we learn that the North-kingdom's long-deserted citadel, further away, now bears the name *Deadmen's Dike* – the once-proud heart of a nation reduced to ruin and superstitious rumour.

Some remnants of old power are still in use. The East Road running from the Grey Havens to Rivendell recalls Roman roads in Britain, still plied by traffic. So does the road through Ithilien, where 'the handiwork of Men of old could still be seen in its straight sure flight and level course', though in places it dwindles to a track.[38] In Tolkien's undergraduate days, walking the 182-mile (293km) Fosse Way – part working road, part track – had been an ambition shared with friends in the inspirational T.C.B.S (see pp.171, Places of War; 178, Craft and Industry). R. Q. Gilson sent him a postcard from Lincoln at its eastern end saying he had 'set foot upon it with a thrill of long-cherished anticipation' and adding, 'Would we were starting now!'[39] G. B. Smith wrote a poem beginning:

> *This is the road the Romans made,*
> *This track half lost in the green hills...*[40]

For Tolkien, it was a never-ending fascination that the Anglo-Saxons called one of Britain's old roads *Watling Street*. It was also their name for the Milky Way, surviving into the time of Geoffrey Chaucer. Judging that some irrecoverable astronomical legend lay behind the name, Tolkien had once pondered recreating just such a 'lost tale', but never pursued it.

The mythological name is a sign of the Anglo-Saxons' amazement at the scale and workmanship of the Roman roads and other edifices that they found in Britain after the imperial withdrawal. *Wansdyke* has a similar origin – the structure was so impressive that the incomers called it 'Wóden's dike' after their chief god. Old English poetry describes such inexplicably huge edifices as the *eald enta geweorc*, 'the old work of giants'.

Both the Riders of Rohan and the hobbits share this same perspective when considering what the Númenórean founders of Arnor and southern Gondor built at the height of their power long ago. The fortress of Helm's Deep seems to them to have been built 'with the hands of giants', and Minas Tirith appears 'carven by giants'.[41] Gigantic masonry and unearthed treasures help to convey what archaeologist Deborah Sabo calls 'Tolkien's trademark view of the past' – that days gone by were poignantly and irretrievably greater than the present.[42] The stone kings on either bank of the River Anduin, the Argonath, are veritable images of the kind of beings capable of building the old works of Gondor and Arnor.

The very name *Orthanc* conjures a parallel line of Old English verse, *orþanc enta geweorc*, 'the cunning work of giants'.

It befits how the tower of Isengard has been fashioned from volcanic rock using forgotten skills (see pp.91–2, Roots of the Mountains). So in a very philological way, the march of the Ents upon Isengard (see pp.169–70, Places of War) is like an extraordinary piece of wordplay, earnest and knotty. The tree-shepherds take their name from the Old English *ent* 'giant'. They have the strength to tear and mould rock with their bare hands, and Treebeard's home at Wellinghall is therefore truly *enta geweorc*, 'the work of ents'. If they could demolish Orthanc (they cannot), they would be dismantling the old work of those other 'giants', the Númenóreans.

Reminiscences of the archaeological remains of civilizations more ancient than Rome have also been noted in the works of the Númenóreans (see p.41, Four Winds). Christina Scull compares the Argonath to Egyptian statuary; and the peculiar three-headed stone Watchers at Cirith Ungol to sculptures from Egypt or Assyria. The headless statue at the Cross-roads in Ithilien recalls for her the statue of Rameses II of Egypt, which once stood sixty-six feet (20m) tall but is now in ruins – the inspiration for the 'vast and trunkless' Ozymandias in Shelley's famous poem, with its 'shattered visage' lying nearby. Tolkien said that he had modelled the Númenóreans on the Egyptians in their obsession with monumental tombs, and Murray Smith notes the similarity between the Noirinan, the royal Valley of Tombs in Númenor itself, and the Egyptian Valley of the Kings.[43]

The Argonath, statues of Gondor's founding fathers (here depicted by Matt Ferguson), capture the idea that giants built the realm's massive monuments.

Relics in Rohan

The tombs of Rohan reflect Tolkien's interest in the burial mounds built by Anglo-Saxons and their Germanic kindred. One of England's greatest archaeological discoveries was made while Tolkien wrote *The Lord of the Rings* – the seventh-century ship burial at Sutton Hoo. At Old Uppsala in Sweden stands a line of three royal barrows. But Tolkien also drew on older, Neolithic barrows, as he had in the Barrow-downs and at Nargothrond. Sabo points out that Théoden's mound, raised over his 'house of stone', is like rock-built Maeshowe in Orkney rather than wood-framed Sutton Hoo.[44] For the arrangements of the kings' mounds at Edoras on either side of the road, seven on the left, nine on the right, she points to a description – in a book translated by E. V. Gordon – of Bronze Age barrows in Denmark 'set in long rows … beside the old travelling routes'.[45] Scull compares an illustration from Stukeley's pioneering book on Stonehenge labelled 'The 7 Kings Barrows' and 'The 6 Old Kings Barrows'.[46]

Also in Rohan, at Dunharrow, stand an avenue of standing stones and a series of crudely carven figures known as Púkel-men, 'huge and clumsy-

The White Horse of Uffington as seen by Eric Ravilious. Tolkien had 'an intense awareness' of the hill with its huge chalk figure.

limbed, squatting cross-legged with their stumpy arms folded on fat bellies'. Stones stand in avenues at Avebury and elsewhere, but the inspiration for the Púkel-men seems harder to place. As Deborah Sabo notes, they convey the enigmatic mood of Easter Island's statues, but look nothing like them. I wonder whether they are Tolkien's attempt to imagine a masculine, non-sexual version of ancient female fertility figures such as the so-called Venus of Willendorf discovered in Austria in 1908. But his masterstroke is to bring us face-to-face later with 'one of those old images brought to life', as Merry sees it – Ghân-buri-Ghân of the Wild Men of Drúadan Forest (see p.116 panel, Tree-woven Lands).[47] It is a marvellous piece of wishful thinking, as if we could meet the makers of Stonehenge itself in some dark corner of England's woodlands.

A ballad of the White Horse

Christopher Tolkien recalls sitting as a young boy beside his father on White Horse Hill near Uffington. 'I think even then I appreciated his intense awareness of that hill,' says Christopher, 'the archaic carving of the white horse in the chalk, the *bones* of the hill. One can see Weathertop in that.'[48] Tolkien himself had probably been visiting it since undergraduate days at Oxford, when in 1912 he walked and sketched in the surrounding Berkshire Downs.

Setting aside its size, age and gravitas, Weathertop perhaps takes its conical shape, 'slightly flattened at the summit', not from White Horse Hill but from its lower neighbour, Dragon Hill.[49] This is the spot where St George, patron saint of England, reputedly slew the dragon, and the bare chalk on its flat top is said to show where the monster's blood was spilled. As Bob Blackham has pointed out, the same motif reappears at the site in the Pelennor Fields where the carcass of the Witch-king's flying mount was burned, leaving the earth 'ever black and bare'.[50]

The White Horse was created sometime between the fourteenth and sixth centuries BC by cutting through the turf to reveal the underlying chalk. Up until the 1930s, it was thought to have been created by the Anglo-Saxons. That may be one

reason why, for *The Book of Lost Tales*, Tolkien planned to make Oxford the capital of one of two legendary founders of England, Hengest and Horsa (see pp.51–2, The Land of Lúthien). The seventeenth-century antiquarian John Aubrey had once argued that 'the White Horse was their Standard at the Conquest of Britain'.[51] In notes for *The Book of Lost Tales*, Oxford belongs to Horsa, and Anglo-Saxonist Maria Artamonova surmises that Tolkien pictured it being cut into the hill 'to remind people that this was Horsa's land – as his sigil'.[52] These associations linger in *The Lord of the Rings* with the banner of Anglo-Saxon-style Rohan, a 'white horse upon a field of green'.[53]

Invisibly, the White Horse also presides over the Shire. In his youth, Tolkien had loved 'the brilliant smash and glitter' of G. K. Chesterton's 1911 poem *The Ballad of the White Horse*. By the time he wrote *The Lord of the Rings* he had reservations about it.[54] Yet, as poet Malcolm Guite and others have noted, his chapter 'The Scouring of the Shire' looks to be named after Chesterton's final canto, 'The Scouring of the White Horse'.[55]

Up until the nineteenth century, the White Horse was ceremonially cleaned, with accompanying festivities, every seven years. It is now done with equal vigour, if less jollity, by volunteers for the National Trust. In Chesterton's poem, King Alfred orders the Horse to be scoured in a symbolic act of national renewal. He has just defeated the heathen Danes, saving England from complete subjection, but he warns,

> *If we would have the horse of old,*
> *Scour ye the horse anew*

and makes plain that the scouring will need to be repeated indefinitely – because weeds will always come back.[56]

So Tolkien's echoic chapter title – yet another way of equating the Shire with England – implies that the routing of Saruman's forces from the Shire may be merely one of many needful 'scourings' over time. As he told Dutch fans in 1958, 'I do not see a Sauron, but I see very many descendants of Saruman!'[57]

WATCH
AND WARD

It was Tolkien's great fortune to grow up around people and places
that could nurture his extraordinary capacity for learning. Then came
the hardest lesson – barbaric war that left peerless archives in smoking
ruins and brilliant minds snuffed out in mud. The 1914–18 war laid the
foundation for his imaginary seats of lore and towers of guard – places
that need each other if they are to stand against the tides of destruction.

SEATS OF LORE

Even at Sarehole before he reached nine, Tolkien's mother taught him
Latin and French, drawing and botany. Then he won a scholarship
that paid for him to go to King Edward's School, Birmingham's best.
At the same time, he was visiting another place of learning daily – the
Birmingham Oratory, home to his guardian, Father Francis Morgan,
a priestly community with a library stocked for lifelong learning.

At Oxford, his great philology tutor Joseph Wright told him the
university was really 'a factory … making *fees*', but Tolkien remained
enchanted by the time-honoured seat of learning.[1] He thought the
Bodleian Library 'an awesome and splendid place' of 'wonderful
manuscripts and books without price'.[2] In his own college, Exeter, he
discovered the Finnish Grammar that inspired him to invent Elvish. Exeter

Broadway Tower
commands views
across the Vale of
Evesham near the
home of Tolkien's
brother Hilary.

marked its six-hundredth birthday in June 1914 –
just before guns fired the first salvo of the Great War.

In Oxford that autumn, almost everyone
he knew had left to serve king and country.
'It is awful,' he said.[3] The university housed
refugees, war-wounded and soldiers in training.
Tolkien drilled with the Officer Training Corps
while despatches brought news of students
and schoolfriends killed in battle. Meanwhile,
Belgium's medieval fortresses fell like ninepins.
At Louvain, German troops paused to torch
the library of the world's oldest Catholic
university, destroying hundreds of irreplaceable
medieval manuscripts.

Foundations of war

On these foundations of war, Tolkien built the
towers, towns and realms of his legendarium.

A poem, *Kôr: A City Lost and Dead*, borrows its
name and its strange brew of desolation, endurance
and blazing heat from Henry Rider Haggard's
She. Tolkien once said, 'I suppose as a boy *She*
interested me as much as anything.'[4] In this 1887
romance, Kôr is a remote African ruin concealing
the subterranean city of immortal Queen Ayesha.
In Tolkien's 1915 poem, it is the shoreland capital
of Elvenhome – grand and timeless yet silent and
empty, its occupants having marched to aid their
kindred in war overseas. Though he changed much
about the city over the years, he always preserved
his original notion that Eärendil the star-mariner
finds it deserted – a memory, as it seems, of Oxford
in wartime.

In 1915, Tolkien left with a first-class degree
and hurriedly enlisted in the army. Returning for
his graduation ceremony in March 1916, he wrote

ABOVE LEFT
The library at
the Oratory,
Birmingham, a seat
of learning as well as
worship.

ABOVE RIGHT
A Tolkien poem
against wartime
complacency refers,
seemingly, to effigies
at Warwick's parish
church like this one
of Robert Dudley.

a poem featuring Oxford and Warwick, where he was just about to marry Edith Bratt. *The Town of Dreams and the City of Present Sorrow* uses the two towns as waymarks on his personal journey – Warwick standing for old self-indulgence, Oxford for present duty.

In Warwick, 'old lords' sleep undisturbed by the war and 'uncomprehending of this evil tide'.[5] Tolkien was probably thinking of Richard Beauchamp, Ambrose Dudley and Robert Dudley (favourite to Elizabeth I), earls whose effigies lie in the Protestant parish church.[6*] Warwick already had a place in the legendarium as the faded remnant of elven Kortirion, where 'old memory is waning' though elves still secretly sing 'a wistful song of things that were' (see pp.48–51, The Land of Lúthien).[7] The 1916 poem laments it as a 'town of dreams, where men no longer sing'.[8*]

By contrast, Oxford is addressed as the embodiment of lore:

> *in thy hall still doth thy spirit sing*
> *Songs of old memory amid thy present tears…*

It keeps alive the ancient literature that still speaks to the present – not least, the Old English *Battle of Maldon*, *The Wanderer* and *Beowulf*. Tolkien ends on a note of hope:

> *While war untimely takes thy many sons,*
> *No tide of evil can thy glory drown…*[9]

So he laid the symbolic foundations for a drama that would be played out repeatedly in Middle-earth. Vigilance and memory, or complacency and forgetfulness – these are the contrary attitudes by which Tolkien's strongholds stand or fall.

From Gondolin to Gondor

Written just a year later, after the Battle of the Somme, Tolkien's earliest Lost Tale shows complacency destroy the most glorious tower of guard.

Elven Gondolin is a seat of lore where the mortal Tuor learns arts, crafts and cosmology.[10] It is also a city of love, where he weds Idril, daughter of the elven king Turgon, and perhaps draws some inspiration from Cheltenham, where Tolkien and Edith had been reunited in 1913 (see p.48, The Land of Lúthien). Above all, Gondolin is a 'city of watch and ward'.

Yet Turgon brushes off a call to arms from Ulmo, Vala of the waters. Hidden in its mountain-ringed valley, the mighty city bathes in a false sense of security. When treachery reveals its location, Gondolin burns. Not Babylon, Nineveh, Troy or Rome 'saw such terror as fell that day', the storyteller in The Book of Lost Tales declares.[11] Intriguing parallels have been pointed out with the fall of Troy, but Gondolin is plainly to be taken as the archetype for all the great fallen cities of history.[12]*

One point of similarity with Troy only became truly significant when Tolkien expanded his legendarium into the Second and Third Ages. In Virgil's *Aeneid*, Aeneas leads Troy's refugees to Italy, becoming the forefather of Rome. In medieval tradition, Troy was a fountainhead of wider European nationhood, with Britain, the Holy Roman Empire and others said to have been founded by Trojan dynasties. Aeneas-like, Tuor leads Gondolin's refugees to safety, becoming the forefather of the kings of Second Age Númenor. In the Third Age, Elendil of Númenor establishes the realms in exile, Gondor and Arnor.[13]* Troy and

LEFT The Tower of Babel as Bruegel the Elder imagined this biblical symbol of hubris.

its after-history provided a general model for a vast history of rises and falls – all determined by the ebb and flow of vigilance and complacency.

Númenor, a land given to mortal men who aided the Elves against Morgoth, achieves a zenith of human arts, crafts, literature and science. Eventually, however, it becomes an imperial power more concerned with subjugating other lands and grasping for longer life. In utter pride and folly, the last king brings Sauron himself as captive to Númenor, then embraces his secret counsels. Succumbing to propaganda that paints Elves and Valar as enemies, the Númenóreans worship Morgoth upon the mountain that had been holy to Ilúvatar, God.

Númenor is modelled on Atlantis; but the temple to Morgoth recalls another epitome of hubris, the Tower of Babel. God 'does not look kindly on Babel-builders', Tolkien wrote in 1945, shortly before a major expansion of his Númenor legend.[14] The circular, domed temple in the 1946 version recalls the archetypal 190-foot (60m) Pantheon of Hadrian

in Rome. But with a dome topping 500-foot (150m) walls, it would approach the scale of the Nazis' truly hubristic scheme for a 950-foot (300m) version of the Pantheon, the Berlin Volkshalle.[15*] Remarkably, in *The Notion Club Papers* of 1945–6, the Bodleian Library's eighteenth-century Radcliffe Camera triggers a near-vision of the temple of Morgoth. But the resemblance is meant to be casual (and probably to raise a laugh among the Inklings).

The mark of Rome on Minas Tirith, Gondor's citadel, is hard to miss, with its imperial history, southern location, seaward influence and massive stoneworks (see p.142, Ancient Imprints). The city, formerly Minas Anor ('Tower of the Sun') has been compared with the Civitas Solis ('City of the Sun') described in a 1602 work by the Italian philosopher Tommaso Campanella. Each is built on a hill and has seven concentric walls that make it almost invulnerable. Campanella writes, 'he who wishes to capture that city must, as it were, storm it seven times.'

Minas Tirith is closer still to the noble castle in Limbo in Dante's *Divine Comedy*, with seven walls *and* seven gates. The virtuous pagans who have won fame honourably during their lives spend their afterlives here. They include Homer, Ovid and other poets; heroes such as Aeneas; statesmen such as Julius Caesar; and philosophers including Aristotle, Socrates and Plato. Tolkien certainly knew his Dante.[16]* As Tom Shippey says, *The Lord of the Rings* is nothing if not 'a story of virtuous pagans'.[17]

Besides being the Tower of Guard, Minas Tirith is a city of lore, cherished by Faramir 'for her memory … and her present wisdom' more than for her martial virtues.[18] Gondor almost falls because the Steward Denethor has left behind 'the days of his wisdom'.[19] So here, for one last time in the annals of Middle-earth, Tolkien revisits the drama of the ideal city that he had first embodied in Oxford in 1916.

The golden hall

The Lord of the Rings enshrines the vital importance of memory in Meduseld, a hall straight out of *Beowulf*. As Shippey has shown, the approach to Théoden's 'golden hall' is modelled step for step upon the approach to Hrothgar's – right down to Legolas's observation that 'the light of it shines far over the land'.[20] Inside, both have woven hangings and many-coloured stone floors. The old verses that men of Rohan still sing – 'Where now the horse and the rider? Where is the horn that was blowing?' – come from the Old English elegy, *The Wanderer*.[21]

In Rohan, Tolkien's story and his characters alike recite the 'songs of old memory' sung by Oxford in *The Town of Dreams and the City of Present Sorrow*.[22] The scenery is all about memory too – wall hangings showing Eorl the Young, Rohan's founding father; the grave mounds of his dynasty; the bright flowers of *simbelmynë* or Evermind that grow on them.

Yet this seat of waking memory is in mortal danger of succumbing to forgetfulness and complacency. King Théoden sits beneath the heroic image of Eorl, mourning his own son's death in battle, yet refusing to act upon warnings of danger. The whisperings of his counsellor, Wormtongue, have left him

as if in a dark dream – like one of Warwick's earls, 'uncomprehending of this evil tide' in their stony sleep.[23] Théoden must be awoken by Gandalf's intervention before he can answer the challenge of his times.

The Golden Wood

Nowhere in Middle-earth embodies the past as fully as the chief elven strongpoint against Sauron, Lothlórien.

Tolkien's Golden Wood grows out of Haggard's Kôr – a most surprising bloom of that subterranean city beneath its volcanic African wasteland.[24]* Both realms are the creations of brilliant, beautiful, charismatic and undying enchantresses with prophetic 'mirrors' of water. In Kôr, Ayesha has preserved an ancient civilization through millennia, keeping at bay all terrestrial enemies as well as time itself. In Lothlórien, Galadriel uses enchantment to

strive against the Enemy's fastness in Mirkwood (see pp.122–3, Tree-woven Lands), and to arrest the natural processes of decay.

Yet the Haggard parallels point to the problem with all this. Trying to hold back the years is a dubious and impossible goal. Ayesha, at her crazed and imperious worst, is what Galadriel might become if she accepted the Ruling Ring – and Ayesha does not live happily ever after. Galadriel embodies what Tolkien meant when he described his Elves as 'embalmers' who want to stop change in mortal Middle-earth so they could 'keep it as a pleasaunce'.[25]

There may be a further warning sign in the way Lothlórien's stately treescape harks back to Warwick (see pp.118–21, Tree-woven Lands), Tolkien's old 'town of dreams'. Lothlórien, which means 'Dreamflower', is all about light and memory rather than dim forgetfulness – but a dream is a dream, and we must all eventually wake up.

ABOVE Meduseld in Rohan as painted by John Howe. Tolkien modelled it directly on Heorot, the golden hall in *Beowulf*.

TWO TOWERS AND MORE

It is widely taken as fact that 'Tolkien's Two Towers' were inspired by two in the small area of Edgbaston, Birmingham, where he lived in his youth. One is the ninety-six-foot (30m), six-storey Perrott's Folly, built by a local gentleman in 1758 to look over his hunting park. Properly 'the Monument', it had been used since 1884 as a pioneering weather-forecasting station. The other, an object of architectural beauty and industrial smoke, is not really a tower but a chimney for Edgbaston Water Works pump-house. Both could be seen from the far end of Stirling Road, Tolkien's home for nearly four years. The claim for inspiration seems to have originated in 1992 and gone viral on the back of Peter Jackson's 2002 *Two Towers* film.[26]*

Yet there is no sign that Tolkien (or anyone else) thought of these landmarks as a pair. And he only reluctantly considered any *Lord of the Rings* towers

The Lighthouse, Withernsea

as a pair. The title *The Two Towers* emerged only because his publisher insisted the huge story must come out in three instalments. He struggled to think of any title to fit the adventures in Rohan as well as the borders of Mordor. He or his publisher suggested *The Two Towers* in desperation. Which two were meant could 'be left ambiguous', Tolkien said. There were no less than five to choose from – Orthanc, Minas Morgul, Cirith Ungol, Barad-dûr and Minas Tirith. Although ultimately he settled on Orthanc and Minas Morgul, looking for 'the two towers' that inspired him is a futile exercise.[27]*

In any case, his imaginative processes were far more interesting, as can be seen from the extraordinary creative journey that led to the creation of one of those five *Lord of the Rings* towers.

Seaward towers

One of Tolkien's earliest towers is the Tower of Seabirds, where Eärendel the star-mariner pines for his wife Elwing, or Elwing pines for him. Given the distinct autobiographical element in the early writings, Michael Flowers may be right to see a connection with Yorkshire's Withernsea lighthouse, 200 yards (180m) from where Edith lodged in summer 1917.[28] She was pregnant and Tolkien was usually elsewhere, on duty or in hospital with trench fever.

Lighthouses, those vital beacons heroically maintained in lonely duty, doubtless contributed to the sense of yearning that Tolkien often attaches to his seashore towers. Approaching the Undying Lands, a mariner will see first the light from the tower in Elvenhome's chief haven. In a Tower of Pearl on the Twilit Isles (in one early poem) an imprisoned figure yearns to sail west like the Elves.[29] In the 1930s *Fall of Arthur*, the exiled Lancelot gazes across the thundering surf from a tower in France, longing for homeland and king.

Then there are the elf-towers looking across the distant sea towards Elvenhome from the high downs west of the Shire – though no hobbit has ever climbed one to see the view. As will become clear, a different inspiration was stirred into the mix that produced these.

The allegory of the tower

In 1933 lectures to Oxford undergraduates, Tolkien celebrated *Beowulf* as a poem of courage, monster-battles and the mortal condition. Lamenting how most critics only wanted to mine its historical, linguistic or archaeological data, he invented a little allegory:

A man found a mass of old stone in an unused patch, and made of it a rock-garden; but his friends coming perceived that the stones had once been part of a more ancient building; and they turned them upsidedown to look for hidden inscriptions...

One of the friends complains, 'He's such a tiresome fellow – fancy using these beautiful stones just to set off common-place flowers.'[30] As an allegory, this is meant to be decoded rather than enjoyed for its own sake. The gardener represents the *Beowulf* poet and the old stone his ancient source material. The rock garden is the poem; the flowers are its artistic beauty. The 'friends' are the latter-day critics. Doubtless Tolkien, a keen gardener in an era when rock gardens were fashionable, identified strongly with his allegorical counterpart. When he rewrote the lectures, sometime between 1934 and 1936, the rock garden stayed.

But then a new impulse struck and he changed the allegory. Now the man uses the old stone to build a *tower*. The others knock it down to search for inscriptions and whatnot, with a final complaint, 'He is such an odd fellow! Imagine his using these old stones just to build a nonsensical tower.' Instead of flowers, there is a poignant final line: 'But from the top of that tower the man had been able to look out upon the sea.'[31]*

This allegory of the tower is now well known. It went into Tolkien's 1936 British Academy lecture *Beowulf: The Monsters and the Critics*, which permanently shook up *Beowulf* scholarship. It is also a standard reference point in studies of Tolkien's own literary work.

But something else has gone unnoticed. The tower allegory emerged at the time of a loud and entertaining controversy about the construction of a nonsensical tower just outside Oxford.

The builder was Lord Berners, a musician, writer, artist and famous eccentric whose friends included Salvador Dalí. When he proposed a folly on a hilltop near his Faringdon estate west of Oxford, planning officials said they 'failed to see the object or benefit' – to which he replied, 'The great point of the Tower is that it will be entirely useless.'[32] Neighbours complained, notably a retired vice-admiral who said the folly would spoil his view – from four miles (6.5km) away through a telescope. But public open days were promised, with fabulous views from the belvedere and turret looking across several counties. Faringdon Folly was opened in 1935 with fireworks, society guests and a full page in *The Tatler*. A vista of the tower, by Berners, was used prominently in Shell advertising in 1936 (see p.23 panel, England to the Shire). A myth has attached to the folly that on a clear day you can see the Bristol Channel from it.[33]

Tolkien can hardly have missed this furore. He must have been struck by how it fitted – and improved – his fable about an imaginative eccentric with unimaginative friends. The new payoff line, 'the man had been able to look out upon the sea', perfectly caught the mood of *Beowulf*, a poem of shorelands and sombre reflection. Besides, Faringdon Folly was national news, so Tolkien could expect a chuckle of recognition.

From allegory to feigned history

The next step also seems to have been overlooked. Evidently pleased with the tower scenario in his *Beowulf* lecture, Tolkien grafted it onto his legendarium. In the process, it changed from coded allegory into plain, poetic story – famously his preference.[34]* And the scenario – the tower, the visionary builder or occupant, and the sceptical outsiders – proceeded to reappear in new guises in different Middle-earth situations. For Tolkien, it became what we might call a meme.

The jump from allegory to story happened in *The Fall of Númenor*, conceived (as I have shown

Faringdon Folly near Oxford played a complex but crucial role in the creation of several of Tolkien's literary towers.

elsewhere) in the weeks after the 1936 British Academy lecture. Towers are built near the western shores of Middle-earth by survivors hoping to catch a vision of Valinor along the Straight Way (see pp.80–1, The Shore and the Sea). But the majority of their compatriots, lacking vision or imagination, 'scorned the builders of towers'.[35]

Then, in 1938 drafts for *The Lord of the Rings*, Tolkien reimagined the Númenórean towers as elf-towers (as his son Christopher has noted) and planted them on the Tower Hills west of the Shire. The downland setting suggests that Tolkien was also now thinking of follies in the Cotswolds – Broadway Tower, looking across the Vale of Evesham near his brother Hilary's home (see pp.15–16, England to the Shire), and Beckford's Tower above Bath, from which the Bristol Channel can be seen. But the full symbolic package from Tolkien's *Beowulf* lecture is still intact – with the hobbits themselves as the unimaginative outsiders:

> *The tallest was furthest away, standing alone on a hill. The hobbits of the Westfarthing said that you could see the Sea from the top of that tower: but no hobbit had ever been known to climb it… They did not go in much for towers.*[36]

Yet at the end of *The Lord of the Rings*, when Sam Gamgee's descendants move to Westmarch beneath the Tower Hills, it means that at least some of the neighbours are free of the old scepticism (see p.59, The Land of Lúthien).

By that time, remarkably, the tall elf-tower had spawned a sibling far away. The process began in 1939 as Tolkien grappled with ways to explain Gandalf's delay during Frodo's journey to Rivendell. He decided that Black Riders would besiege the wizard in the tallest elf-tower – a drama glimpsed by Frodo in a dream. The Riders do indeed look up at the topmost chamber with 'mocking laughter', though it is Gandalf they mock, not the tower.[37]

In 1940, Tolkien came up with the definitive reason for the delay. Gandalf is still held captive on top of a tower, and in Frodo's dream about it there is even a 'crying of fell voices' from below.[38]* But this is a new tower belonging to a new character – the renegade wizard Saruman – and the creatures are those of Isengard. In Christopher's words, 'the earlier conception of the Western Tower … changes into Orthanc'.[39]

So, with a final creative twist, we arrive at one of those iconic towers in *The Lord of the Rings*. Orthanc is not much like Faringdon Folly, but both are topped by observation platforms (Saruman's is for stargazing), accessible only by a long stairway. And the faintest hints of the *Beowulf* allegory can still be discerned in Frodo's dream – the good man, the tower and the sound of hostile voices.

PLACES
OF WAR

Like Merry and
Pippin at Isengard,
soldiers in 1916
relax incongruously
against the Somme
landscape. Beyond
lies Ovillers-la-
Boisselle, where
Tolkien first saw
battle.

Tolkien's early bereavements, separations and moves culminated in the most violent uprooting of all – one that was universally shared. The Great War of 1914–18 turned Europe into a battle zone and brought his generation marching into a landscape akin to hell. It was in this world of disaster that Middle-earth, like a flower in No Man's Land, first burgeoned and bloomed.

MYTH AND WAR

Tolkien recalled that much of the early legendarium was devised 'in grimy canteens, at lectures in cold fogs, in huts full of blasphemy and smut, or by candle light in bell-tents, even some down in dugouts under shell fire'. This was no mere escape to fairyland. Then and later, he wrote to express his '*feeling* about good, evil, fair, foul in some way: to rationalize it, and prevent it just festering'.[1]*

He was a man whose instinct was 'to cloak such self-knowledge as he has, and such criticisms of life as he knows it, under mythical and legendary dress'.[2] To a surprising degree, this suited the bizarre and estranging experience of the trenches. Phantasmagorical and mythical elements also appear in war writings by other soldier-writers brought up on classical myth and Arthurian legend, from Wilfred Owen to David Jones. It was a world of 'reinvigorated myth', according to Paul Fussell, who writes, 'The experiences of a man going up the line to his destiny cannot help seeming to him like those of a hero of medieval romance if his imagination has been steeped in actual literary romances or their equivalent.'[3]

But Tolkien also shows a complementary tendency towards realism, especially in depicting landscape. Rather than looking at remote figures in a tapestry, we seem to walk with his heroes through the world of lived experience.

Their impressions are so vivid that the blasted desolations, cramped and twisting tunnels and scenes of renewed natural wonder sometimes seem to reflect what is going on inside head and breast. So landscape becomes a way to chart interior as well as exterior journeys.

All this is especially true in the stories about hobbits who are pitched, like the Edwardian Englishmen they resemble, into a wider world at war. Sam Gamgee, said by Tolkien to have been inspired by 'the memory of the privates and my batmen that I knew in the 1914 War … grafted on the village-boys of early days', might be a Sarehole gardener walking voluntarily into No Man's Land beside 'Captain Frodo'.[4]

Preludes

The opening salvoes of war in 1914 reverberate in one of Tolkien's earliest-known pieces of landscape writing. Having arrived in Cornwall in August just as Britain declared war on Germany (see pp.62–4, The Shore and the Sea), he wrote The Tides: On the Cornish Coast that December, when the scale of the war had become clear.[5]* Cornwall was too far west to hear anything like the 'gunnery practice out at sea' that wakes the dead in Thomas Hardy's 1914 poem Channel Firing. Instead Tolkien depicts a coastal storm in which 'the thunder of great battles shook the World beneath my rock'.[6] The storm is mythologized as a military assault by the sea in which

his armies rose to war
And swept in billowed cavalry toward the walled
and moveless shore

of an inviolable England.[7]

But behind this stands the real war, and its thunderclap impact on Tolkien.

Nature and war are fused again in Kortirion among the Trees (see pp.118–20, Tree-woven Lands), written in Warwick during army leave in autumn 1915, when Tolkien's peers were beginning to be cut down on the battlefields of Europe. It describes autumn as an armed attack by Winter,

his blue-tipped spears
Marching unconquerable upon the sun…

The elm leaves are 'mourning multitudes', turning pale with fear; wildflowers in profusion are lopped by the harvester.[8] Another poem, Habbanan beneath the Stars, completed en route to the Somme in 1916, imagines the souls of mortal men encamped near immortal Valinor in an Elysian limbo 'where all roads end however long'.[9]* Like the naturally recurrent sea-tempest and autumnal imagery of the two earlier poems, this is a consolatory image from a man who had not yet seen battle.

More ominous is an untitled painting from 1915 or the following years. This is no recognizable legendarium landscape. We look into the gaping entry of a weirdly distorted structure like a railway hall or tunnel, receding towards violent bursts of light in the distance. Silhouetted against flames, mountains stand beyond, black and blood red.[10]

To the front

Tolkien arrived on the Somme battlefield in July 1916 after several days' march across the Picardy countryside with his battalion, the 11th Lancashire Fusiliers. A constant boom and rumble of big guns drew ever nearer as the British artillery sought to pulverize the enemy trenches of the 'Big Push'. At night, the horizon ahead was lit by flares and

An untitled Tolkien painting from 1915 or soon afterwards hints at dire journeys into danger.

explosions, like Frodo and Sam's view towards Mordor: 'In the East there was a dull red glare under the lowering cloud: it was not the red of dawn.'[11]

War's desolation was first revealed when Tolkien's battalion reached the village of Bouzincourt on 3 July. A nearby hill was his equivalent of the bleak Emyn Muil of *The Lord of the Rings* – a vantage point across fields of death and decay. Ahead was a rolling landscape of fields and woods on chalk downland much like south-east England. But it was scored by trenches and marked with pockmarks and puffs of white from ongoing explosions. Binoculars might pick out a multitude of dark dots on the rising ground beyond the River Ancre – unburied bodies from the 20,000 British soldiers killed two days earlier on the first day of the battle.

A BATTLEFIELD BOTH ANCIENT AND MODERN

The war-haunted Old Forest and Barrow-downs recall the Picardy landscape as much as the Cotswold Hills or Berkshire Downs (see p.139, Ancient Imprints). On the Somme, the Ice Age and its meltwater had created what battlefield historian Peter Barton describes as 'a region of rolling hills identical to the downland of south-east England'.[1] It had its own ancient tumuli too, such as the Butte de Warlencourt, an ancient barrow for which tens of thousands lost their lives in 1916. But Edmund Blunden felt that even the bones of the dead from 1914, occasionally unearthed by shell-burst or spadework, seemed like relics as old as 'the defences of Troy'.[2]

Being buried alive – almost the fate of the hobbits – was one of the terrors of trench warfare. Tolkien's closest officer friend in the 11th Lancashire Fusiliers, Leslie Huxtable, was sent home wounded after a shell burst brought the trench wall down on top of him. Even the scene where the hobbits struggle across the giant ruts and 'sunken roads' of the Old Forest will seem oddly familiar to anyone who has clambered among the old, overgrown Somme trenches.[3] Every trench map had its 'sunken road', a valuable defensive feature or fearsome obstacle.

Tolkien went into the trenches with his battalion many times between July and October 1916. The sun would set over green fields and, after a night march of several miles, rise the next morning over ruinous waste.

Such sudden and harsh contrasts seem to have stimulated the kind of double-exposure vision he had experienced as a child (see p.12, England to the Shire) – but now doubling England with France, and rural peace with desolating war. So there are hints of war in the Land of Willows, as much like the Ancre as Oxford's Cherwell (see pp.105–6, Rivers, Lakes and Waterlands).

Journeys to the trenches were marked by ominous symbols of old order overturned. In Albert, the nearest town to the front line, a golden statue of the Virgin Mary hung precariously by twisted metal from a church spire that had been struck by enemy shells. The crucified Christ presided over many road junctions; and such a calvary had once stood en route to the front line from Bouzincourt, at a tree-girt cross-roads that soldiers called Crucifix Corner. Similarly, en route to Mordor, Frodo and Sam see the old stone king at the Cross-roads in Ithilien – his head knocked off by orcs yet still whole.

Tolkien's description of the Cross-roads trees, 'gaunt and broken, as if tempest or lightning-blast had swept across them', suggests Western Front scenes like the one in the 1918 painting *We Are Making a New World* by Paul Nash (see pp.120–1, Tree-woven Lands).[12] An undated watercolour by Tolkien

Tolkien's painting *London to Oxford through Berkshire* has been likened to a Somme scene of blasted trees.

titled *London to Oxford through Berkshire*, showing pollarded trees like fingerless fists in silhouette, has been compared by Wayne Hammond and Christina Scull to 'a memory of wasted No Man's Land'.[13] Tolkien spent two stints in the trenches of Thiepval Wood in August and September, between which it was reduced to what Edmund Blunden calls 'a black vapour of smoke and naked tree trunks or charcoal'.[14]

Trench life

The trenches themselves might have been calculated to leave an ineradicable imprint on any soldier, especially 'a young man with too much imagination', as Tolkien described himself.[15] They may be a prime reason why he housed his hobbits in safe and comfortable holes and yet created so many settings of claustrophobic danger and terror.

Pressed on the inspiration for hobbit-holes, Tolkien pointed to the comforts of thatched cottages (see pp.21–2, England to the Shire) but added, 'We found German trenches which were often very habitable indeed…'[16]

It may seem surprising that there is a little of the Western Front in the Shire, but his generation was the first since prehistoric times to live in holes.

Trench soldiers could enjoy the night displays of star shells, flares and artillery as much as hobbits enjoy fireworks. Even Tolkien's sensitive, artistic friend Robert Quilter Gilson found guns firing in the darkness 'beautiful – if they were not so terrible'.[17] But all soldiers were happy to retreat to the shelter of funk-holes carved beneath trench parapets, or down the stairs to dugouts carved in the deeper chalk.

Tolkien knew personally how a hole can mean comfort and security, a place to try and shut out all dangers. Officers' dugouts were meticulously positioned, engineered for safety, built and maintained by each unit's dedicated carpenters, blacksmiths, bricklayers and miners. An amazingly efficient supply network supplied their needs, from food to post. The Somme chalk made them both solid and bright. A British officers' dugout could be an enviable snug, as well furnished as a student room at Oxford – a place of camaraderie,

humour, civilized conversation. The German dugouts seized and occupied by Tolkien's battalion were deeper, bigger, safer and better equipped, with stoves and excellent ventilation.

It hardly needs saying that this cosiness is only part of the picture. The 'troglodyte world' of the trenches (as one soldier dubbed it) was also a place of suffocating squalor, exhaustion, boredom and terror.[18] To reflect this dichotomy, Tolkien used a favourite technique – creating contrasting opposites. The plucky, home-loving Hobbits are ranged against the even more subterranean Orcs, who have no life except soldiering. These goblins know their way through the labyrinthine tunnels of the Misty Mountains 'as well as you do to the nearest post-office' – or indeed as well as soldiers knew the maze of trenches.[19]

The underground world often shows touches of the Somme. Moria begins to be seriously disturbing when hidden enemies are heard sending what sounds 'disquietingly like signals' – in fact, much like Morse.[20] The scene in the

Chamber of Mazarbul (like the troll cave in *The Hobbit*) might be a captured enemy dugout, with the remains of dead defenders and a war diary to decipher. The floor trembles to an incessant *doom-boom* 'as if huge hands were turning the very caverns of Moria into a vast drum' – or as if Tolkien remembered the sound of artillery 'drumfire' detonating beyond his dugout.[21]

Likewise, Smaug's fury on the mountainside brings stone crashing around Bilbo and the dwarves as they cower in a tunnel. A direct hit from above or a blast from an explosive-packed enemy sap beneath could destroy a dugout; or enemies might attack down the stairs with bayonet, grenade or flamethrower. Sleeping in a Misty Mountains cave, Bilbo has dugout nightmares – a crack opening in the wall, or the floor giving way beneath.

Underground or overground, fear in Middle-earth is as invisible as the rush of wind from an explosion or the poison gas that could turn the Somme's very air deadly. Tolkien embodies fear in fog on the Barrow-downs, the Black Breath of the Nazgûl,

The Ancre valley, epicentre of Tolkien's Somme activities, is turned to mud and flood by autumn 1916 rains.

and the grey vapour that flows from the Paths of the Dead. Pippin Took, racing through the blazing streets of besieged Minas Tirith to find Gandalf – like one of the runners whom Tolkien commanded as signal officer – forces himself forward 'against a gust of fear and horror' when the city gate is broken with 'a great shock, and a deep echoing boom'.[22]

At times, however, the frontline offered sights of destructive power expended harmlessly. Tolkien's Somme contemporary Siegfried Sassoon describes a cloud of artillery smoke against the blue sky looking like 'a hooded giant with clumsy expostulating arms', which eventually collapses and 'dissolves into nothingness'.[23] Hugh Brogan makes the striking comparison with the scene at the downfall of Sauron when his shadow rises huge in the sky, stretches out 'a vast threatening hand, terrible but impotent', and is then blown away by the wind.[24]

No Man's Land

During Tolkien's time on the Somme, the battlefield was transformed by war and weather. When Tolkien said the Dead Marshes 'owe something to Northern France after the Battle of the Somme' (see p.189, Appendix), he meant after the autumn rains had turned the chalky clay to claggy mud and slime.[25]

In the Marshes, we are in a world unlike anything else in Middle-earth, but remarkably like the battlefield Tolkien knew, with its desolation, its smoke and gas barrages, and its deadly observers in the sky and to the east. Mists curl upward from the pools and the air is filled with a perpetual 'reek' – an English and Scottish dialect word for smoke or (in this case) vapour that looks like it. The travellers cower from flying Ringwraiths and, for the first time, Frodo stoops to avoid the unseen Eye of Sauron. They tread with extreme caution lest they 'go down to join the Dead ones' – a real hazard for Somme soldiers if they slipped from the duckboards criss-crossing the waste.

The dead of the Marshes are the victims of no recent war, but spectral after-images from the

Last Alliance of Elves and Men against Sauron, three millennia ago. This is reality reworked by a mythmaker. Gollum explains that the Dead Marshes have grown and 'swallowed up the graves' from the ancient battle.[26] So it was on the Somme, where the swollen Ancre inundated the makeshift cemeteries around it, and rain filled the shellholes where soldiers had crawled to die.

Alan Lee's visualization of the Dead Marshes, with their submerged dead faces echoing Somme experience.

In trench memoirs, it is the faces of the dead that horrify most. In *The Lord of the Rings* we see them with Sam as if 'through some window, glazed with grimy glass', like the dying gas victim seen through a gas mask in Wilfred Owen's poem *Dulce Et Decorum Est*,

> Dim, though the misty panes and thick green light,
> As under a green sea...[27]

Like the cemeteries of the Somme, the flooded graves of the Last Alliance lie to the west and rear of the military advance. Then the ground rises into barren Noman-lands (a clear echo of Great War language), leading to the upland of the Dagorlad (Sindarin, 'Battle Plain') at the gate of Mordor. A book by Hugh Cecil (son of Tolkien's Inklings friend Lord David Cecil) surveying British fiction about the Great War opens not with Blunden or Owen or any other conventional soldier-writer, but Tolkien's description of the Dagorlad.[28] This is the epicentre of desolation:

The gasping pools were choked with ash and crawling muds, sickly white and grey, as if the mountains had vomited the filth of their entrails upon the lands about. High mounds of crushed and powdered rock, great cones of earth fire-blasted and poison-stained, stood like an obscene graveyard in endless rows... a land defiled, diseased beyond all healing – unless the Great Sea should enter in and wash it with oblivion.[29]

Those whites and greys are the colour of the chalky Somme mud. The land has been scorched and tainted by forces beyond the hobbits' understanding. Recalling the real battlefield, Tolkien said, 'I remember miles and miles of seething, tortured earth, perhaps best described in the chapter about the approaches to Mordor. It was a searing experience.'[30] The comparison to endless lines of gravestones suggests a ghastly parody of the overwhelmingly vast Commonwealth war cemeteries in France or Belgium.

The desolation outside Mordor is recapitulated on the plateau of Gorgoroth within, the long-ago

Cheap prefabricated huts on torn-up land, one of Tolkien's training camps looks ahead to the orc-stations of Mordor.

scene of the Last Alliance's siege of Barad-dûr. Again, Tolkien jettisons all fantastical and faëry elements and lets memory speak directly, as if there is no escape for imagination. Here are no demons, Miltonic lakes of fire or Dantesque titans – only a modern hell, bitter and drearily oppressive.

Gorgoroth (Sindarin, 'horror, dread') is a plain 'pocked with great holes, as if, while it was still a waste of soft mud, it had been smitten with a shower of bolts and huge slingstones'.[31] Whether from Mount Doom's volcanic ejecta or the war of the Last Alliance, the effect recalls the Somme, especially as seen in aerial trench photographs.[32]

In this desert, the scant water tastes 'at once bitter and oily' and the air itself has a 'bitter tang that dried the mouth'.[33] Thirst was a problem on the Somme, where the chalk terrain drained rain so efficiently from the upland. Water, in jerrycans, was always 'petrol-tainted', said Charles Carrington, while 'the smell of burnt and poisoned mud' was inescapable.[34]

The orc camps of Gorgoroth form 'straight dreary streets of huts and long low drab buildings'.[35] In England in 1915–16, Tolkien had trained in Rugeley and Brocton camps, utilitarian blots on Staffordshire's otherwise beautiful Cannock Chase. In France, he saw the newly-invented corrugated steel half-tubes of Nissen huts sprouting in what historian Peter Barton calls 'rashes of encampments' along roads and around villages.[36]

Many desolations

Desolations akin to the Somme had first emerged in *The Book of Lost Tales*, begun in 1917 during convalescence in Great Haywood, Staffordshire – the village that Tolkien mythologized as Tavrobel of the Lonely Isle (see pp.49–51, The Land of Lúthien). An epilogue, supposedly written by his fictional alter ego Eriol at Tavrobel, tells how men at war have driven the elves away and left the nearby High Heath 'blackened with the reek of fires'.[37] This must refer to Cannock Chase. So, much as he would later have the hobbits return to find the Shire industrially blighted (see p.182,

TANKS AT GONDOLIN

Tolkien never wanted his rich mythological creations to be reduced to mere codes. He rightly refuted claims that the Ring was an allegory for the atom bomb, which it predated; and that Orcs represented Britain's wartime enemy. 'I've never had those sort of feelings about the Germans,' he said. 'I'm very anti that kind of thing.'[1] But he was also very anti-machine, and modern armouries had a clear impact on his imagination.

In *The Fall of Gondolin*, written straight after the Somme, the fire that traps and engulfs defenders in the narrow streets of the elven city seems to evoke the raw terror of the portable German *Flammenwerfer* or flamethrower. It is wielded by demonic Balrogs or spewed by strange dragon-engines.

These monsters or engines of war crawl ponderously on 'iron so cunningly linked that they might flow … above all obstacles before them' or smash through the defences by sheer weight.[2] Their armour is proof against fire, and orc troops climb out of their clanging 'hollow bellies'.[3] All these features recall the tank, first unleashed in September 1916 on the Somme in a bid to break the mutual siege of trench warfare. Early reports typically compared the machine to a monster. Though Smaug and Glaurung are fully fledged characters, dragons in the unfolding legendarium remain a secret weapon devised by Morgoth to overcome elven defences where conventional attack has failed.[4]*

Talking of dragons outside his legendarium, Tolkien said in 1938: 'Poison-gas is a sweet breath to them (they invented it).'[5] *The Hobbit* similarly speculates that goblins, who always loved explosions, invented our 'ingenious devices for killing large numbers of people at once'.[6] In *The Lord of the Rings*, explosions are the 'devilry' of Saruman.[7] Under the influence of Sauron, the Númenóreans in the 1937 story *The Lost Road* build steel ships that outrun the wind, with long-range firepower. The warplane, which Tolkien also first saw on the Somme, later inspired a doodled insignia for the 'Mordor Special Mission Flying Corps', obviously a sardonic reference to the Nazgûl.[8]

Craft and Industry), Tolkien transferred the horror of the Somme to the very refuge he had reached after the battle.

In the story of Túrin Turambar, which survived into *The Silmarillion*, a swathe of destruction is scored across the fair elven lands of Beleriand by Glaurung, father of dragons. In a 1927 painting, the dragon is flanked by trees half-consumed by fire. Glaurung is also in the forefront of the Battle of Sudden Flame, in which lava from Morgoth's mountains transforms the lush grassland of Ard-galen (Sindarin, 'Green Region') into Anfauglith, the Gasping Dust. In the *Lay of Leithian* it is a place

> *of blistered stones and gasping sand,*
> *of splintered bones…*[38]

Anfauglith is later the scene of Tolkien's closest rendition of the Somme – the slaughter he called Nirnaeth Arnoediad, 'Unnumbered Tears'. He had initially conceived the battlefield as a 'Valley of Weeping Waters' (see p.106 panel, Rivers, Lakes and Waterlands).[39] *Unnumbered Tears* can be construed as the grimmest of puns on *la Somme*, name of the largest river on the battlefield but also a soundalike for *la somme* 'sum, amount'. Like the Battle of the Somme, the Nirnaeth is a grand assault by allies with high hopes of victory, but mischance and miscommunication lead to losses beyond comprehension.

Morgoth's victorious orcs heap up the vast numbers of their defeated foes to create a Hill of Slain. Mounds of corpses were known on the Somme and doubtless exaggerated by rumour. A July 1916 news report from the village of Ovillers, a German stronghold newly seized with the help of Tolkien's battalion, claimed one of its roads was blocked by 'a terrible rampart' of eight hundred German bodies.[40]

The Hill of Slain is symbolically quite different from the Dead Marshes, with their message of horror and despair. No orc dare tread on the mound, the only place where grass grows in the war-scoured desolation of Anfauglith. Túrin finds it 'bedewed as by drops of drooping tears'.[41] As Simone Bonechi says, Morgoth has built a monument to inspire terror but nature has transformed it into 'a symbol of grief, but also of unyielding hope'.[42] Like the Mounds of Mundburg raised in Gondor after the Battle of the Pelennor Fields, it becomes a fit Middle-earth equivalent of the Commonwealth war cemeteries created after the Great War.

For *The Hobbit*, which Tolkien initially set in the *Silmarillion* regions before transferring the action to specially invented Wilderland, he effectively cloned Anfauglith to produce the dragon-desert of the Withered Heath (in the same way that he cloned the Forest of Night to create Mirkwood, see pp.122–4, Tree-woven Lands). In addition, of course, the Lonely Mountain is surrounded by the Desolation of Smaug, with 'neither bush nor tree, and only broken and blackened stumps to speak of ones long vanished'.[43] A similar 'dragon's playground' appears in the short story *Farmer Giles of Ham*.[44] For Tolkien, they epitomize environmental destruction by war or other means (see pp.179–84, Craft and Industry). 'A dragon made a desert,' he said.[45]

In *The Lord of the Rings*, the fate of Anfauglith is reiterated in the gardens of the Entwives, as Treebeard recalls: 'We crossed over Anduin and came to their land: but we found a desert: it was all burned and uprooted, for war had passed over it.'[46] What remains are the Brown Lands, glimpsed by the Fellowship of the Ring from the Great River.

In the Ents' destruction of Isengard, Tolkien turned conventional war on its head, portraying a war to halt just this kind of destruction. His avowed inspiration was youthful disappointment over Shakespeare's 'shabby' work in *Macbeth*, where the

The destruction of Isengard by the Ents, here envisioned by Ian Miller, takes its cue from both Shakespeare and the Somme.

prophesied coming of 'Great Birnam wood to high Dunsinane hill' turns out to be soldiers carrying branches lopped from the wood for camouflage.[47] But far more than literary anger propels the march of the Ents and Huorns, trees conscious and mobile. In a grim and terrifying piece of wish fulfilment, Tolkien equips the Ents with the power to tear stone apart far more effectively than any quasi-explosive 'devilry' of Saruman. And it is not a

mechanical process but a hyper-organic one – they do exactly what tree roots can do, except far, far faster.

The result, strangely enough, is Tolkien's most realistic description of the immediate aftermath of modern battle – acres of masonry reduced to complete ruin as if by bombardment; pits flooded; machinery smouldering. The drowning of Isengard to trap Saruman and drive out his forces recalls how, in 1914, Belgium

THE MARSH OF TODE

The Dead Marshes have a precursor in *Knocking at the Door*, a poem about the man-eating Mewlips who live

> *a long and weary way,*
> *Down in mouldy valleys where trees are wet and grey,*
> *By the dark pools' borders…*

To visit these creatures is to dice with death:

> *You sink into the bog, who dare*
> *To knock upon their door,*
> *While fireworks flicker in the air*
> *And shine upon the shore.*[1]*

Tolkien pretended all this was about knocking on the door of 'an exalted academic person' – a satirical joke befitting *The Oxford Magazine*, which published the poem in 1937. But the landscape of this fantasia on fear is like nowhere on earth except the Western Front at night, with its drowning mud, its bursts of artillery fire and flares. There are also those 'spider shadows' that Tolkien seems to have linked with war terrors. Perhaps 'the marsh of Toad' (spelt 'Tode' in *The Mewlips*, a rewrite for Tolkien's 1962 verse collection *The Adventures of Tom Bombadil*) is a pun on German *Tod* 'death'.

The rather Gollum-like Mewlips are also reminiscent of a trench rumour that No Man's Land after the battle was peopled (as another writer said) 'with wild men, British, French, Australian, German deserters, who lived there underground, like ghouls among the mouldering dead, and who came out at nights to plunder and to kill'.[2] The Mewlips gather their victims' bones beneath weeping willows like the Ancre's (see p.106 panel, Rivers, Lakes and Waterlands). The most bizarre detail, that they are 'cased like armadilloes', suggests a surreal fusion between man and tank.

Pauline Baynes' illustration for *The Mewlips*, from Tolkien's Middle-earth verse anthology *The Adventures of Tom Bombadil*.

opened the sea sluices on the River Yser to block the German advance. The hobbits Pippin and Merry disport themselves in the ruins like victorious soldiers enthusiastically scavenging food and tobacco to enjoy in freshly seized trench dugouts.

The tortuous journey home

For all his horror at environmental destruction, Tolkien was concerned, too, by the damage that war, loss and dreadful duty could do to the heart and mind – at its extreme, what others have called shell shock, war trauma or post-traumatic stress disorder. He mapped it in the journeys taken by his wounded, war-weary and sorrow-stricken characters through landscapes that threaten to entrap, entangle or engulf them.

Woods on the Somme 'left indelible marks upon the souls of survivors', says Barton.[48] Before Thiepval Wood was destroyed, rising and falling flares gave a semblance of night-time motion to its trees, the epicentre of furious action. Blunden called it 'horrible and mad'.[49] In *The Silmarillion*, the No Man's Land of Anfauglith is also overlooked by a forest of despairing insanity – Taur-nu-Fuin, the 'Forest under Night' (see p.122, Tree-woven Lands). Tangled tree roots, 'groping in the dark like claws', clutch at wanderers who are 'pursued to madness by phantoms of terror'.[50]

Another forest of bewilderment appears in an early 1930s poem, *Looney*, a dream vision about a mortal who returns grievously altered from otherworld shores. A sudden dark cloud drives him into a silent, leafless wood to walk with bent back or 'sit, wandering in wit'.[51] Returning home by sea, like Tolkien from war in 1916 (see p.62, The Shore and the Sea), he is alienated from his own people and speaks only to himself. Verlyn Flieger has compared how returning Great War veterans found it nearly impossible to express their experiences to people at home. *Looney*, she suggests, speaks for soldiers such as Tolkien himself, whom the Somme bereaved of the close fellowship of former schoolfriends, the Tea Club and Barrovian Society, or T.C.B.S.[52]

Might the wood in *Looney* reflect a specific place? In July 1916, fresh from combat, Tolkien learned that Rob Gilson of the T.C.B.S. had been killed. But duties meant that he was given no time to think until his battalion went into rest at Bus-lès-Artois three weeks later. Here, he sat out in the wood for two nights, weary, hungry and lonely, with 'intense feelings more than ideas but very powerless', as he said in a letter to TCBSite Geoffrey Bache Smith the next day.[53] Tolkien's urge would have been familiar to Sassoon, who described how 'thoughts you've gagged all day' would drive you 'out to jabber among the trees'.[54]

Tolkien's close friends G. B. Smith and (below him) R. Q. Gilson both died on the Somme battlefield.

Tolkien also refers to those nights at Bus-lès-Artois in *The Forest Walker*, an unpublished poem written in a dugout two weeks later.

In Frodo's journey, and those of the First Age heroes Beren and Túrin, Tolkien charts the progress of the war-damaged individual. Significant overlaps seem to point once again to the Somme.

When Beren's father and war band are massacred in his absence (see pp. 116–7, Tree-woven lands), Beren dreams of almost drowning before rising

> through slime beside the brim
> of sullen pool beneath dead trees

where carrion birds caw with bloody beaks.[55] Escaping through the Mountains of Terror, Beren passes through the haunted valley of Nan Dungortheb, where demonic spiders spin webs of 'clinging black despair'.[56]

Tolkien had already imagined despairing night as a spider before he arrived at the trenches, but perhaps Bob Blackham is right to compare his fictional spiderwebs with the barbed wire that fatally entangled so many young men in No Man's Land.[57] At any rate, after Beren finally emerges from the valley 'grey and bowed', he never speaks of his journey 'lest the horror return to his mind'.[58] His recovery comes – like spring after winter – in the autobiographically inspired encounter with Lúthien Tinúviel, dancing in the woods of Doriath (see p.117–8, Tree-woven Lands).

Túrin is driven almost out of his wits in Taur-nu-Fuin after inadvertently killing his friend Beleg in the desolate flats of Anfauglith. He meets no spiderwebs but his mind is 'meshed in darkness' and he seems robbed of the power of speech.[59] In one version he traverses the same haunted valley as Beren. Only the guidance of a stalwart companion, the elf Gwindor, brings Túrin to the 'dancing water' of Ivrin (see p.102, Rivers, Lakes and Waterlands), where he is able to speak and live again.[60] Even so, at times he plunges again into

mental darkness, and we might be with Tolkien in the trenches:

> in gloomy hour
> of night's watches,   when down narrow winding
> paths of pondering   he paced wearily...[61]

In his turn, Frodo meets phantoms in the Somme-inspired Dead Marshes, as well as earlier in the Barrow-downs (see pp.139–41, Ancient Imprints). He passes through another haunted valley, Morgul Vale, with its poisonous stream, and into another spider-ravine, Shelob's lair. In the desolation of Gorgoroth he is reduced to almost complete dependency on the loyal Sam. After their rescue, Frodo laughs again at the sunlit field of Cormallen; but inside he remains damaged. *The Adventures of Tom Bombadil* includes *The Sea-bell*, a hobbit poem linked with 'the dark and despairing dreams' that afflict Frodo on the anniversaries of his wounds from the Witch-king and Shelob.[62] This was a rewritten version of *Looney*, complete with the wood of wandering wit. For Frodo, only departure west over the Sea to the Lonely Isle (see p.81, The Shore and the Sea) offers any hope of healing.

Tolkien's own version of a spider bite came from one of the lice that were an inescapable part of frontline life. In October 1916, he fell ill with louse-borne trench fever, and a few weeks later he was carried back to England by hospital ship. It was the beginning of an odyssey in and out of hospitals that dominated the rest of his war – Gézaincourt, Le Touquet, Birmingham, Harrogate (where he probably wrote part of *The Fall of Gondolin*), Hull (where he first wrote the stories of Beren and Túrin), Blackpool. So the Houses of Healing, where Merry and Éowyn are treated in *The Lord of the Rings*, almost complete the picture of a soldier's journey to recovery – a picture mythologized from real life.

CRAFT AND INDUSTRY

'Mordor, a wasteland of furnaces and factories – Birmingham by any other name.'[1] So broadcaster Ian Hislop sums up the city of Tolkien's youth. His move here from rural Sarehole is often seen as an exile from Eden. Yet both village and city played their parts in shaping the ideal of craft at the heart of his legendarium.

CRAFT

His boyhood world up to 1900 was much like the one that Laurie Lee recalls in *Cider with Rosie*: 'Man and horse were all the power we had – abetted by levers and pulleys.'[2] Sarehole's watermill 'dominated my childhood', said Tolkien, who used to peer inside with his brother at the whirring gears and pulleys and the men at work.[3] This is what sets the technological limit for hobbits, who dislike 'machines more complicated than a forge-bellows, a water-mill, or a hand-loom'.[4]

There is little sign of Mordor in Tolkien's life in Birmingham. In 1903, his mother reported that he and Hilary had been in town and 'done all my Xmas shopping – Ronald can match silk lining or any art shade like a true "Parisian Modiste".'[5] In his teens, he made the most of the city's upbeat, whirligig bustle. Memorably – using the familiar shortening of its alternative name *Brummagem* – he dubbed it 'giddy old Brum'.[6]

Victorian wharves at Gas Street Basin, Birmingham, on Tolkien's daily route to school.

A four-year
project to turn
Tolkien's artworks
into tapestries at
Aubusson, France,
begun in 2017,
celebrates his ideals
of craft.

It may be Tolkien's 1970s biographer, Humphrey Carpenter, who first popularly equated 'industrial, smoky, desolate Birmingham' with Sauron's realm of Mordor.[7] Maggie Burns has argued that Carpenter was simply showing an Oxford bias, further coloured by the depressed Birmingham of his own day. Burns's view of Tolkien's Birmingham could hardly be more different – a leafy hive of 'craftsmanship … in thousands of small workshops'.[8] The truth lies somewhere between.

The artisan heyday was a century before Tolkien's time. He found everything grimier, smokier and noisier than Sarehole, of course; and he saw areas of heavy industry and crowded back-to-back houses. It would be no surprise if, like Worcestershire author Francis Brett Young, he saw the countryside and Birmingham as opposed forces, 'the green and the black'.[9]

Yet there was also an ideal Birmingham, rooted in the city's manufacturing history, to which its artisans, artists and architects continued to aspire. Industrialization appalled Tolkien for the same reasons that artisan community appealed to him.

Birmingham's shining self-image celebrated the same virtues as his writing – small-scale craft and the joy of making. Alongside power and mortality, this is his key theme – the use and abuse of creativity.

The great toy shop

Birmingham's most effective invention was itself. With few natural resources and no big river for transportation, in the sixteenth century it was just a market town. Over the next two hundred years it built an industry to sidestep these obstacles. Metal, pre-rolled elsewhere into thin sheets, was brought to the town's many small forges. There, craftsmen transformed it into small items transportable to distant markets – tools and fripperies ranging from sugar tongs to clocks, and above all buckles and buttons. Birmingham pushed ahead of its rivals with new technologies to create fashionable novelties – pearl jewellery, enamelled snuffboxes, silk-covered buttons, silver buttons, gilt buttons.

These are exactly the knick-knacks that a well-to-do hobbit appreciates. Bilbo Baggins has a clock on his mantelpiece and brass buttons on his waistcoat.

LEFT Near King's Norton, Birmingham, 1906, this is canal life as Tolkien would have seen it in his youth.

BELOW A particular definition of *toy* earned Birmingham the nickname of 'toy shop of Europe'.

After his escape through the goblin gate, his litany of losses includes 'his buttons and his friends'.[10] In the end, his rise in the world is signalled by new buttons – of gold. Tolkien does not explain which hobbit hive of industry made them.

But he does give the provenance for other trinkets much loved by hobbits – the toys distributed at Bilbo's birthday, marked DALE. In its industrious exuberance, 'the merry town of Dale' is a close match for 'giddy old Brum'.[11] The waterways that Glóin extols to Frodo are another link. To make up for its lack of a decent river, Birmingham had built more miles of urban waterway than Venice. Tolkien's walk to school would have taken him across the Birmingham Canal were it opened into Gas Street Basin, its wharves ahum with business.

As Burns points out, Dale's most telling connection with Brum is characteristically linguistic – the word *toy*. In Birmingham, famously dubbed 'the toy shop of Europe', *toys* meant the whole panoply of small metal goods manufactured there. The idea of a whole town as a 'toy shop' – that was something to conjure with! 'The toy market of Dale was the wonder of the North,' recalls Thorin.[12] But Dale's toys are the kind that children enjoy. Those given out on Bilbo's birthday leave the hobbit-children 'so excited that for a while they almost forgot about eating' – in hobbit terms, a truly remarkable feat.[13]

TOY MAKERS.

An infinite Variety of Articles that come under this Denomination are made here, and it would be endless to attempt to give a List of the Whole, but for the information of Strangers we shall here observe, that these Artists are divided into several Branches as the Gold and Silver Toy Makers, who make Trinkets, Seals, Tweezer and Tooth Pick cases, Smelling Bottles, Snuff Boxes, and Fillegree Work, such as Toilets, Tea Chests, Inkstands, &c. &c. The Tortoise Toy maker, makes a beautiful variety of the above and other Articles; as does also the Steel, who make Cork Screws, Buckles, Draw and other Boxes; Snuffers, Watch Chains, Stay Hooks, Sugar Knippers, &c, and almost all these are likewise made in various Metals, and for cheapness, Beauty and Elegance no Place in the World can vie with them.

The Arts and Crafts ideal

When Tolkien was growing up in Birmingham, the artisans' ideal of the city had been revitalized and transformed by the Arts and Crafts Movement and its pioneers. The influence of its central figure, William Morris, can be seen in his writings (see p.189, Appendix), decorative artwork and calligraphy. The associated Pre-Raphaelite Brotherhood inspired Tolkien's early ideal of creative community, which he saw as part of his youthful friendship circle, the Tea Club and Barrovian Society or T.C.B.S. The Arts and Crafts ethos shaped the ideal of creativity at the heart of his legendarium and also, arguably, his idea of Middle-earth architecture. These influences were pervasive in the Britain of his formative years, but Birmingham was a nexus for them all.

The Gothic Revival, inspired by the writings of John Ruskin and forming a prologue to Arts and Crafts, was all around Tolkien at King Edward's School. The 1838 building in New Street, designed by Charles Barry and furnished by Augustus Pugin, was a seminal essay in Victorian Gothic. More than an architectural movement, Victorian Gothic was a wholesale reaffirmation of the values of King Arthur and the Round Table – nobility, chivalry and honour as counterpoints to hurtling industrialization. The fluted columns and traceried vaults of King Edward's gave Tolkien a foretaste of medieval and revivalist Oxford. They may also have nurtured the taste for cathedral-like architecture that he expresses here and there in Middle-earth (see pp.130–1, Tree-woven Lands).[14]*

Another Ruskin-inspired style, Venetian Gothic, was familiar from the architecture of Birmingham's university clock tower, the city's art school and Highbury Hall, the mansion on the hill above Tolkien's home in Kings Heath around 1901. He did not travel to Italy until after finishing *The Lord of the Rings*, but found Venice 'like a dream of Old Gondor, or Pelargir of the Númenórean ships'.[15] Feasibly, Venice and Gondor both fitted an idea of Venetian Gothic acquired in Birmingham. Similarly, the throne room at Minas Tirith, with its marble columns, carven capitals and dull gold vaulting, has a Romanesque air reminiscent of the church at the Birmingham Oratory, which Tolkien saw built during his teens.

Such estimates of influence can only be vague. Tolkien's writing leaves much to the imagination, and so do his few pictures of the buildings in his legendarium. Illustrators tend to visualize a kind of elven Art Nouveau, all organic curves and imagery

'Big School', the largest classroom at King Edward's School, the Gothic revival masterpiece where Tolkien was a pupil.

from nature. They are probably thinking primarily of the tree-house of Galadriel and Celeborn, an oval chamber pillared by a living tree and walled and roofed as with its foliage and blossom (see p.118, Tree-woven Lands).

What can be said with confidence is that the Elves, representing words 'beauty and grace of life and artefact', embody the Arts and Crafts way that Tolkien first imbibed in Birmingham.[16] The movement sprang from the 'Birmingham Set' orbiting Morris and Burne-Jones, a Brummie. Morris's horror at Birmingham working conditions led him to conclude that 'real art is the expression by man of his pleasure in labour'.[17] Rejecting mass production, the Arts and Crafts Movement promoted the idea of simple, useful and beautiful objects made from natural, local materials by the same person who designed them. Such views were embraced by the artisans of Birmingham, where they had their heyday in

Tolkien's formative years. They left their mark especially in Edgbaston, where he spent his teens. They also left their mark on Rivendell and Lothlórien, which provide the Fellowship with artefacts of grace and utility; and especially on Gondolin – a veritable college of crafts, from masonry and metalwork to 'weaving and spinning, broidure and painting'.[18]

No building, boat, city or sword in Tolkien's world embodies these ideals better than the world itself. It is designed by the Creator-God Ilúvatar with the angelic Valar, who then live in it and shape its raw materials into startling beauty. From them, craft and creativity flow down via the Elves to the Númenóreans and thence to Gondor. A separate line of inspiration flows from Aulë, the smith of the Valar, via the Dwarves to those illustrious toy-makers of Dale. Beneath the Creator, they are all 'sub-creators', like Tolkien himself.

INDUSTRY

In 1944, just as he was resuming Frodo's journey to Mordor, Tolkien went to pay his respects to his old school building – demolished by commercial developers in 1935–6 after the school relocated to airier Edgbaston to escape noise and congestion. German bombs had dropped on New Street, but Tolkien wrote, 'Except for one patch of ghastly wreckage … it does not look much damaged: not by the enemy. The chief damage has been the growth of great flat featureless modern buildings. The worst of all is the ghastly multiple-store erection on the old site.'[19]

ABOVE A wallpaper design by William Morris, one of Tolkien's chief inspirations as a writer and artist.

RIGHT Pages from Morris's 1896 romance *The Well at the World's End*, decorated by himself and illustrated by Edward Burne-Jones.

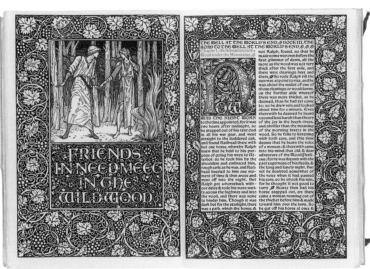

David Blissett, Sir Charles Barry's biographer, calls the old school a loss to Britain and to Victorian Gothic heritage. 'If that New Street building still stood today, you wouldn't be able to demolish it,' he says. 'It would be recognized as a national monument.'[20] The only part that survives is a beautiful corridor, transported to Edgbaston and converted into the school chapel. The corridor once ran between the biggest classroom and the library in which Tolkien and his friends first formed their all-important T.C.B.S. (see pp.142, Ancient Imprints; 171, Places of War). The war memorial on its walls carries the names of several members, including G. B. Smith and R. Q. Gilson, two of Tolkien's dearest friends.

Mounting traffic noise and congestion had been a blight upon Oxford since the 1920s. Tolkien – who never saw a motor car during his Sarehole childhood – called it 'a centre of the motor industry: that fantastic lunacy'.[21] Local manufacturer William Morris (no relation of the Morris whom Tolkien admired) had brought Henry Ford's mass-production ideas to Britain; his Cowley motor works made Oxford the third-fastest-expanding British town that decade. Its High Street, with the only Thames crossing for miles, was a major route for heavy goods vehicles.

In 1931, an Oxford Noise Abatement Society was formed to campaign against the traffic blight. The same week, the *Oxford Magazine* editor, active in the campaign, published a Tolkienian barrage against the motor vehicle. *Progress in Bimble Town*, set in a fictional seaside resort (see pp.72–4, The Shore and the Sea), is clamorous with cars, motorbikes and motor coaches. Above the racket, late at night, the sea can occasionally be heard – churning the litter on the beach. And the next day will bring

> *more folk to Godknowswhere*
> *and Theydontcare, to Bimble Town...*

To the tourist crowds swollen by the rise of mechanized transport, whatever made the town unique is irrelevant – so long as it has cigarettes, gum and postcards. The poem ends sardonically with the contemporary Shell advertising slogan *See Britain First!*[22]

When his success as the *Hobbit* author gave him a new platform, with a 1938 talk in Oxford about dragons, Tolkien showed no hesitation in using fantasy to attack reality. 'When you wake up and hear a screech and a roar, and see strange flashings and feel your house shake,' he said, 'it is probably not a dragon attacking Oxford but some great man's heavy lorries using the roads through sleeping houses for a railway.' He lamented the new tarmac black of Oxfordshire's country roads, formerly the colour of the local land. 'If you want to see a *dragon-trail* just go and look,' he said.[23]*

In 1950 the Tolkiens moved to an old house in Holywell, in the city's heart. Wartime petrol rationing ended and the street, five feet (1.5m) from their door, became clogged with through traffic. The house was 'uninhabitable – unsleepable-in, unworkable-in, rocked, racked with noise, and drenched with fumes,' he complained. 'Such is modern life. Mordor in our midst.'[24] An unpublished Tolkien satire, *The Bovadium Fragments*, describes the worship of the *motores* (cars) manufactured by the Dæmon of Vaccipratum (a Latinization of 'cow-field', or Cowley) that jam the streets of Bovadium ('ox-ford' in Latin), asphyxiate its inhabitants, and explode.[25]

Trains and aeroplanes were further targets of Tolkien's ire. Late in the Second World War, he told his publisher he could not write a sequel to *Farmer Giles of Ham* (see pp. 17–18, England to the Shire); 'The heart has gone out of the Little Kingdom, and the woods and plains are aerodromes and bomb-practice targets.'[26]

The swallowing of Sarehole

The fate of Sarehole was more bitter still. 'I always knew it would go – and it did,' Tolkien recalled in old age.[27] 'The country in which I lived in childhood was being shabbily destroyed before I was ten.'[28] The railway reached Sarehole in 1908, and Birmingham swallowed the hamlet whole. When Tolkien drove through in 1933, he got lost nearby in 'a huge tram-ridden meaningless suburb', once a neighbouring village. But eventually he came to 'what is left of beloved lanes of childhood, and past the very gate of our cottage, now in the midst of a sea of new red-brick'. The house of one of the two 'ogres' (Sarehole Farm) was a petrol station. The 'bluebell lane' was 'a dangerous crossing alive with motors and red lights', and the elms beyond it had gone. 'How I envy those whose precious early

Maps from 1905 and 1956 record the obliteration of rural Sarehole that inspired 'The Scouring of the Shire'.

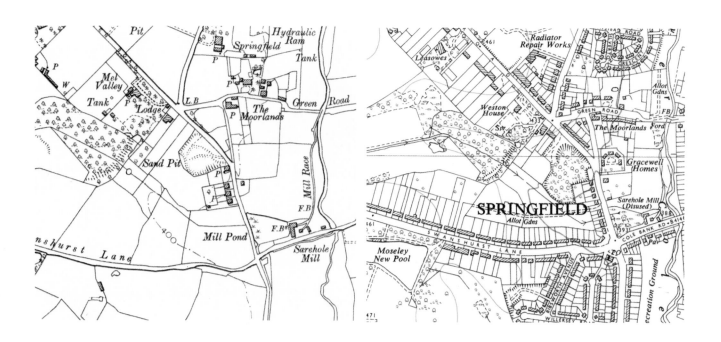

The Soho Manufactory, the world's first
assembly-line factory, built in the 1750s by
Matthew Boulton after he left Sarehole Mill.

scenery has not been exposed to such violent and peculiarly hideous change,' wrote Tolkien.[29]*

His beloved West Midlands had also been the very cradle of the global industrial revolution that fuelled some of his darkest and angriest scenarios. The mass production of iron using coal-fired furnaces began at Coalbrookdale in Shropshire. The world's first iron bridge, over the Severn, gives nearby Ironbridge its name. In Birmingham, industry received a major injection from the scientific curiosity of the eighteenth-century Lunar Society. Members included Joseph Priestley, who first isolated oxygen as a gas; James Watt, the steam engine pioneer; and industrialist Matthew Boulton – the man who invented the modern factory.

In the 1750s, Sarehole Mill (see p.13, England to the Shire) had been one of the 'flatting mills' supplying sheet metal for Boulton's Birmingham button and buckle business. But Sarehole had no mill pool at that time, so Boulton moved his flatting operation to the other side of Birmingham. There, he swiftly rebuilt his new mill as the Soho Manufactory, where he pioneered assembly-line mass production. By the end of the 1760s it was Europe's biggest manufacturing site, with a thousand workers. After installing coal-fired steam engines, he declared to a visitor, 'I sell here, Sir, what the world desires to have – power.'[30]

In *The Hobbit*, Hobbiton's mill only appears twice, as Bilbo leaves and returns – a mark of comfort, prosperity and order. This is Tolkien's Sarehole childhood projected into a remote prehistory, 'long ago in the quiet of the world, when there was less noise and more green'.[31]* But *The Lord of the Rings* makes the mill the very symbol of industrialization – of more noise and less green. True to Tolkien's experience, the damage is done while we look elsewhere. The heroes return to Hobbiton to encounter after-images of Tolkien's 1933 visit to his vanished Sarehole. Trees have been wantonly cut down. Cosy hobbit-holes and gracious old buildings have given way to 'shabby houses'.[32] But this is not just urban sprawl. It is as if Matthew Boulton had stayed at Sarehole Mill and turned it into his 'manufactory'. The Hobbiton mill has been replaced by a red-brick building, belching black smoke as if coal-fired, pouring pollution into the Water.

Chief culprit is Saruman, who is doing to Hobbiton what he has already done to his own home, Isengard. Tom Shippey has suggested that Tolkien consciously linked the wizard's name with *Sarehole*, which perhaps contains the same initial element, Old English *searu* 'device, design, contrivance, art'. Shippey also illuminatingly translates *Isengard* as 'Irontown', recalling Charles Dickens's Manchester-inspired Coketown.[33]* Isengard has been turned from a parkland of green groves into a lifeless waste of rubble and steaming pit shafts. Farmer Cotton has not seen Isengard, but he is spot on when he complains, 'If they want to make the Shire into a desert, they're going the right way about it.'[34] Sam goes a step further. 'This is worse than Mordor!' he reflects – worse because it is home and he remembers it before it was ruined.[35]

The Black Country

The region immediately west of Birmingham, rich in coal, iron and clay, has been known as the Black Country since the nineteenth century because of what heavy industry has done to it. Tolkien never said Mordor was inspired by any such area, yet the Elvish name does mean 'the Black Country', and both are blighted, benighted landscapes.[36]*

Visiting England's Black Country in 1824, Thomas Carlyle wrote, 'A dense cloud of pestilential smoke hangs over it for ever, blackening even the grain that grows upon it; and at night the whole region burns like a volcano spitting fire from a thousand tubes of brick.'[37]* In 1940, Francis Brett

RIGHT The Black Country in its hellish mid-nineteenth-century heyday, undoubtedly one inspiration for Mordor.

BELOW Inside a Black Country rolling mill, from an 1890s illustration.

Young could still write that 'the Black Country smouldered beneath its perpetual smoke-pall'.[38]

There is more than a hint of industry in the slag heaps of the Dagorlad (see p.166, Places of War); in the noise 'as of great engines throbbing and labouring' in the guts of Mount Doom; in the roiling fumes that it belches.[39] The cesspool stench and 'greasy' waters of the Dead Marshes (see p.165, Places of War) go back at least partly to Tolkien's plan to describe them 'like green pools and rivers fouled by modern chemical works'.[40]

Such descriptions were still years away when, in *The Fall of Númenor* (1936–7), Tolkien coined the name *Mordor*, using the Elvish elements *mor-* 'black' and *dor* 'land'. The general sense would obviously suit any realm ruled by evil, and the sonorous sound satisfyingly recalls Old English *morðor* 'murder' and Arthurian *Mordred* (see p.35, Four Winds).

With the similarity of name and (in *The Lord of the Rings*) of landscape, it is hardly plausible that Birmingham-grown Tolkien was unaware of the parallels. Though he did explicitly compare Mordor with the landscape of the Somme (see p.166, Places of War), I think it plain that the local Black Country of his youth must have been an ingredient too. To paraphrase his comments about names like 'the Hill' (see p.18, England to the Shire), his fictional Black Country will have been made out of every blasted, poisoned and fume-filled country he had ever seen, but especially out of the Black Country which, for him, first embodied the phrase. Yet he would almost certainly have denied all specific connection – determined that each reader should feel free to see his or her own idea of a 'Black Country' in Mordor.

A mythology for the world

It is easy to mock Tolkien as reactionary, misty-eyed and impractical in his opposition to industry and the machine. Indeed, there was a time when no self-respecting opinion-maker would miss the chance to do so.

Even admirers who embrace an environmental message in Tolkien's works can sometimes underestimate the strength of feeling behind it. The attack on Isengard by the Ents strikes Anne C. Petty as 'one of the most satisfying acts of retribution committed to paper', yet she is at pains to defuse any power it might have beyond mere literary pleasure. 'Although his stance on defending nature, and trees in particular, was notoriously embraced by the "green" activists

of the sixties and several more aggressive ecology movements since then,' she writes, 'you won't find any evidence that he supported these groups.' She seems to have overlooked a comment from Tolkien in support of far more radical action. 'There is only one bright spot and that is the growing habit of disgruntled men of dynamiting factories and power-stations,' he said. 'I hope that, encouraged now as "patriotism", may remain a habit!'[41]

This was 1943, and context suggests he was talking about dissident acts of sabotage in totalitarian regimes. Even so, these are the authentic tones of an old soldier from the generation that fought partly – as Great War recruiting posters make clear – to preserve the British rural landscape. Looking back, fellow soldier-writers such as Siegfried Sassoon characterized England as a lost paradise, too. To them, the old landscapes called out from a lost past. As Tolkien pointed out, nostalgia is not 'mere regret'; it is an '(aching) desire to go home'.[42]* Patrick Curry has described Tolkien's mood as one of 'radical nostalgia' that sees a problem and can inspire change – 'an emotionally empowering nostalgia, not a crippling one'.[43]

The values that Tolkien saw in old Sarehole – community, peace, freedom, craft and intimacy with nature – speak eloquently to people worldwide when embodied in the Shire. So does his ideal of craft, not least because he put it so superbly into practice himself.

Whether he was re-envisioning England as a rural haven or as a medieval kingdom, Tolkien was not alone. He and other writers were responding to the immeasurable changes wrought by the Industrial Revolution. Laurie Lee claimed to belong 'to that generation which saw, by chance, the end of a thousand years' life', but the same went for Tolkien, a generation older.[44]

That there was also foresight in his vision need hardly be said in a world where the stakes – for the environment and the human condition – seem to get higher every year. Middle-earth was created to reflect what he most loved and detested in his own world. It folds into itself a multitude of real landscapes and locations, ancient or modern, wild or nurtured or despoiled. Indeed, you might say that upon the pages of Tolkien's legendarium, landscape itself has written an impassioned message. That is why this is not ultimately a mythology for England or for Britain only, but for a planet that sorely needs every inspiration to save itself.

Love of countryside helped motivate Britain's volunteer soldiers in the Great War.

LEFT The Milky Way
over Kynance Cove,
Cornwall, visited by
Tolkien just before he
began his mythology.

APPENDIX

1. LYDNEY, THE VYNE RING AND TOLKIEN

Tolkien made one direct contribution to archaeological inquiry – writing a note on the Celtic divine name *Nodens* for the report of 1928–9 excavations at the Roman temple at Lydney, Gloucestershire. From this has sprung a myth – but it is at least nine-tenths a myth *about* Tolkien, rather than by him.

A tablet found at Lydney is inscribed with the complaint of a man called Silvianus, saying he has lost a ring and calling upon the god Nodens to curse 'those who are called Senicianus' unless it is returned to the Lydney temple. This has been linked by some historians with a ring found at Silchester, Hampshire, carrying a Christian inscription including the name *Senicianus*.

Whether or not the ring mentioned in the tablet is anything to do with the Hampshire one, the Lydney inscription offers a glimpse of a time when Roman occupiers fostered native British gods, even as Christianity took hold. Except in inscriptions at Lydney and perhaps Cockersand Moss in Lancashire, Nodens is unknown.

The ring has been dubbed by newspapers 'the Hobbit ring' and the 'ring that inspired Tolkien'.[1] A BBC article, calling it the 'J. R. R. Tolkien ring', says that archaeologist R. E. M. Wheeler 'is believed to have discussed the ring with Tolkien after realizing its connection to the curse' and that Tolkien 'repeatedly visited the temple'.[2] All this seems to come from a press release issued by the Vyne, the Hampshire National Trust property where the ring is exhibited. Wikipedia's entry for the ring uncritically repeats the claims.[3] To unravel all this, along with other arguments for Lydney as an inspiration for Tolkien, would take a chapter.[4*]

Between the Lydney and Vyne artefacts and Tolkien's Ruling Ring, medieval scholar Lynn Forest-Hill detects a common pattern of loss, recovery, theft and malediction. But she concedes that it has no bearing on *The Hobbit* as written near the time of his work on *Nodens*.[5] The original chapter 'Riddles in the Dark', published in 1937, differs drastically from the one now famous. Gollum, as polite as any cannibal can be, concedes defeat in the riddle game, apologizes to Bilbo when he cannot find the ring he has pledged as prize, and shows him the way out of the goblin tunnels. Gollum's curse on 'the Baggins' only emerged in a riddle scene rewritten to fit *The Lord of the Rings* and published in 1951.[6]

In initial notes and drafts for *The Lord of the Rings*, from early 1938, we can see Tolkien identify Bilbo's ring and the Necromancer (Sauron) as the two most promising loose ends left over from *The Hobbit*. The obvious way to tie them together was to make Sauron a giver of rings, the traditional role of a lord in Germanic tradition. Tolkien had first given that tradition a sinister twist in the *Lay of Leithian* – in spring 1928 before his Lydney involvement – when the Necromancer himself calls Morgoth 'the greatest giver of gold and rings'.[7] To my eye, the story of Sauron's Ring – its loss and recovery by Gollum, its theft by Bilbo and Gollum's curse – came together in a painstaking jigsaw process from sheer plot necessity. Resemblance to the Lydney curse and Vyne ring is only apparent once the pieces were in place, and that makes coincidence look more likely than imitation, conscious or unconscious.

Tolkien's involvement with the Lydney excavations seems to have been blown out of all proportion, and the sense of a powerful nexus of inspiration seems illusory. It was not Wheeler who made the connection between the Lydney and Vyne artefacts, which had been done in 1888.[8*] There is no evidence that Tolkien met Wheeler or visited Lydney; and such an excursion was entirely unnecessary for his note on *Nodens*.

The note itself hardly goes beyond summarizing and refining the existing consensus that linked *Nodens* with Irish and Welsh mythological figures Nuada and Nudd. Tolkien's innovation is to interpret *Nodens* as meaning 'the Catcher'. He writes, 'Whether the god was called the "snarer" or the "catcher" or the "hunter" in some sinister sense, or merely as being a lord of venery [game-hunting], mere etymology can hardly say.'[9]

At the end of a fine summary of the Lydney–*Nodens* story, John D. Rateliff argues that in his later *Annals of Aman*, Tolkien was inspired by 'the catcher' to create a sinister Huntsman figure who would chase and devour straying elves in their earliest beginnings.[10] If so, he took some twenty years getting round to it, and ignored all the other catchers and snatchers of story and folklore.

It is at least as attractive – though equally impossible to prove – that Tolkien had already thought about the *Nodens* problem in 1926 when he gave the epithet 'the Hunter' to Thû (later the Necromancer Sauron) in his *Sketch of the Mythology*.[11] Historian-archaeologist R. G. Collingwood, Tolkien's colleague from 1925 to 1935 at Pembroke College, Oxford, had been engaged since 1919 on becoming the leading authority on Roman inscriptions.[12*] His Oxford history *Roman Britain and the English Settlements* acknowledges that Tolkien helped 'untiringly with problems of Celtic philology'.[13*] Elsewhere Collingwood declares Lydney (which he did visit) to be 'the most interesting Temple in Britain'.[14*] It was almost certainly Collingwood who recommended Tolkien – a Germanist rather than a Celticist – to analyse *Nodens* for Wheeler. So it would not be a major surprise if Collingwood and Tolkien discussed the *Nodens* inscription prior to that.

2. UNRIDDLING TOLKIEN ON WILLIAM MORRIS AND THE WESTERN FRONT

The only time Tolkien wrote down his debt to the landscapes of the Great War, he muddied the waters. The passage runs:

> *Personally I do not think that either war (and of course not the atomic bomb) had any influence upon either the plot or the manner of its unfolding. Perhaps in landscape. The Dead Marshes and the approaches to the Morannon owe something to Northern France after the Battle of the Somme. They owe more to William Morris and his Huns and Romans, as in* The House of the Wolfings *or* The Roots of the Mountains.[15]

The statement has led to some head-scratching among the few Tolkien readers who have actually read these Morris romances. Tom Shippey presumes Tolkien meant to say that Great War soldiers found Morris 'more realistic … than the genteel novels favoured by literary critics'.[16] That would be reasonable if either of these Morris tales described anything like the Dead Marshes or the Battle Plain. But as Jessica Yates points out, 'neither book has a comparable wasteland'.[17] And, transparently, the Western Front did.

Holly Ordway has tried to discern likenesses between the landscapes towards Mordor and towards Silver-dale in *The Roots of the Mountains*.[18] But similarities are too slight to bear the strain. The wide tracts of the Dead Marshes and their ancient spectral armies cannot be equated with a boggy patch and a brace of recent murder victims in Morris.

Undoubtedly, what Tolkien actually meant was that the heroic journey of the Burgdalers to Silver-dale influenced the Ride of the Rohirrim to Minas Tirith. In each case, a large armed force travels in haste to liberate its allies from a cruel occupying enemy – the Huns in Morris, Mordor in Tolkien. On the eve of battle, the Burgdalers conceal themselves among the trees of Wood-dale and the Rohirrim shelter in the Grey Wood in Stonewain Valley. Here both forces learn of the enemy's merciless slaughter of non-combatants – in Tolkien's version, the errand-riders of Gondor.[19*]

Everything becomes clear if we recognize that Tolkien's comment is just unclearly punctuated. He meant that in its plot, *The Lord of the Rings* owed more to Morris's two romances than to the world wars; but (parenthetically) that the landscapes approaching Mordor were indeed indebted to the Somme. It is baffling, anyway, how the Marshes or the Battle Plain (or any landscape) can be indebted to Morris's 'Huns and Romans'.

I would insert editorial brackets thus: 'Personally I do not think that either war (and of course not the atomic bomb) had any influence upon either the plot or the manner of its unfolding. [Perhaps in landscape. The Dead Marshes and the approaches to the Morannon owe something to Northern France after the Battle of the Somme.] They owe more to William Morris and his Huns and Romans, as in *The House of the Wolfings* or *The Roots of the Mountains*.'

So the *they* in the final sentence refers to the plot and its unfolding, not to the Marshes and Dagorlad. The pattern 'owe something to' and 'owe more to', is merely a sign of haste in a very short letter dashed off to a fan.

When I put this to Tom Shippey, he graciously responded: 'I too was taken in by the way Tolkien did not indicate an aside – I think your comment is completely convincing.'

Introduction (pp. 6–7)

1 *Letters*, no. 211.
2 *Lord of the Rings*, 259.
3 *Lord of the Rings*, 291.
4 *Letters*, no. 181.

England to the Shire: main text (pp. 10–23)

1 Norman.
2 Resnick.
3 *Letters*, no. 163.
4 *Lord of the Rings*, 1030.
5 *On Fairy-Stories*, 75.
6 Foster.
7 *Letters*, no. 178. Sarehole, in Worcestershire when the Tolkiens lived there, was reassigned to Warwickshire in boundary changes of 1911.
8 *On Fairy-Stories*, 282
9 Ezard.
10 *Hobbit*, 252.
11 Ezard.
12 Ezard.
13 Ezard.
14 Brace 1968.
15 Ezard.
16 *Reader's Guide*, 8.
17 Brace 1968.
18 Hilary Tolkien 12, 16.
19 *Biography*, 29.
20 Charlotte and Dennis Plimmer, 'The Man Who Understands Hobbits', *Telegraph Magazine*, 22 March 1968.
21 Ezard.
22 Brace 2001.
23 The similarity of *Bombadil* to Francisco *Bo(m)badilla*, an adversary of Christopher Columbus, and Captain *Bobadil* in Ben Jonson's *Every Man in His Humour*, seems irrelevant. The similarity to *Bumble Dell* is curious, but the sound-shape was a Tolkien favourite. Bimble Bay was a fictional locale of several poems he wrote for the children (see p.73). *Tumble Hill* was his nickname for a height above Lyme Regis – perhaps Timber Hill, above the shore east of the town (*Artist and Illustrator*, 30), or perhaps some other local hillside that was tumbling to ruin, as many do there. It would be little surprising if *Bindbole Wood* (visible on the Shire map and in the distance in *The Hill: Hobbiton across the Water*) was meant to be pronounced like Bimble. Place-names are often so worn that they no longer sound how they look, as *Magdalen College* in Oxford and *Bicester* to its north testify – 'Maudlin' and 'Bister' respectively.
24 *Letters*, no. 19.
25 Maria Artamonova, interview.
26 *Adventures of Tom Bombadil*, 277. The king's name comes from Welsh ('noble') and *ond* is 'stone' in a real pre-Celtic language that is otherwise almost entirely unrecorded (John Rhys, *Celtic Britain* [London: Society for Promoting Christian Knowledge, 1882], 266). In his legendarium, Tolkien made *ond* and *gon(d)* the Elvish words for 'stone'.

27 *Letters*, no. 122.
28 Brin Dunsire, 'Of Ham, and What Became of It', *Amon Hen*, no. 98 (1989), 17.
29 *Letters*, no. 36.
30 *Reader's Guide*, 335–6.
31 *Hobbit*, 34.
32 *On Fairy-Stories*, 82.
33 *Letters*, no. 190.
34 Edmund Weiner to the author.
35 Christopher Tolkien thought Nobottle meant 'the village was so poor and remote that it did not even possess an inn' (*Treason of Isengard*, 424). In fact it means 'new building'.
36 Draft of Tolkien's 'Nomenclature of The Lord of the Rings', in *The Lord of the Rings Companion*, 56; *Reader's Guide* 171. Source-spotters should take *Bumble Dell* as fair warning that Tolkien sometimes used unofficial names for places he knew. His 1933 diary entry about a visit to Sarehole refers to 'the bluebell lane', 'the mill lane' and 'the White Ogre's house' (*Biography*, 125). Blackham notes that *Green Hill* (like the Shire name *Green Hill Country*) was the local name for a rise at the end of Ashfield Road, Kings Heath, where Tolkien stayed with his Suffield grandparents on first arriving in England (*The Roots of Tolkien's Middle-earth*, 15).
37 Shippey, 114.
38 Gilliver et al, 129.
39 Maria Artamonova, interview.
40 Paul H. Vigor, 'Questing for "Tygers": a historical archaeological landscape investigation of J. R. R. Tolkien's real Middle-earth', *Mallorn* no. 48 (Autumn 2009), 33.
41 *Artist and Illustrator*, 17.
42 *Artist and Illustrator*, 40; online Addenda and Corrigenda to *Artist and Illustrator*, www.hammondandscull.com/addenda/artist.html
43 *Lord of the Rings*, 100.
44 Gelling, *The Place-Names of Oxfordshire*, 93. Names elsewhere in the county refer to the god Woden (by the name *Grim*); to ghostly hauntings; to a dragon-hoard. *Poppets Hill* originally meant 'goblin-pit hill', containing *puca*, related to *Puck* and *púkel*, used by Tolkien in *Púkel-men*, the mysterious carven stones of Dunharrow.

England to the Shire: panels

Buckland, Wales (p.19)

1 Seamus Hamill-Keays, 'Tolkien in Buckland: An Analysis of the Evidence', *Brycheiniog* (Journal of the Brecknock Society) no. 69 (2018) (condensed online at http://www.talybont.com/); 'Tolkien and the Wines of Jerez', *Beyond Bree*, March 2019. For a discussion by another local, see https://calmgrove.wordpress.com/tag/seamus-hamill-keays/.

Sam and Other Sketches from Life (p.21)

1 *Letters*, no. 303.
2 *Farmer Giles of Ham*, 30.
3 *Letters*, no. 257. Gamgee was a Birmingham name for the surgical cotton wool invented by Sampson Gamgee. His surgeon son Leonard had been

an imposing figure at the Birmingham hospital where Tolkien was sent from the Somme in 1916. Coincidentally, as it seems, Tolkien sat beside Leonard Gamgee at a governors' meeting for King Edward's School, Birmingham, in February 1938, just after introducing Gaffer Gamgee into the story.
4 Tolkien to H. Cotton Minchin, 16 April 1956, sold at auction and reproduced at the Tolkien Gateway website, http://tolkiengateway.net/wiki/Letter_to_H._Cotton_Minchin_(16_April_1956). Tolkien's military papers do not identify any of these men.
5 *Peoples of Middle-earth*, 52. H. C. O'Neill's 'The True Love of Barnabas Butter and Betty Kick' (*Devonshire Idyls*, 1892) purports to be the true story of a man of that name who is buried at a fictional 'Leaworthy' in Devon.
6 Guy Davenport, 'J. R. R. Tolkien, RIP', *National Review*, 28 September 1973, quoted in Bratman, 'Hobbit Names Aren't from Kentucky', *The Ring Goes Ever On: Proceedings of the 2005 Tolkien Conference* vol. 2 (Tolkien Society, 2008), 164.
7 Tolkien papers, Bodleian Library; private correspondence with Barnett's family.
8 Bratman, 168.

The Hill (p.23)

1 David Hinton, 'Lord of the Hrungs', *British Archaeology*, no. 65, June 2002 (with thanks to Charles Noad and Jessica Yates).
2 'German Planes visiting Cassel by Sir William Orpen', www.tolkienguide.com, 4 September 2016.
3 *Chronology*, 17 January 1937, suggests it was drawn after pictures previously submitted to George Allen & Unwin had been accepted (7 January). Tolkien told C. A. Furth on 13 August that he had made a painting of the scene.
4 On sources for *The Trolls*, *Bilbo Awoke with the Early Sun in His Eyes*, *Beorn's Hall* and *Lake Town*, see *Artist and Illustrator*, 110–11, 120–4 and 132–3, and Douglas A. Anderson in *The Annotated Hobbit* 74–5, 160, 170–1 and 244–5.

Four Winds: main text (pp. 24–41)

1 *Lord of the Rings*, 418.
2 Tolkien's *Sellic Spell*, a 1940s retelling of *Beowulf* as a fairy-story, begins identically: 'Once upon a time there was a King in the North of the world and in his house there was a young lad who was not like other young lads.' *Beowulf: A Translation and Commentary*, 387.
3 *The Red Fairy Book*, ed. Andrew Lang (London: Longmans, Green & Co., 1890) 357; *On Fairy-Stories*. 55.
4 Andrew Wawn, *The Vikings and the Victorians: Inventing the Old North in Nineteenth-Century Britain* (Cambridge: D. S. Brewer, 2000), 27–9. Gray's 1768 *The Fatal Sisters* translates a poem from *The Saga of Burnt Njal*.
5 *Lost Tales II*, 290.
6 *Monsters and the Critics*, 18.
7 *Beowulf: A Translation and Commentary*, 226.
8 *Letters*, no. 19.
9 *Lost Tales II*, 290.

10   *Letters*, no. 19.

11   *Lost Tales II*, 290.

12   'Tolkien Talking', *Sunday Times*, 27 November 1966,
     9. Language invention began before his mother's
     death, perhaps around the age of eight or nine
     (*Reader's Guide*, 631).

13   Claims that the Burren in County Clare inspired
     Middle-earth landscapes are groundless. Another
     claim, that Tolkien said he could sense an evil in the
     Irish soil, comes from George Sayer, who admitted he
     sometimes had difficulty catching his friend's rapid,
     choppy mumble. Tolkien himself wrote that he was
     'always happy' in Ireland (*Reader's Guide*, 729).

14   On Tolkien's Celtic sources, I am indebted to the
     work of Verlyn Flieger, Dimitra Fimi, Marjorie Burns,
     Charles Huttar, Carl Phelpstead, Kris Swank, David
     Doughan and Yoko Hemmi.

15   Marjorie Burns, 53.

16   *Lord of the Rings*, 388. For how Tolkien did indeed
     plan for Lórien to be timeless, see Verlyn Flieger,
     A Question of Time: J. R. R. Tolkien's Road to Faërie
     (Kent, Ohio: Kent State University Press), 89–107.

17   *Letters*, no. 131.

18   David Doughan, 'An Ethnically Cleansed Faery:
     Tolkien and the Matter of Britain', *Mallorn* no. 32
     (1995), 23–24. Astolat, home to the tragic Elaine in
     Sir Thomas Malory's *Le Morte D'Arthur*, may have
     given shape to a *c.* 1931 Quenya word, *Astulat*
     'Bony ridge' (Tolkien, *Declension of Nouns*, in *Parma
     Eldalamberon*, no. 21 (2013), ed. Christopher Gilson,
     Patrick H. Wynne, and Arden R. Smith). Malory
     identifies Astolat with Guildford in Surrey, which
     lies below an imposing ridge of land called the Hog's
     Back.

19   *On Fairy-Stories*, 55.

20   Draft Valedictory Address, Tolkien papers,
     Bodleian Library.

21   For a fuller discussion of Longfellow and Tolkien,
     see my paper '"The road from adaptation to
     invention": How Tolkien came to the Brink of
     Middle-earth in 1914', *Tolkien Studies*, vol. 11
     (2014), 18–21, 28–30, 32–5.

22   Shippey, 127.

23   *Letters*, no. 294.

24   *Letters*, no. 142.

25   Cited in Garth, *op. cit.*

26   *Letters*, no. 227.

27   *The War of the Ring*, 229.

28   Judy Ann Ford, 'The White City: The Lord of the
     Rings as an Early Medieval Myth of the Restoration of
     the Roman Empire', *Tolkien Studies* vol. 2 (2005), 54.

29   *Letters*, no. 131.

30   *Lost Tales II*, 262.

31   *Letters*, no. 78.

32   *Letters*, no. 71.

33   *Letters*, no. 61 (18 April 1944). The chapter
     introducing Ithilien and ending with the Haradrim
     ambushed was written between then and 30 April.

34   *Lord of the Rings*, 650. As Christopher Tolkien notes
     (*War of the Ring*, 134) it was the need to describe
     Sam's cooking of rabbits that prompted his father

to launch into an exploration of the aromatic flora
of Ithilien. Claims that Tolkien was inspired by the
Hogsback area (not to be confused with the landmark
in Surrey, England, mentioned in note 18) in the
Eastern Cape are groundless.

35   *Lord of the Rings*, 661.

36   See Margaret Sinex, '"Monsterized Saracens",
     Tolkien's Haradrim, and Other Medieval Fantasy
     Products', *Tolkien Studies*, vol. 7, 2010; as well as
     Brian McFadden, 'Fear of Difference, Fear of Death:
     The *Sigelwara*, Tolkien's Swertings, and Racial
     Difference', in *Tolkien's Modern Middle Ages*, ed. Jane
     Chance and Alfred K. Sievers (Basingstoke: Palgrave
     Macmillan, 2005), 156; and Jane Chance, 'Tolkien
     and the Other: Race and Gender in Middle Earth',
     op. cit.

37   Tolkien, 'Sigelwara Land', *Medium Ævum*, vol. 3,
     no. 2 (1934), 110.

38   Tom Shippey, *Author of the Century* (London:
     HarperCollins, 2000), 86.

39   *Lord of the Rings*, 670.

40   *Letters*, no. 297. At the same time, Tolkien insisted
     that Gondor's Stone of Erech had nothing to do with
     the biblical city of the same name.

41   The 1876 translation (by photography pioneer and
     amateur philologist Henry Fox Talbot) was wrong in
     almost every way. The similarity with Tolkien's story
     was spotted and first investigated by Peter Gilliver. I
     give a full account and discussion in 'Ilu's Music: The
     Creation of Tolkien's Creation Myth', in *Sub-Creating
     Arda*, ed. Dimitra Fimi and Thomas Honegger
     (Zürich: Walking Tree, 2019).

42   Interview with Denys Gerould, BBC Radio, 1965.

43   W. B. Yeats, *The Song of Wandering Aengus*, from
     The Wind among the Reeds (1899). For comment
     and further suggested parallels, see Marie Barnfield,
     'Celtic Influences on the History of the First Age',
     Mallorn, no. 28 (1991).

44   Nansen, vol. 2, 383.

45   Languages in the Semitic family (such as Arabic and
     Hebrew) derive words from triconsonantal bases,
     such as КТВ 'to write', by vowel insertion and affixion.
     Tolkien also used Semitic as the model of Khuzdul,
     the language of the Dwarves.

46   *Letters*, no. 131.

47   *The Travels of Sir John Mandeville* (London:
     Macmillan, 1900), 46.

Four Winds: panels

Where It All Began (p.27)

1   *Letters*, no. 5 (August 1916).

2   *Sauron Defeated*, 236. Tolkien first chose the name,
    spelt *Loudham*, for a portrayal of his loudmouthed
    Inklings friend Hugo Dyson. In a radical shift of plot
    and character, *Lowdham* (spelt like the village near
    Gedling) became a self-portrait.

Elves, Finns and England (p.28)

1   Andrew Higgins, '"Those Who Cling in Queer
    Corners To The Forgotten Tongues and Memories
    of an Elder Day": J. R. R. Tolkien, Finns and Elves',
    Journal of Tolkien Research, vol. 3, no. 2 (2016).

2   Andrew Higgins, unpublished PhD thesis.

3   Thomas William Shore, *Origin of the Anglo-Saxon
    Race* (London: Elliot Stock, 1906) 127–8.

A Hostile World (p.30)

1   *Monsters and the Critics*, 18.

2   *Monsters and the Critics*, 18.

3   *Monsters and the Critics*, 20.

4   *Beowulf: A Translation and Commentary*, 163-164.

Peoples of the North (p.32)

1   *The War of the Jewels*, 282.

2   *Lord of the Rings*, 1136.

3   Shippey, 117.

Elvish and Welsh (p.33)

1   *Monsters and the Critics*, 197. Tolkien once wrote
    that Welsh had been in Britain so long it 'belonged
    to the land in a way with which English could not
    compete', and yet 'stirs deep harp-strings' even for
    English speakers who do not understand ('English
    and Welsh', *Monsters and the Critics*, 177, 194).
    Yoko Hemmi points out that *The Lord of the Rings*
    recreates this situation when Frodo and company
    meet Elves in the Shire ('Tolkien's *The Lord of the
    Rings* and His Concept of Native Language: Sindarin
    and British-Welsh', in *Tolkien Studies*, no. 7, 2010).
    Their Sindarin speech, lingering mainly in Lindon
    (see p.58), is far more ancient than hobbit Common
    Speech; and to the hobbits the Sindarin hymn they
    sing seems 'to shape itself in their thought into words
    … only partly understood' (*Lord of the Rings*, 79).

The Land of Lúthien: main text (pp. 42–59)

1   *Lord of the Rings*, 2.

2   *Letters*, no. 236.

3   *Qenya Lexicon*, 42.

4   Reprinted in Garth, 2003, 145.

5   *Lost Tales II*, 160. Christopher Gilson, Bill Welden,
    Carl F. Hostetter and Patrick Wynne (*Early Noldorin
    Fragments*, 96) note that Gnomish *baros* in *Celbaros*
    means 'hamlet'. They take the tree for a weeping
    willow, but Tolkien associated willows with Oxford.
    The laburnum was the inspiration for Laurelin, the
    golden tree of Valinor (*Morgoth's Ring*, 157–8), and
    for its offshoot in Gondolin.

6   *Qenya Lexicon*, 36. On *Erinti* as Edith, see
    Christopher Gilson, '*Narqelion* and the Early
    Lexicons', *Vinyar Tengwar* no. 40 (1999), 9.

7   Gilson et al (*Early Noldorin Fragments*, 94) wonder
    whether *tram nybol* means 'snowy bridge' (Gnomish
    nib 'snowflake'). Indeed, the winter of 1916–17
    was long and cold, with several heavy snowfalls in
    December and January. But Tolkien was only just
    inventing Gnomish, and much flux is to be expected.
    I would compare his poem *The Grey Bridge at Tavrobel*
    and perhaps Gnomish *nim* 'pale blue' (*Gnomish
    Lexicon*, 60).

8   Further echoes of Great Haywood in *The Book of
    Lost Tales* have been argued by David Robbie after
    close research that also led to the development of
    walks in Tolkien's footsteps as well as a successful
    touring exhibition (with librarian Scott Whitehouse)
    about Tolkien in Staffordshire.

9   *Lost Tales I*, 13.
10 *Lost Tales II*, 291, 288.
11 *Lost Tales II*, 289.
12 *Lord of the Rings*, xxiv.
13 *Lost Tales II*, 288–9.
14 *Lost Tales I*, 34.
15 *On Fairy-Stories*, 67.
16 Thomas Honegger, 'A Mythology for England? Looking a Gift Horse in the Mouth', in *Myth and Magic: Art According to the Inklings*, ed. Eduardo Segura and Thomas Honegger (Zürich: Walking Tree, 2007). Honegger's paper gives a fuller and somewhat different account of what I have called Tolkien's successive reboots or world-pictures.
17 *Lost Tales II*, 290.
18 The compiler of the Lost Tales was still Eriol in March 1920, and maybe also in October, when Tolkien's second son Michael was born – some of the final jottings about the quasi-autobiographical Eriol give him a second son, too. From that month, Tolkien spent two academic terms living alone in Leeds, only returning to Oxford for weekends. A change of scene, with solitary evenings – it seems a likely point for a rethink.
19 *Lost Tales II*, 313.
20 *Lost Tales II*, 313.
21 *Lost Tales II*, 314. Dimitra Fimi argues that Ælfwine's Celtic mother is 'the first missing piece' in the merging of Celtic and Anglo-Saxon traditions ('Tolkien's "'Celtic' type of legends": Merging Traditions', *Tolkien Studies*, vol. 4 [2007], 53) but the role of place is as important.
22 *Lost Tales II*, 313.
23 Trans. Shippey, 373. The father's name is Déor, and the Old English poem *Déor* was part of Tolkien's 1920–21 Leeds syllabus.
24 *Lost Tales II*, 313.
25 *Shaping of Middle-earth*, 39.
26 *Shaping of Middle-earth*, 134.
27 *Lost Road*, 33. None of the few islands that Tolkien now envisaged surviving Beleriand's destruction (such as Himling and Tol Fuin) are prehistoric British Isles.
28 *Lord of the Rings*,
29 *Lord of the Rings*, 276. Gandalf refers to Hollin.
30 A handwritten note by Tolkien on a printed *Lord of the Rings* map for artist Pauline Baynes (McIlwaine, 382–3) begins by saying Hobbiton is on the latitude of Oxford (cf. *Letters*, no. 294). With a meridian line drawn through it, Hobbiton seems to be his starting point when he says Minas Tirith (roughly on the latitude of Ravenna) 'is 900 miles east of Hobbiton more near Belgrade'. By projecting the Middle-earth map on to Google Earth, Brandon Rhodes manages to locate Hobbiton at Oxford and Minas Tirith at Belgrade ('Google Earth and Middle-earth', 30 September 2009, https://rhodesmill.org/brandon/2009/google-earth-and-middle-earth/), though Didier Willis's calculations using the same data put Hobbiton in the Netherlands (http://tolkiengateway.net/wiki/Middle-earth). Doubtless it depends on the map projection you use.

31 Tolkien was perfectly capable of superimposing his myth on his daily life, as demonstrated by a letter from this very spot, Clevedon, on a 1952 visit. Tolkien sent his son Christopher a sketch, saying it was 'not a vision of Tirion [the capital of Elvenhome], but an attempt to catch Cardiff caught in a rainbow across the Severn Sea' (*Reader's Guide*, 246).

The Land of Lúthien: panels
Tales that Grew in the Telling (p.44)
1   *Tales from the Perilous Realm*, 286.
A Mythology for England (p.47)
1   *Letters*, no. 131.
2   *Letters*, no. 131.
3   Angela Bartie, Paul Readman et al, 'Commemoration through dramatic performance', in *The Age of Anniversaries: The Cult of Commemoration 1825– 1925*, ed. T. G. Otte (London: Routledge, 2018), 195; 'Warwick Pageant', *The Times*, 3 July 1906, 12.
4   *Lost Tales I*, 33. It is not entirely unlikely that Tolkien attended the Warwick Pageant at 14 with his guardian, Father Francis Morgan, a man partial to theatricals. Special rail services had been laid on all the first week of July 1906 from Birmingham, London and elsewhere. In 1913, Tolkien visited Pageant House, the event's former headquarters, and drew the gardens that had been laid out with pageant profits.
5   *Letters*, no. 131, to Milton Waldman, probably 1951.
Twin Towns in Faërie (p.54)
1   *Lost Road*, 203, 380. Here, in the c. 1937 'Etymologies', *Tavrobel* is also the name of the village where the hero Túrin Turambar makes his home in the Forest of Brethil. Christopher Tolkien sees a possible 'echo' of Great Haywood, suggesting that his father 'did not wish finally to abandon this old and deep association of his youth'; and compares the confluence of the nearby rivers Taiglin and Sirion with that of the Sow and the Trent (413). Tavrobel appears sporadically for the place in Brethil even in 1950s writings (*War of the Jewels*, 148, 157, 186). In 1937 Tolkien revised *Kortirion among the Trees*, his old poem about Warwick, but it is entirely unclear how he saw it fitting into the legendarium – if he did at all.
What's in a Name? (p.56)
1   *The Mistress of Vision*, from *New Poems* (1897); repr. *The Poems of Francis Thompson: A New Edition*, ed. Brigid M. Boardman (London: Continuum, 2001), 97.
2   When first applied to England, around 1919, Gnomish *Lúthien* is given the Quenya equivalent *Lósien* (*Qenya Lexicon*, 2), perhaps recalling one of Tolkien's earliest Gnomish names for the Lonely Isle, *Gar Eglos*, 'Land of Release' (*Lost Tales I*, 13, 21).
3   Tinúviel was first named *Lúthien* in 1924. Much later translations of *Lúthien* (Tinúviel) as 'enchantress' (around 1937, *The Lost Road*, 370) or 'daughter of flowers' (1960s, *Words, Phrases and Passages*, 11) are unhelpful for understanding Tolkien's intentions when he coined these names in the 1920s.
4   *Lost Tales I*, 13, 250.
5   *Lays of Beleriand*, 120.

6   The reason for the root-connection between *free* and *friend* is actually far from sentimental. In Germanic and Celtic cultures, the only members of a household who were not slaves were the head's family – so the loved ones were also the free ones. 'To love' was still the sense of Old English *fréon* – the source of the modern English word *friend*. The closely related *fréogan* 'to release' led to *free* in its modern English senses.

The Shore and the Sea: main text (pp. 60–81)
1   W. H. Lewis, *Brothers and Friends: The Diaries of Major Warren Hamilton Lewis* (New York: Harper & Row, 1982), 206.
2   *Adventures of Tom Bombadil*, 34.
3   *Family Album*, 18, gives the Indian Ocean in error for the Atlantic.
4   The *Guelph* (launched less than a year earlier and put into service in October) left Tenerife on the morning of 14 April, Madeira at lunchtime the next day and Lisbon at 4 p.m. on 17 April. *Hampshire Advertiser*, 24 April 1895, 3; and *The Times*, 22 April, 6.
5   Bill Cater, 'We talked of love, death and fairy tales', *Daily Telegraph*, 4 December 2001, 23.
6   Tolkien, 'The Lonely Isle', *Leeds University Verse 1914–1924*, 57; reprinted in Garth 2004, 145.
7   Garth 2004, 145.
8   Weather historians attribute this 'year without a summer' – with one of the coldest Augusts on record – to the eruption of Mount Katmai in Alaska (Kington, 396).
9   Tolkien papers, Bodleian Library. Lizard Town is reputed to be named for a medieval colony of lepers or 'lazars' there (*Kelly's Directory of Cornwall 1914*, 176), but the name actually comes from the Cornish for 'high court; court in a high place'.
10 *Biography*, 71.
11 *Biography*, 70.
12 *Kelly's Directory of Devonshire and Cornwall*, vol. 3 (London: Kelly's Directories, 1914), 176.
13 *Shaping of Middle-earth*, 214.
14 *Shaping of Middle-earth*, 217.
15 *Shaping of Middle-earth*, 216.
16 *Lord of the Rings*, 1030.
17 The visit spanned at least 5–16 August. Weather reports show clear evenings in the latter part, except the stormy 14th. The moon was waning from the 7th and low in the east. Astronomical observations are my own, using Stellarium software.
18 *Lost Tales II*, 268.
19 The theory is summed up here by B. Symons in *Grundriss der Germanischen Philologie* vol. 2, part 1 (ed. Hermann Paul [Strassburg: Karl J. Trubner, 1891-93], 62–3), which Tolkien borrowed from Exeter College Library in June 1914. The passage was translated for me by Allan Turner. Müllenhof's original theory is in *Deutsche altertumskunde* (Berlin: Weidmannsche Buchhandlung, 1870), 30–46. Much later, Tolkien alluded to it when he theorized that the Old English elegy *The Seafarer* had 'at one time recognizable references … to a mariner-

adventurer a northern Ulysses-like character in his old age' (1964–5 notes, quoted in Stuart Lee, 'Tolkien and The Wanderer', *Tolkien Studies* vol. 6 [2009], 199).

20 *Lost Tales II*, 262.

21 *Family Album*, 18.

22 Nansen, vol. I, 156, 284. C. S. Lewis later adapted the same traditions for the island of the Three Sleepers in *The Voyage of the Dawn Treader*.

23 Nansen, vol. I, 192, 363.

24 *Lost Road*, 24. The Quenya name simply means it is near Valinor. Later, in the form *Avallónë*, Tolkien made this the name of the haven on Tol Eressëa, rather than the whole island.

25 *Morgoth's Ring*, 365.

26 Nansen, vol, I, 375.

27 *Adventures of Tom Bombadil*, 90. In an episode in the *Navigatio* of St Brendan the sea-beast (though referred to as a 'fish') is evidently a whale – as it is in Tolkien's first version of *Fastitocalon*, first published in the *Stapeldon Magazine* (Exeter College, Oxford, June 1927) and reprinted in the 2014 edition of *Adventures of Tom Bombadil*. In his second version, Tolkien made the creature a turtle because he recognised that the medieval name *Fastitocalon*, though used for a whale, actually derives from *aspido-chelōne*, 'turtle with a round shield (of hide)' (*Letters*, no. 255).

28 *Lost Tales II*, 262.

29 George MacDonald, *At the Back of the North Wind* (1871).

30 Lecture to students, 1920s–30s (*Beowulf: A Translation and Commentary*), 151. See Shippey, 170–1.

31 *Beowulf: A Translation and Commentary*, 152.

32 *Lost Road*, 77. Conceived in 1937, this would have been one of a series of historical episodes hinting at the existence of Valinor in the distant past.

33 Nansen's arguments seem largely forgotten these days, though not even the 1960 discovery of Norse relics at L'Anse-aux-Meadows, Newfoundland, proves that this was Vinland rather than one of the other, less fanciful regions named in the sagas, Helluland or Markland.

34 In a new book on the sagas, Craigie defended the historical basis of the 'much discussed and disputed' Vinland account (*The Icelandic Sagas*, Cambridge: Cambridge University Press, 1913, 58).

35 November 1914 talk to an Oxford student society (*Story of Kullervo*, 68).

36 Revision of 1914 *Kalevala* talk, 1919–23 (*Story of Kullervo*, 113–14). Christopher Tolkien and his son Adam kindly checked Tolkien's copy of Nansen's *In Northern Mists* for me. The first volume is inscribed 'John Reuel Tolkien, November 1921'.

37 In his lecture *On Fairy-Stories* (29, 88), Tolkien complains that 'the magic land of Hy Breasail in the West had become the mere Brazils'. Hy Breasail was an 'isle of bliss' from Irish fable, but in the Age of Discovery it appeared on the maps that helped spur explorers like John Cabot and Christopher Columbus westward. Nansen argues that *Hy Breasail*, perhaps from Irish *bress* 'good fortune, prosperity', gave rise

to the real place-name *Brazil* by confusion with Portuguese *brasile* 'red dye-wood'.

38 Though principally about Thorfinn, the text Tolkien read is more widely known as *The Saga of Erik the Red*, Leif's father. *The Saga of the Greenlanders* also gives a somewhat different account of the Vinland voyages.

39 The drawing is titled *I Vene Kemen*, a Quenya pun meaning both the Shape of the World and the Ship of the World.

40 *Valinor*, *Valar*, *valin* are all related to *vald-* 'good fortune, blessedness, happiness' (*Qenya Lexicon*, 99). Later, Tolkien reconsidered the meaning, so *Valar* means 'the Powers'.

41 *Lays of Beleriand*, 40, 112 (from the early 1920s).

42 Nansen, vol. I, 1.

43 Nansen, vol. I, 195.

44 *The Lord of the Rings*, 1041–2.

45 Several months later, Tolkien recorded the holiday dates as 6–27 September. Wayne G. Hammond and Christina Scull suggest he misremembered, pointing out that the moon reached full on 2 September and weather caused coastal damage on 5 September ('High tides and rough seas', *The Times*, 7 September 1925, 12). But another possibility for the storm seems to be 19 September, when 'wind rose to gale force on exposed parts of the southern and eastern coasts and heavy rain fell locally … e.g., 55mm (2.18in) occurred at Filey', according to the Meteorological Office monthly UK weather report. On 6 September, the moon rose over the sea at 8.35 p.m., still near enough full.

46 Carpenter (*Biography*, 38) claims he 'supposed' it to be a dragon jaw. In print, Tolkien said he was introduced to palaeontology as early as fairy-stories, and enjoyed the 'gleam of fantasy' surrounding prehistoric beasts, but 'did not like being told that these creatures were "dragons"' (*On Fairy-Stories*, 81).

47 *Qenya Lexicon*, 47; *Gnomish Lexicon*, 40; *Treason of Isengard*, 312. Given Tolkien's taste for puns, especially in his youth, it may have been the similarity between Lyme Regis's *Cobb* and the English word for a male swan, *cob*, that led Tolkien to think of Swanhaven in the first place.

48 *Letters*, no. 257.

49 Davies's poem *Lamorna Cove* was written in 1928.

50 In 1958 Wrenn spoke on 'Saxons and Celts in South-West Britain' for Oxford's annual O'Donnell Lecture in Celtic Studies. Tolkien had delivered the inaugural lecture, 'English and Welsh', in 1955.

51 Predannack is within walking distance (*Lost Road*, 50).

52 S. Baring-Gould, *Cornwall* (Cambridge: Cambridge University Press, 1910), 29.

53 *Letters*, no. 257.

54 *Reader's Guide*, 246.

55 Tolkien, *The Lay of Aotrou and Itroun*, ed. Verlyn Flieger (London: HarperCollins, 2016), 15. Broceliande is traditionally associated with the small Forêt de Paimpont in the middle of Brittany.

56 *Letters*, no. 257.

57 *Letters*, no. 332.

58 For the date of the conception of Númenor, see

my blog post, 'When Tolkien reinvented Atlantis and Lewis went to Mars', https://johngarth.wordpress.com/2017/03/31.

59 *Silmarillion*, 279.

60 *Lord of the Rings*, 1037.

61 *Sauron Defeated*, 264. The poem began as *The Death of St Brendan* in *The Notion Club Papers*, and was published as *Imram* in 1955.

62 *Silmarillion*, 304.

63 *Lord of the Rings*, 1030.

64 *Lord of the Rings*, 1030.

65 *Silmarillion*, 304.

66 *Lord of the Rings*, 1030.

The Shore and the Sea: panels

From Great Yarmouth to Belfalas (p.65)

1 *Adventures of Tom Bombadil*, 31.

2 Tolkien's friend Christopher Wiseman wrote to him on 16 September 1913 saying he had heard Tolkien was about to visit Norwich. A list of expenses written by Tolkien on the envelope includes 'fares Norwich'. (Tolkien family papers, Bodleian Library.) A note on a yet-unpublished poem, *The Lonely Harebell*, says it was inspired at Cromer in Norfolk in 1914. For Tolkien's visits to Whitby, Yorkshire, in 1910 and 1945, and a stay in Hove, East Sussex, in 1904, any comparable impact remains to be identified.

Where on Earth is Dorwinion? (p.69)

1 *Hobbit*, 153.

2 *Lays of Beleriand*, 11, 111–12.

3 Late notes for *The Lord of the Rings* translate *Dorwinion* as 'Young-land country' (*Words, Phrases and Passages*, 54), evidently from *dor* 'country' and Sindarin *gwin* 'youth' (191). The latter goes right back to *gwinwen* 'youth, freshness' in the 1917 *Gnomish Lexicon*, 45.

4 Roger Echo-Hawk, *Tolkien in Pawneeland: The Secret Sources of Middle-earth* (Charleston: CreateSpace, 2013) 8–13; 'Night the Spider', tolkienland.wordpress.com (2 October 2018). Echo-Hawk also notes some of the connections between Valinor and Vinland of the Norse sagas in Tolkien's earliest Éarendel outline.

5 *Lost Road*, 334.

6 *Lord of the Rings*, 1030.

7 *Fall of Arthur*, 55.

In a Cave by the Sea Lived A… (p.72)

1 *Annotated Hobbit*, 119.

2 *Hobbit*, 68.

3 *Gulum* is the Gnomish equivalent to Quenya *Ulmo* in an early list of names in *The Fall of Gondolin* (*Early Noldorin Fragments*, 101). Contemporary notes derive *Ulmo* from a stem ULU 'pour, flow fast' (*Qenya Lexicon*, 97), which may have a similar glugging inspiration.

4 *Annotated Hobbit*, 119.

5 Helen Armstrong, 'Whence We Hobbits', *Amon Hen* no. 187 (May 2004), 31. She cites Katharine Briggs's 1976 *A Dictionary of Fairies* – a paraphrase of Henderson that is far less hobbity than the original.

The word *hobbit* has inspired vast speculation. Tolkien thought he had made *hobbit* up, though he conceded that 'buried childhood memories might suddenly rise to the surface long after' (*Letters*, no. 319). After his death it was noticed that the word appears (without description) in a huge list of supernatural creatures in *The Denham Tracts*, a nineteenth-century folklore collection. There is no evidence that Tolkien saw the list. Alternatively, he may have come across *hobbit* as an obsolete unit of measurement or an old word for howitzer; but even if he did, such things suggest little of what *hobbit* now means to us.

6   William Henderson, *Folk-lore of the Northern Counties of England and the Borders* (London: Folk-lore Society, 1879), 264.
7   Edmund Weiner to the author.
8   *Lord of the Rings*, 54.

The Curse of Porlock (p.75)

1   The 1937 walk is known to have been in the Quantocks, but may have been part of a longer hike to Minehead, between Porlock and Watchet on the Somerset coast. In a 1957 letter, Tolkien said 'the last really long walk I did (years ago) was from Lyme Regis to Minehead, largely cross-country. Not in one day!' (*Reader's Guide*, 755). The hike would have covered fifty miles (80km) or more – a distance that Tolkien seems unlikely to have undertaken without the indefatigable Lewis. In a postcard from the Quantocks in 1937, Tolkien told his daughter Priscilla they were hiking twenty miles (32km) a day. It seems quite possible that her memory, some four decades later, was hazy when she said he had joined Lewis for a *separate* walking tour to Lyme Regis (Humphrey Carpenter, *The Inklings* [London: George Allen & Unwin, 1978] 57). There were few available years for a Lewis–Tolkien walking tour after 1937. In 1938 they walked in Hampshire; in 1947 near Malvern, seemingly Tolkien and Lewis's last walk together before they drifted apart. There were no wartime walks; only 1939 and 1946 are uncertain.

What's in a Name? (p.78)

1   *Broseliand* seems never to have been translated, and *Beleriand* not until 1937 (when it is connected with the Bay of Balar, *Lost Road*, 350).

Shipwrecks (p.79)

1   J. C. Trewin, *Up from the Lizard* (London: Anthony Mott, 1982; first pub. 1948), 196.
2   *Adventures of Tom Bombadil*, 254. *Looney* was later rewritten for this 1962 collection as *The Sea-bell*.
3   *Monsters and the Critics*, 214.
4   Claudian, 'The First Book against Rufinus', in *Claudian*, trans. Maurice Platnauer (London: Heinemann, 1921), 35. See Hersart de la Villemarqué (ed.), *Barzaz-Breiz: Chants Populaires de la Bretagne*, vol. 1 (Paris: Franck, 1846), 259–60; and Procopius, *History of the Wars*, Book 8, Chapter 20.
5   *Lost Tales II*, 283, 285.

Roots of the Mountains: main text (pp. 82–99)

1   *Letters*, no. 306.
2   Tolkien was collected by relatives from school on

26 July. Guestbook entries show the party visited the Ober Steinberg guesthouse above Stechelberg on 5 August and the Cabane de Bertol south of Arolla on on 25 August (Alex Lewis and Elizabeth Currie, *Tolkien's Switzerland: A Biography of a Special Summer*, privately published 2019). On 17 August 1911, Tolkien's friend Christopher Wiseman replied to two cards received that day from Tolkien, who he said was 'on the other side of the valley' from Gletsch (Tolkien papers, Bodleian Library). That probably meant somewhere in the Rhône valley, or possibly the Grimsel Pass.

3   *Lost Tales II*, 261.
4   *Letters*, no. 109.
5   *Letters*, no. 78. Tolkien consistently spells *moraine* as *morain*.
6   Sally Pehrsson to the author.
7   *Letters*, no. 96.
8   *Hobbit*, 47.
9   *Letters*, no. 306.
10 *Hobbit*, 48.
11 *Art of The Hobbit*, 41–8; *Art of The Lord of the Rings*, 56, 180.
12 *Letters*, no. 306.
13 I am grateful to geologist Sally Pehrsson on these points. Tolkien may well have attended a talk by his mountaineering headmaster, Robert Cary Gilson, about a trip to Skye (*King Edward's School Chronicle*, March 1906, 10).
14 'Four deaths on the Eiger', *The Times*, 23 July 1936, 15.
15 *Lord of the Rings*, 792.
16 *Lord of the Rings*, 791.
17 *Art of The Lord of the Rings*, 163–4.
18 *Letters*, no. 306. Tolkien recollected that this was from the Aletsch glacier but commentators believe it must have been from the Arolla area.
19 Killed in a Himalayan avalanche in 1895, Mummery had been the 'ever-to-be-lamented friend' and climbing companion of Tolkien's headmaster Robert Cary Gilson (*Old Edwardians Gazette*, March 1902, 121), father of Rob Gilson of Tolkien's T.C.B.S. The ghost account appears in Mummery's *My Climbs in the Alps and Caucasus* (London: Fisher Unwin, 1895, 30–4) – a mountaineering classic recommended by the headmaster in a talk on 'out-of-doors literature' to the school Literary Society, which Tolkien frequented, in January 1911.
20 *Reader's Guide*, 770.
21 Brookes-Smith describes the route marked on school inspector Dorothy Le Couteur's '1911 map of the tour'. He says that after the Aletsch glacier and Brig they went to Stalden, over a pass westward to St Niklaus and so to Gruben in the Turtman valley; then west again over the Forcletta Pass to Grimentz; then south-south-west to Les Haudères and Arolla.
22 Brookes-Smith, 2.
23 *Letters*, no. 306.
24 *Letters*, no. 232.
25 Tolkien to Hermione Jolles (daughter of his schoolmaster R. W. Reynolds), 6 March 1964, courtesy of Arnold Jolles. The photo on p. 84, labelled the Grimsel Pass on the back and once owned by

Colin Brookes-Smith, appears in *Family Album* (31) captioned as the Aletsch Glacier. But a visit to the Arolla Glacier is confirmed by the new-found Cabane de Bertol guestbook entry (see note 2). This must by the 'high hut of the Alpine Club' Tolkien recalls reaching roped, with the Matterhorn in the distance. His memory of arriving in Zermatt, late and bedraggled, to 'the lorgnette stares of the French bourgeoises dames' (*Letters*, no. 306), suggests they may have crossed via the Col de Bertol from Arolla – '10–11 hours, fatiguing but repaying' (Baedeker's 1909 *Switzerland*, 393) – a route broadly surmised by Nancy Martsch ('Tolkien's Trip to Switzerland', *Beyond Bree*, November 2011, 2). Brookes-Smith is hazy beyond Arolla: 'How long we stayed there I do not remember but we were nearing the end of our holiday and must have walked down the Val d'Herens to Sion' – where they caught the train for home.

26 *Artist and Illustrator*, 116, 200. The undated painting, in an early style, appears on the final page of a sketchbook of juvenilia, following a picture of Golden Cap near Lyme Regis (*Artist and Illustrator*, 12). Tolkien's last certain holiday there was in 1907.
27 Rateliff, 36–7. If Tolkien imagined the Lonely Mountain around the position of the yet-to-be-invented Hill of Himring (as suggested by Rateliff, 19–20), then Hithlum would be a reasonable starting point for a quest heading east. In 1920s poetry, Tolkien referred to its 'misty hills' (*Lays of Beleriand*, 37). The phrase was first capitalized 'the Misty Mountains' at Rivendell (111), but he may have carried the adventure right through the mountains to the Eagle eyrie before finally devising the familiar setting in which they are the western rim of Wilderland (see p.123).
28 Shippey, 74, 81. Auden puts these lines as 'Over the misty mountains, / The fells of the troll-folk', in a translation dedicated to Tolkien (Paul B. Taylor and W. H. Auden, *The Elder Edda*, London: Faber, 1969, 119).
29 Longfellow, Canto IV; *The Lord of the Rings*, 502.
30 Lars Gustafsson, 'Den besynnerlige professor Tolkien' ('Tolkien, the Peculiar Professor'), *Dagens Nyheter*, 21 August 1961; trans. Morgan Thomas and Shaun Gunner, 'Two Swedish Interviews with Tolkien', in *Hither Shore* 9 (2012).
31 *On Fairy-Stories*, 55.
32 *Lord of the Rings*, 555.
33 W. G. Collingwood and Jón Stefánsson, *A Pilgrimage to the Saga-Steads of Iceland* (Ulverstone: W. Holmes, 1899) 154–6. The co-author's son, R. G. Collingwood, was a friend and colleague to Tolkien at Pembroke College, Oxford, for more than a decade. Tom Shippey has pointed out that Tolkien must have known Collingwood senior, or at least his work on Northern archaeology and this particular Icelandic travel book. The tradition of Borgarvirki ('the Burg-work') is recounted too by William Morris and Eiríkr Magnússon in *The Story of the Ere-Dwellers with The Saga of the Heath-slayings* (London: Bernard Quaritch, 1892), xl–xliii.

34 J. W. Dunne, *An Experiment with Time* (3rd ed., London: Faber and Faber, 1934), 34. Dunne does not claim he actually saw a vision of the Pelée disaster, but judges that he probably read the report first and then his subconscious manufactured a false memory of dreaming. He is mistaken in thinking that water intrusion caused the Krakatoa eruption.

35 Verlyn Flieger, *A Question of Time: J. R. R. Tolkien's Road to Faërie* (Kent, Ohio: Kent State University Press, 1997), 66.

36 *Lost Road*, 52.

37 *Sauron Defeated*, 251.

38 *The Voyage of St Brendan*, in *Sauron Defeated*, 295.

39 *Silmarillion*, 22. The passage is from version 'C' of *Ainulindalë*, written c. 1948–51 (*Morgoth's Ring*, 16).

40 Richard Plotz of the Tolkien Society of America claimed that Tolkien had reported seeing Stromboli during his 1966 Mediterranean cruise and 'said he's never seen anything that looked so much like Emyn Anar' ('An Edited Transcript of Remarks at the December 1966 TSA Meeting', *Niekas*, no. 19 [December 1968], 40). Even if this is an accurate report, and granting a possible error for *Amon Amarth* (Sindarin 'Mount Doom'), it would mean Stromboli had reminded him of Mount Doom, not inspired it. Some online discussions misattribute the claim to Clyde S. Kilby, whose unrelated comments are reported on the same pages of *Niekas*.

41 For various parallels between Verne's book and *The Hobbit*, see Mark T. Hooker, *The Tolkienaeum* (CreateSpace Independent Publishing Platform, 2014), 1–11.

42 Organ, 110.

43 Comment by Stephen Tempest (18 April 2018) at www.quora.com/When-writing-The-Hobbit-did-Tolkien-take-Erebos-the-Greek-god-of-darkness-as-an-inspiration-for-Erebor. Probably sensibly, Tempest dismisses comparisons with Erebus as god of darkness or region of hell in Greek mythology.

44 *Letters from Father Christmas*, 23.

45 *Lays of Beleriand*, 33.

46 *Lays of Beleriand*, 309.

47 All *Times* quotations are from 'Hekla in eruption', 26 April 1947, 5, and 'Iceland volcano in eruption', 31 March 1947, 6.

48 'After 102 years: Mount Hekla in eruption', *Times*, 2 April 1947, 6.

49 *Lord of the Rings*, 949.

50 Richard Fortey, *The Earth* (London: HarperCollins, 2005), 151.

51 *Letters*, no. 187.

52 *Shaping of Middle-earth*, 214.

53 The 1867 excursion was by the Geological Section of the British Association, which was meeting in Dundee (Archibald Geikle, *A Long Life's Work: An Autobiography* [Cambridge: Cambridge University Press, 2012], 117–18).

54 Anon., 'A geotourist at the Rock and Spindle', *New-Cleckit Dominie* blog, 20 August 2013 (newcleckitdominie.wordpress.com). Tolkien would have noted that this *Rock* is the old word for distaff,

the cleft staff used (together with a spindle) in spinning wool or flax.

55 *Shaping of Middle-earth*, 217.

56 The phrase *geological cycle* seems to have appeared first in G. A. Mantell and G. F. Richardson, *The Wonders of Geology*, 1838.

57 Calculated by Archbishop Ussher in the seventeenth century, the date 4000 BC was one 'to which, with the pride and courage of Englishmen, we adhere as stoutly as to the text itself' (R. S. Watson, *Cædmon: The First English Poet* [London: Longman, Green, 1875], 30).

58 *Lost Tales I*, 106.

59 Hynes, 22.

60 *Shaping of Middle-earth*, 240.

61 *Shaping of Middle-earth*, 239.

62 *Letters*, no. 257.

63 *Times*, 12 August 1929, 8 (report on a meeting of the British Association for the Advancement of Science); *Letters*, no. 324.

64 *Times*, 29 September 1931, 9 (also on a British Association meeting).

65 *Letters from Father Christmas*, 86. For this point I am indebted to David Llewellyn Dodds, '"Kubla Khan" and Father Nicholas Christmas?', www.superversivesf.com/inklings/2018/11/07/.

66 Mitch Liddell, 'Tectonics of Middle-Earth' LondonMoot 2018 (unpublished), citing W. A. S. Sarjeant, 'The Geology of Middle-earth', in *Proceedings of the J. R. R. Tolkien Centenary Conference*, ed. Patricia Reynolds and Glen GoodKnight (Milton Keynes: Tolkien Society, 1995) 334–9.

67 For a recent large-scale study, see Chris Ingles and Lindy A. Orthia, 'A New Synthesis on the Geology of Middle-earth: Genesis, Orogeny and Tectonics' (manuscript prepared for *Journal of Hobbitlore*, 2016). For a smaller-scale study, see Neil Holford's 'The Geology of the Northern Kingdom' (*Mallorn* no. 29, August 1992, 2–5).

68 *On Fairy-Stories*, 58.

69 *Letters*, no. 26.

70 Joseph O'Neill, *Land Under England* (Woodstock, NY, 1985), 49–51.

71 *Letters*, no. 321.

72 Ernest A. Baker and H. E. Balch, *The Netherworld of Mendip* (Clifton: J. Baker and Son, 1907), 92.

73 *Silmarillion*, 93.

74 *Lord of the Rings*, 547–8.

75 *Lord of the Rings*, 548.

Roots of the Mountains: panels
The Mountains of Paradise (p.90)

1 Denis Bridoux, 'Over Snows by Winter Sown and Under Mountains of the Moon' (unpublished presentation, Oxonmoot 2016).

2 *Lost Tales II*, 292.

3 *tún* 'mound, bare hill' appears in the 1920s 'Noldorin Word-lists' (*Early Noldorin Fragments*, 154); Noldorin *tund, tunn* 'hill, mound' appears in the c. 1937 'Etymologies' (*Lost Road*, 395).

4 C. W. R. D. Moseley (trans.), *The Travels of Sir John Mandeville* (London: Penguin, 1983), 183. Cf. A. Keith

Kelly and John Livingston, '"A far green country": Tolkien, Paradise and the End of All Things in Medieval Literature', *Mythlore* vol. 27, no. 3 (2009), 95–6.

5 Longfellow, Canto IV.

Rivers, Lakes and Waterlands: main text (pp. 100–11)

1 *Silmarillion*, 252.

2 *Lays of Beleriand*, 62.

3 Elias Lönnrot, *Kalevala*, trans. W. F. Kirby (London: Dutton, Everyman's Library, 1907), vol. 2, 113.

4 Charles Marriott, *The Romance of the Rhine* (London: Methuen, 1911) 77.

5 The story has acquired the timelessness of folklore but began with an 1801 ballad by Clemens Brentano and was made famous by Heinrich Heine's 1924 poem *Die Lorelei*.

6 *Amon Hen* no. 68 (Tolkien Society), 22.

7 Barnfield, 7–9. Neither *Lauterbrunnen* ('clear spring') nor *Lütschine* appears to mean 'Loudwater'.

8 Blackham 2006, 31, and interview; Brace 1968; Acocks Green History Society, 'The river Cole in Yardley, and its fords and bridges', aghs.jimdo.com/waters-of-yardley/river-ford-bridges.

9 McIlwaine, 154.

10 *Lost Tales II*, 297.

11 *Lost Tales II*, 153–4.

12 *Lost Tales II*, 154.

13 William Henderson, *Folk-lore of the Northern Counties* (London: Folk-lore Society, 1879), 265.

14 John Milton, *Comus: A Masque*; see John Bowers, 'Tolkien's Goldberry and Maid of the Moor', *Tolkien Studies* no. 8 (2011), 29.

15 *Lord of the Rings*, 129.

16 *Lord of the Rings*, 339.

17 *Treason of Isengard*, 222, 238–9.

18 The name is naturally interpreted 'even course', but Ekwall (162) explains it as 'Eowla's passage or ferry' (Eowla being a personal name).

19 *Lord of the Rings*, 317.

20 Hilary Tolkien, 6.

21 *Lord of the Rings*, 373.

22 A. H. Smith, *The Place-names of the East Riding of Yorkshire and York* (1937, repr. London: Cambridge University Press, 1970), xv–xvi, 129. Smith cites the legal term *vǽt-vangr*, nothing to do with English wet.

23 E. Maule Cole, 'On the Place-name Wetwang', *Saga-Book of the Viking Club*, vol. 4 (1904–5), 104.

24 *Nomenclature*, 779.

25 *Chronology*, 685.

26 Longfellow, Canto 9, 'Hiawatha and the Pearl Feather', *Song of Hiawatha*.

27 *Lord of the Rings*, 626.

28 *Lord of the Rings*, 627.

29 *Beowulf: A Translation and Commentary*, 52. The comparison is made by Rod Giblett, *Environmental Humanities and Theologies: Ecoculture, Literature and the Bible* (Routledge, 2018), 33.

30 *Beowulf: A Translation and Commentary*, 52.

31 *Beowulf: A Translation and Commentary*, 52; illustrations in *Artist and Illustrator*, 54–5.

32 *Beowulf: A Translation and Commentary*, 54.

33 *Unfinished Tales*, 264.

34 Arthur L. Salmon, *Dorset* (Cambridge: Cambridge University Press, 1915) 38.

35 Denis Bridoux to the author.

36 *Unfinished Tales*, 263.

37 Nigel Holmes and Paul Raven, *Rivers: A Natural and Not-So-Natural History* (London: Bloomsbury, 2014).

38 Karen Wynn Fonstad, *The Atlas of Middle-earth* (revised ed., Boston: Houghton Mifflin, 1991) 120–1.

39 *Peoples of Middle-earth*, 39, 67. England's *Malvern* is an old British name related to Welsh *Moel-fryn*, 'bare hill'.

40 Tolkien, *Names and Required Alterations*, in *Parma Eldalamberon*, no. 15 (2004), ed. Patrick H. Wynne, 16.

Rivers, Lakes and Waterlands: panels
Castle and Carrock (p.103)

1 *Silmarillion*, 120.

2 *Lays of Beleriand*, 227.

3 *Hobbit*, 100.

4 Karl Baedeker, *The Rhine* (17th ed., London: Fisher Unwin, 1911), 231. The Elvish element *lam-* had always meant 'tongue', but around the time he was writing *The Hobbit* Tolkien invented related words for echo (*Lost Road*, 358 GLAM, 367 LAM, and 405–6).

5 *Treason of Isengard*, 268–9, 287.

Rivers of War (p.106)

1 Garth 2003, 207–8.

2 *Lost Tales II*, 287.

3 *Lost Tales I*, 240.

River-Names (p.108)

1 *Lost Tales I*, 205.

2 Shippey, 123. He connects *Cher-* with Old English *cierran* 'to turn'.

3 Jason Fisher, 'The Poros and the Bosphorus', *Lingwë – Musings of a Fish*, 9 October 2011 (lingwe.blogspot.com/2011/10/). Greek *Bosphorus* literally means 'ox-ford', which would have appealed to Tolkien, as Fisher points out. C. S. Lewis's brother Warnie, a member of the Inklings, kept a boat named the *Bosphorus* on the Thames at Oxford.

4 Translation from Old English: Orchard, 229.

Tree-woven Lands: main text (pp. 112–31)

1 *Biography*, 47.

2 *Story of Kullervo*, 21 (and see Verlyn Flieger's note, 57).

3 *Lost Tales I*, 183–9; see also Garth, 2003, 95–100.

4 *Lord of the Rings*, 1115.

5 Andy Slater, 'Moseley Bog: A Journey through Time', 11 February 2018. https://andyunderscore.com/2018/02/11/moseley-bog-through-time/

6 *Lord of the Rings*, 255.

7 *Hobbit*, 129–30.

8 Rateliff, 334–5. The butterflies are black (Mirkwood's signature colour) but *The Hobbit* says they may be 'a kind of "purple emperor", a butterfly that loves the tops of oak-woods'. Rateliff observes that although purple emperors are now confined to the very south of England, at the time of writing they ranged up to Oxford and may have been present around Birmingham in Tolkien's childhood.

9 'Philology: General Works', *Year's Work in English Studies, 1925*, ed. F. S. Boas and C. H. Herford (London: Oxford University Press, 1927), 32.

10 *Lord of the Rings*, 650. Tolkien's first-published Oxford poem (*Stapeldon Magazine*, Exeter College, Oxford, 1913), written soon after he arrived as an undergraduate in 1911, is a paean to the river beginning 'From the many-willow'd margin of the immemorial Thames'.

11 *On Fairy-Stories*, 55.

12 *Silmarillion*, 165.

13 C. A. Johns, *Flowers of the Field*, vol. 1 (London: Society for Promoting Christian Knowledge, 1853), 255.

14 Flowers, 127–32.

15 See Shippey, 247–8, and Lee and Solopova, 243.

16 *Legend of Sigurd and Gudrún*, 73-74

17 *Lost Tales I*, 33. The lines quoted here survive (36) in *Kortirion among the Trees* as Tolkien retouched it in 1937, the year he began *The Lord of the Rings*.

18 R. H. Richens, *Elm* (Cambridge: Cambridge University Press: 1983), 55.

19 *Gnomish Lexicon*, 32. In Tolkien's much later writings, an *elm*-like sound persists in *ele*, the exclamation the Elves are said to have made on first seeing the stars – and the source of the Quenya words *elen*, 'star' and *Eldar* '"star-folk", Elves' (*War of the Jewels*, 360).

20 *Lord of the Rings*, 377.

21 *Lost Tales I*, 33, 35.

22 *Lost Tales I*, 95.

23 Ethelfleda's Mound (or Mount) was the focus of an elm avenue planted in the 17th century or earlier across the Temple Park. Under 18th-century landscape gardener Capability Brown, more than 1200 elms were planted in this pleasaunce south of the River Avon (David Jaques, 'Warwick Castle Grounds and Park, 1743–60', *Garden History*, vol. 29, no. 1 (2001) 51, 60. Lord Brooke's Clump, now part of a plantation, stood alone in Tolkien's youth, before Castle Park was sold to commercial interests and thus lost its purpose as a complement to the castle.

24 As discussed elsewhere (see p.193, 'Curse of Porlock' panel), this 1937 hike may be the walk Tolkien remembered as going from Lyme Regis to Minehead. That would most likely have followed the western side of the Quantock Hills, where the Seven Sisters stand on Cothelstone Hill (visible across most of Somerset and even from South Wales).

25 *Lord of the Rings*, 350.

26 *Lays of Beleriand*, 255.

27 Tolkien recalled 'a very big gap' in writing at this point when he 'really didn't know how to go on' (1957 radio interview for *Carnival of Books* with Ruth Harshaw, quoted in Anderson, 8). Rateliff (228–9) gives the plot notes mentioning Mirkwood, and describes a matching break in the manuscript at the Eagles' eyrie but (overlooking this 1957 comment) thinks it shows a pause of 'probably no more than a single night'.

28 *Letters*, no. 289.

29 Anderson, 210.

30 On Gondor, the 'Northmen' of Rhovanion, and the Wainriders of Rhûn, see *The Lord of the Rings* 1045–9, *Unfinished Tales*, 288–95, and Tom Shippey, *Roots and Branches: Selected Papers on Tolkien* (Zürich: Walking Tree, 2007), 117–18.

31 *Legend of Sigurd and Gudrún*, 131.

32 *Farmer Giles of Ham*, 10, 57.

33 *Return of the Shadow*, 29 (and the forest is 'dubious' in a plot outline too, 42).

34 They discussed Bournemouth, Dorset, as part of their upcoming Easter 1938 walk (C. S. Lewis, *Collected Letters, Volume 2: Books, Broadcasts and War 1931–1949* [London: HarperCollins, 2004], 222). In the event, they walked between Basingstoke and Alton (as indicated by a spoof quiz written by Tolkien reproduced in McIlwaine, 244–5), and probably further. From one of these Hampshire towns to Bournemouth was seventy miles (113km) – not impossible by Lewis's normal standards – and would have entailed crossing the New Forest. It seems unlikely they actually made such a trek, however; Lewis had a bad foot and Tolkien would not have hiked so far in any case.

35 *Lord of the Rings*, 265.

36 *Lord of the Rings*, 265. Oronzo Cilli records the Warwickshire saying and gives many nineteenth-century examples of its use (*Tolkien's Library: An Annotated Checklist* [Edinburgh: Luna Press, 2019] xxv–xxvi). In their 1925 edition of the Middle English poem *Sir Gawain and the Green Knight*, 94, Tolkien and E. V. Gordon cite the similar saying 'From Blacon Point to Helbree / A squirrel may leap from tree to tree'; but Hilbre in the Dee Estuary is an island, so this seems to refer instead to loss of land (now under water) rather than merely to loss of trees.

37 Jacquetta Hawkes, *A Land* (London: HarperCollins, 2012; first published 1951), 144.

38 *Unfinished Tales*, 263. R. G. Albion, *Forests and Sea Power: The Timber Problem of the Royal Navy 1652–1862* (Cambridge, Massachusetts: Harvard University Press, 1926) gives a persuasive picture of the impact of naval timber demand on English woodlands, though since 1986 it has been downplayed influentially by Rackham (91–2).

39 *Lord of the Rings*, 131.

40 *Lord of the Rings*, 462.

41 *Lord of the Rings*, 459.

42 *Lord of the Rings*, 469.

43 *Lost Tales II*, 327–8.

Tree-woven Lands: panels
The King's Oak (p.115)

1 *Lord of the Rings*, 170.

2 *Black and White Ogre Country*, 6. Hilary's memory, jotted down in old age, confuses Charles I for his son and locates the oak in Sarehole, whereas the Lickey Hills near Rednal are more likely to have an oak with such a legend attached. The fugitive Charles II passed them on 10 September 1651 on the road from

Quinton to Bromsgrove. Trees where he is claimed to have hid from pursuers exist 'all along the route of his escape' (J. Simpson and S. Roud, *A Dictionary of English Folklore* [Oxford: Oxford University Press, 2000] 164).

3   Letter to Baronne A. Baeyens, 16 December 1963 (from the website of the Manhattan Rare Books Company).

4   *Lord of the Rings*, 702.

Woods and Wild Men (p.116)

1   Shippey, 74. The standard etymology of the place name *Woodhouse* is simply 'house in the wood'.

2   *Sir Gawain and the Green Knight, Pearl and Sir Orfeo*, 38.

3   *Nomenclature*, 765.

4   *Lord of the Rings*, 831.

Forest of Thunder (p.123)

1   Tolkien papers, Bodleian Library (Tolkien A15/2). Tolkien also connects *Hercynia* with the Old English *fyrgen*, source of the name of the Firien-wood of *The Lord of the Rings*. James Frazer, in his influential study of comparative religion, *The Golden Bough*, notes that the oak was sacred to a whole array of European thunder-gods: Zeus (Greek), Jupiter (Roman), Perkúnas (Lithuanian) and Thor (Norse).

2   *Fall of Arthur*, 19–20.

Hollin and the Doors of Durin (p.129)

1   Charles Kingsley, *Hereward the Wake, 'Last of the English'* (1866). The word is one of many identified by Edmund Weiner as evidence of Tolkien's debt to this book (Peter Gilliver, Edmund Weiner and Jeremy Marshall, 'The Word as Leaf: Perspectives on Tolkien as Lexicographer and Philologist', in *Tolkien's The Lord of the Rings: Sources of Inspiration* [Zürich: Walking Tree, 2008], 69).

Forests and Cathedrals (p.131)

1   François-René de Chateaubriand, *Genius of Christianity, or the Spirit and Beauty of the Christian Religion*, trans. Charles White (Baltimore: John Murphy, 1871) 386.

2   Lyons, 196.

3   *Lord of the Rings*, 470.

Ancient Imprints: main text (pp. 132–45)

1   *Lost Road*, 51. Alboin is quizzically encouraged in his intellectual pursuits by his schoolmaster father Oswin, a part-portrait of Tolkien's guardian, Father Francis Morgan (Diana Pavlac Glyer and Josh B. Long, 'Biography as Source: Niggles and Notions', in Fisher, 197). Though he did not share Tolkien's intellectual passions, Fr Francis had grown up among keen amateur archaeologists – notably his uncle, Thomas Morgan, whose 1886 book *Romano-British Mosaic Pavements* is an important survey (José Manuel Ferrández Bru, *'Uncle Curro': J. R. R. Tolkien's Spanish Connection* (Edinburgh: Luna Press, 2018), 13.

2   Tolkien, 'Philology: General Works' 1924, 64.

3   *Beowulf: A Translation and Commentary*, 33.

4   *Lord of the Rings*, 512.

5   *Sauron Defeated*, 206.

6   B. C. A. Windle, *Remains of the Prehistoric Age in England* (London: Methuen, 1904, revised 2nd ed.,

1909), 134–5. Windle's diverse writings also include *Life in Early Britain* (1897). Tolkien surely knew his work and, as a child, may have crossed paths with this prominent Birmingham Catholic scientist. Until he left the city in 1904, Windle had been part of the same small, tight circle as the Oratory priests. He had converted from Anglicanism under the influence of Oratory founder Cardinal Newman; been president of Birmingham's Catholic Literary Society, which Father Francis Morgan attended (*Tablet*, 10 March 1888, 35); and was a close friend to Oratory provost H. D. Ryder (whose Latin dictionary Tolkien inherited).He was made a Knight of St Gregory the Great by Pope Pius X in 1909 and a knight of the realm in the New Year's Honours, 1912. By then, Tolkien was good friends at Oxford with Max Windle (John Garth, *Tolkien at Exeter College* [Oxford: Exeter College, 2014], 12–13, 46), whose father was cousin to the illustrious man. Nevill Coghill, Tolkien's later Inklings friend, was a remoter relative.

7   John Rhys, *Celtic Folklore: Welsh and Manx*, vol. 2 (Oxford: Clarendon Press, 1901), 679–80.

8   B. C. A. Windle, introducing his edition of Edward Tyson's 1699 *Philological Essay Concerning the Pygmies of the Ancients* (London: David Nutt, 1894), xv. Tyson himself had not anticipated the aboriginal pygmy theory.

9   Andrew Lang, introduction to his edition of Robert Kirk's *Secret Commonwealth of Elves, Fauns and Fairies* (London: David Nutt, 1893), xxi.

10   *On Fairy-Stories*, 254 (a passage from 'Manuscript B' written either for his 1939 St Andrews lecture or in revisions from 1943).

11   On the word *eorðcyning* in *Beowulf*, Tolkien writes, 'I can scarcely refrain from seeing a reminiscence in this rare compound of the tradition that made Finn not the Frisian but the aboriginal king.' It should not be translated 'king of the land' but 'King of the Underworld because of the common mining and digging propensities of dwarves', he adds (Tolkien papers, Bodleian Library). Tolkien drew the Sylt reference from John Earle's translation *The Deeds of Beowulf*, which he was reading in 1914, but it had featured in MacRitchie's 1890 case for aboriginal 'fairies'.

12   *Lays of Beleriand*, 68; *Art of The Hobbit*, 84.

13   See further, *Artist and Illustrator* 59–61, 124–8; and *Art of The Hobbit*, 77–89. Other pictures in these same years provide the two elven strongholds with arched doorways instead.

14   Simon J. Cook, 'Concerning Hobbits: Welsh Fairies in Oxford' (2013), connects hobbits with John Rhys's arguments in particular. www.tolkienlibrary.com/press/1100-concerning-hobbits-welsh-fairies-in-oxford.php

15   Scull, 1993, 48.

16   *The Hobbit*, 31.

17   Joseph Holden Pott, *An Essay on Landscape Painting* (1782), quoted in Nick Groom, 'Gothic Antiquity: From the Sack of Rome to The Castle of Otranto', in D. Townshend (ed.), *Terror and Wonder: The Gothic*

Imagination (London: British Library, 2014), 49.

18   The resemblance to the image in *An Introduction to Old Norse* was first pointed out by William H. Green in 1969, then independently by J. S. Ryan in 1990. The full pedigree was uncovered by Carl F. Hostetter, Arden R. Smith and Douglas A. Anderson. See Rateliff, 260–1, 284–5; Anderson, 171; *Art of The Hobbit*, 66–70.

19   *Hobbit*, 165.

20   Herodotus, *The Histories*, trans. Aubrey de Sélincourt (London: Penguin, 1954, rev. 1972), 285.

21   *Hobbit*, 165.

22   See Scull, 1993, 40–1; Anderson, 244–5; Rateliff, 448–50.

23   Denis Bridoux, 'Laketown: How a Mythology for Switzerland Came to Contribute to a Mythology for England' (unpublished presentation, Oxonmoot 2013, with assistance from Marc-Antoine Kaeser, director of the Laténium Archaeological Museum in Neuchâtel, Switzerland).

24   During his fourteen months in Holderness, Tolkien surely visited Hull library and its adjacent museum, curated by Thomas Sheppard, the prolific local historian who found the Sand-le-Mere lake-dwelling. For an alternative explanation of *Tol Withernon*, see Garth (2003), 236. Hobbit name spotters may like to know that Skipsea had been the fief of one Drogo de la Bouerer under William the Conqueror; and in earlier Anglo-Saxon times a man named Fróda had given his name to North Frodingham, four miles (6.5km) away.

25   On 6 April 1931, for example, *The Times* published a letter from the discoverer of the Glastonbury site, Arthur Bulleid, summing up 39 years of Somerset lake-village excavations and appealing for public support for a volume on Meare to complement the two volumes already published on Glastonbury.

26   Sir John Evans' archaeological collection, donated to the Ashmolean in three tranches (1909, 1927 and 1949) included the lake-village model he commissioned in 1870 (Deborah Sabo, 'Lake-town and Lake-village Archaeology: Romantic Nationalism at the Edges of The Hobbit', unpublished paper, International Congress on Medieval Studies, Kalamazoo 2010).

27   Sabo, *op. cit.* Nowadays it is accepted that the pile-supported settlements originally labelled 'lake-villages' were actually built on flood-prone marshland, not out in the middle of lakes.

28   *Letters*, no. 19; *Adventures of Tom Bombadil, 127*.

29   Alexandra Harris, *Romantic Moderns: English Writers, Artists and the Imagination from Virginia Woolf to John Piper* (London; Thames & Hudson, 2010, paperback edition 2015), 209.

30   *Lord of the Rings*, 114. Old English charters refer to many a sunken road or *hola weg*, whence modern English *holloway* – a lane created through centuries of use by feet, hooves and wheels, and usually overhung by trees that have populated the steep banks.

31   R. E. M. Wheeler, 'Maiden Castle', *Times*, 1 March 1935, 15.

32 R. E. M. Wheeler, 'Maiden Castle', *Times*, 26 February 1937, 17.

33 *Lord of the Rings*

34 R. E. M. Wheeler, 'Maiden Castle', *Times*, 25 February 1938, 17, 20.

35 An underlined and unused five-word memo, 'Mortimer Wheeler and the Belgae', appears among early notes for his lecture *English and Welsh* (Tolkien papers, Bodleian Library). The Belgae were important latecomers from the continent before the Romans, and Wheeler judged that they seized Maiden Castle from the Durotriges just a few years before Vespasian's AD 43 invasion.

36 *Beowulf: A Translation and Commentary*, 163–4. Tolkien borrowed Andrew Lang's term *barrow-wight* for the Old Icelandic *draugr* (Gilliver, et al, 215).

37 *Lord of the Rings*, 143.

38 *Lord of the Rings*, 649.

39 R. Q. Gilson to Tolkien, 8 July 1913 (Tolkien papers, Bodleian Library).

40 'Songs on the Downs', in *A Spring Harvest*, edited by Tolkien and Christopher Wiseman (London: Erskine Macdonald, 1918), 48.

41 *Lord of the Rings*, 528, 751.

42 Sabo, 96.

43 Murray Smith, 'The Wonderful Things of Tutankhamen, Thorin II and Bard', *Amon Hen* no. 252 (2015), 22.

44 *Lord of the Rings*, 976.

45 Haaken Shetelig and Hjalmar Falk, *Scandinavian Archaeology*, trans. E. V. Gordon (Oxford: Clarendon Press, 1937), 144.

46 Scull, 1993, 47.

47 *Lord of the Rings*, 832.

48 Dickinson.

49 *Lord of the Rings*, 183.

50 *Lord of the Rings*, 845.

51 Philip Schwyzer, 'The Scouring of the White Horse: Archaeology, Identity, and 'Heritage'', *Representations*, no. 65 (winter 1999), 45; Schwyzer discusses the tradition further, 59–60. The idea that the White Horse was made by the Anglo-Saxons remained unchallenged until Stuart Piggot in 1931 compared it to Iron Age Celtic art with similarly disjointed horses. A 1995 study with new scanning technology revealed it was actually first cut around 1000 BC.

52 Maria Artamonova interviewed by the author.

53 *Lord of the Rings*, 838.

54 *Letters*, no. 80. When Tolkien called the ending 'absurd', perhaps he was thinking of the breathlessly brief account of Alfred's taking of London, rather than in the Scouring of the White Horse that precedes it.

55 malcolmguite.wordpress.com/2011/10/10/. The phrase had also been used as the title of an 1859 novel by Thomas Hughes (his next after the *Tom Brown's School Days*) describing the renovation of the chalk horse to the accompaniment of traditional folk games.

56 G. K. Chesterton, *The Ballad of the White Horse* (London: Methuen, 1911; 6th ed. 1920), 171.

57 Daniel Helen, 'Lost Tolkien voice recording discovered', Tolkien Society website, 22 May 2014. www.tolkiensociety.org/2014/05/lost-tolkien-voice-recording-discovered/

Ancient Imprints: panels
Doom-Rings (p.142)

1 *The War of the Jewels*, 282–3.

Watch and Ward: main text (pp. 146–57)

1 *Letters*, no. 250.

2 McIlwaine, 152.

3 *Biography*, 72.

4 Henry Resnick, 'An Interview with Tolkien', *Niekas* no. 18 (1967), 40.

5 *Lost Tales II*, 296.

6 The parish church is the Collegiate Church of St Mary's, not to be confused with the Catholic church of St Mary Immaculate, where the Tolkiens married.

7 *Lost Tales I*, 33–4.

8 *Lost Tales II*, 296. The poem (also called *The Wanderer's Allegiance*) seems independent of the legendarium, though Tolkien later adapted its prelude to become part of a *Song of Eriol*.

9 *Lost Tales II*, 297.

10 *Lost Tales II*, 160.

11 *Lost Tales II*, 196.

12 Alexander M. Bruce, 'The Fall of Gondolin and the Fall of Troy: Tolkien and Book II of *The Aeneid*', *Mythlore* vol. 30, no. 3 (2012), 103. Among other parallels, Bruce compares Ulmo's guardianship of the elven city with Neptune's protection of Troy; and the metallic monsters bringing enemy troops into Gondolin (see p.168 panel) with the Trojan Horse.

13 Tolkien compared the return of the king in *The Lord of the Rings* to 'the re-establishment of an effective Holy Roman Empire with its seat in Rome' (*Letters*, no. 294).

14 *Letters*, no. 102.

15 Hitler's architect, Albert Speer, opened his Nuremberg Trials defence in June 1946 by describing 'his dreams as a young artist to build the greatest buildings in the world under Hitler's eager patronage' (*Times*, 21 June 1946, 4).

16 Minas Tirith's structure was conceived in an outline apparently from 1944 (*War of the Ring* 260–1) and fleshed out in prose in 1946. Tolkien joined the Oxford Dante Society in 1945. In the Inklings, he had long been among Dante experts – Charles Williams (who had published *The Figure of Beatrice* in 1943), C. S. Lewis and Colin Hardie. Lewis, with his philosophical expertise and planetological interests, doubtless knew Campanella's Civitas Solis, with its seven circles denoting the seven planets of medieval cosmology.

17 Shippey, 199.

18 *Lord of the Rings*, 672.

19 *Lord of the Rings*, 856.

20 *Lord of the Rings*, 507; *Beowulf: A Translation and Commentary*, 49. See Shippey, 124–5.

21 *Lord of the Rings*, 508.

22 *Lost Tales II*, 297.

23 *Lost Tales II*, 296.

24 In the Rivendell chapters written shortly beforehand, Tolkien had finally changed the name of Elvenhome's capital from *Kôr* to *Tirion*. Thus he suppressed the explicit echo of *She* just in time to borrow from Haggard's book again with Lothlórien.

25 *Letters*, no. 154.

26 The connection began as a joke among Tolkien Society officers reconnoitring Birmingham in August 1991 to prepare bus tours for the following year's Tolkien Centenary Conference (Denis Bridoux to the author). It was promoted by Peter Leather, an expert on Birmingham buildings who conducted the tours (Chris Arnot, 'Lord of the ring road', *Guardian*, 5 August 2003). (Since I wrote this chapter, it has been suggested to me that Birmingham broadcaster Carl Chinn talked about the city's 'two towers' in the 1980s, and that historian Chris Upton referred to them in a booklet published in time for the 1992 conference.) Another Edgbaston tower some distance away, the Joseph Chamberlain Memorial Clock Tower at Birmingham University, has been pinned as the inspiration for Barad-dûr. No doubt this is because of a passing likeness to the column-shaped Dark Tower of the movies, with the clock as the flaming Eye of Sauron. But Tolkien's illustrations show a much more pyramidal Barad-dûr, and the Eye in *The Lord of the Rings* is a mostly unseen threat (Wayne G. Hammond and Christina Scull, *The Art of The Lord of the Rings* [Boston: Houghton Mifflin Harcourt, 2015] 187, 220).

27 *Letters*, no. 140. Tolkien was reluctant for his epic, already complete by this point, to be split into volumes at all. His dustjacket sketches depict the 'two towers' either as Minas Tirith and Barad-dûr or as Minas Morgul and Orthanc (*Artist and Illustrator*, 180–1). Tolkien said in print at the at end of vol. 1, *The Fellowship of the Ring* (1954), that the two towers were Minas Morgul and Orthanc.

28 Flowers, 136–8.

29 See *The Happy Mariners*, 1920 version reprinted in Garth, 2003, 90–1; 1923 version reprinted in *Lost Tales II*, 273–4.

30 *Beowulf and the Critics*, 68.

31 *Monsters and the Critics*, 8. Almost all the other emendations to the ink manuscript are in ink, most probably made at the time of writing. The pencil changes to the allegory make it the most reworked passage of all.

32 Mark Amory, *Lord Berners: The Last Eccentric* (London: Pimlico, 1999).

33 Christopher Hayhurst-France, 'Lord Berners' Folly', publication unknown, 1989.

34 'I cordially dislike allegory in all its manifestations, and always have done so since I grew old and wary enough to detect its presence. I much prefer history, true or feigned' (*Lord of the Rings*, xxiv).

35 *Lost Road*, 28.

36 *Return of the Shadow*, 312–13.

37 *Treason of Isengard*, 34.

38 *Lord of the Rings*, 127. Frodo's dream of the elf-tower partly survives, separately (108).

39 *Treason of Isengard*, 130.

Places of War: main text (pp. 158–73)

1 *Letters*, no. 66. He was advising his son Christopher, then training in the RAF during the Second World War, to try something similar. Tolkien wrote or revised poems in the trenches but did not write any of *The Book of Lost Tales* there (see Garth, 2003, 186).

2 *Letters*, no. 163.

3 Fussell, 124, 146.

4 Letter to H. Cotton Minchin, auctioned by Sotheby's, www.sothebys.com/en/auctions/ecatalogue/2013/books-manuscripts-n09066/lot.226.html. See further my article 'Sam Gamgee and Tolkien's batmen', johngarth.wordpress.com/2014/02/13/. *Lord of the Rings*, 106.

5 Tolkien's first letter to Edith Bratt from Cornwall is dated 5 August.

6 *Artist and Illustrator*, 45 (from the 1915 version, *Sea Chant of an Elder Day*).

7 *Shaping of Middle-earth*, 216 (from the 1917 version, *The Horns of Ulmo*; the 1914 version remains unpublished).

8 *Lost Tales I*, 34.

9 *Lost Tales I*, 91. Habbanan was renamed *Eruman* in *The Book of Lost Tales* and *Araman* in *The Silmarillion* (where, however, it is not a resting-place for mortal souls).

10 The untitled watercolour follows paintings dated 1915 in the sketchbook that Tolkien called *The Book of Ishness*.

11 *Lord of the Rings*, 699.

12 *Lord of the Rings*, 701.

13 *Artist and Illustrator*, 66.

14 Blunden, 65.

15 *Letters*, no. 43.

16 Norman.

17 John Garth, 'Robert Quilter Gilson, T.C.B.S.: A Brief Life in Letters', *Tolkien Studies* no. 8 (2011), 93.

18 John Brophy, quoted in Fussell, 70.

19 *Hobbit*, 59.

20 *Lord of the Rings*, 313.

21 *Lord of the Rings*, 323.

22 *Lord of the Rings*, 827.

23 Siegfried Sassoon, *The Complete Memoirs of George Sherston* (London: Faber and Faber, 1972), 277.

24 *Lord of the Rings*, 949; see Hugh Brogan, 'Tolkien's Great War', in *Children and their Books, A Celebration of the Works of Iona and Peter Opie*, ed. Gillian Avery and Julia Briggs (Oxford: Clarendon Press, 1989), 353–4.

25 *Letters*, no. 226.

26 *Lord of the Rings*, 628.

27 *Lord of the Rings*, 627. Wilfred Owen, *Collected Poems of Wilfred Owen*, ed. Cecil Day Lewis (London: Chatto & Windus, 1963), 55.

28 Hugh Cecil, *The Flower of Battle: British Fiction Writers of the First World War* (London: Secker and Warburg, 1995).

29 *Lord of the Rings*, 631–2.

30 Brace 1968.

31 *Lord of the Rings*, 913.

32 *Silmarillion*, 294.

33 *Lord of the Rings*, 921, 922.

34 'Charles Edmonds' (Charles Carrington), *A Subaltern's War*, 110. Charles Carrington, *Soldier from the Wars Returning*, 142.

35 *Lord of the Rings*, 923.

36 Barton, 36.

37 *Lost Tales II*, 287.

38 *Lays of Beleriand*, 280.

39 *Lost Tales I*, 239.

40 *Northern Daily Telegraph*, 19 July 1916, 7.

41 *Lays of Beleriand*, 58.

42 Simone Bonechi, '"In the Mounds of Mundburg": Death, War and Memory in Middle-earth', in *The Broken Scythe: Death and Immortality in the Works of J.R.R. Tolkien*, ed. Roberto Arduini and Claudio A. Testi (Zürich: Walking Tree, 2012), 143.

43 *Hobbit*, 173–5.

44 *Farmer Giles of Ham*, 58.

45 1938 talk on dragons, *Reader's Guide*, 310.

46 *Lord of the Rings*, 476.

47 *Letters*, no. 163.

48 Barton, 185.

49 Blunden, 95.

50 *Silmarillion*, 155.

51 *Adventures of Tom Bombadil*, 254.

52 See Verlyn Flieger, *A Question of Time: Tolkien's Road to Faërie* (Ohio: Kent State University Press, 1997), 224. The Tea Club and Barrovian Society was named from the group's practice of brewing tea in the school library office and meeting at the tea-room of Barrow's department store in Birmingham.

53 *Letters*, no. 5.

54 *Repression of War Experience*, in *Collected Poems* (London: Faber, 1983), 84.

55 *Lays of Beleriand*, 340.

56 *Lays of Beleriand*, 175.

57 Robert S. Blackham, *Tolkien and the Peril of War* (Stroud: History Press, 2012), 84.

58 *Silmarillion*, 165, 164.

59 *Lays of Beleriand*, 58.

60 *Lays of Beleriand*, 65.

61 *Lays of Beleriand*, 77.

62 *Adventures of Tom Bombadil*, 34.

Places of War: panels

A Battlefield both Ancient and Modern (p.162)

1 Barton, 36.

2 Blunden, 12.

Tanks at Gondolin (p.168)

1 Norman.

2 *Lost Tales II*, 170.

3 *Lost Tales II*, 176.

4 'The Gnomes deem the siege of Angband cannot be broken, but Morgoth ponders new devices, and bethinks him of Dragons' (the earliest *Annals of Beleriand*, from the mid-1930s, in *Shaping of Middle-earth*, 297). In later accounts of the origin of dragons (*War of the Jewels*, 46) Tolkien stressed that they were creatures bred rather than 'devices' invented; but this was because he had arrived at the philosophical view that the Enemy 'can only mock, it cannot make', as Frodo says of orcs (*Lord of the Rings*, 914).

5 Tolkien papers, Bodleian Library.

6 *Hobbit*, 60.

7 *Lord of the Rings*, 537.

8 *Artist and Illustrator*, 189.

The Marsh of Tode (p.170)

1 *Adventures of Tom Bombadil*, 210–12. A yet earlier version of *Knocking on the Door* probably dates from the late 1920s, at the time of the Bimble Bay poems (Rateliff, 377, citing Douglas A. Anderson).

2 Ardern Beaman, *The Squadroon*, London: Bodley Head, 187.

Craft and Industry: main text (pp. 174–85)

1 *Ian Hislop's Olden Days: The Power of the Past in Britain*, episode 3, 'Green Imagined Land', BBC Two, 2014.

2 Laurie Lee, *Cider with Rosie* (London: Vintage, 2014) 212.

3 *Letters*, no. 303.

4 *Lord of the Rings*, 1.

5 *Biography*, 28.

6 Garth (2003), 206.

7 Humphrey Carpenter on BBC Radio 4 *Woman's Hour*, quoted in 'Old Brum', *The Listener*, 30 June 1977, 853.

8 Burns, 26, 28.

9 Quoted in Hall, 18.

10 *Hobbit*, 83.

11 *Hobbit*, 28.

12 *Hobbit*, 28; cf. Burns (2010), 29–30.

13 *Lord of the Rings*, 27.

14 Barry and Pugin went on to build the Palace of Westminster. As a Catholic, Tolkien never worshipped in older English churches (though there is no reason to think he avoided them).

15 *Reader's Guide*, 580–1.

16 *Letters*, no. 73.

17 Morris, 'The Art of the People', 1879 speech at Birmingham Town Hall.

18 *Lost Tales II*, 163.

19 *Letters*, no. 58.

20 Elliander Pictures, *Birmingham's Lost Masterpiece – The Charles Barry Building* (2011) vimeo.com/20017714.

21 Letter to Ronald Ashton, 12 March 1927 (Michael Silverman, *Catalogue Twenty-Seven*, London, 2009).

22 *Oxford Magazine*, 15 October 1931, 22; reprinted *Annotated Hobbit*, 254.

23 Talk on dragons, 1 January 1938, the University Museum, Oxford (Tolkien papers, Bodleian Library). Tolkien originally wrote that the lorries belonged to Lord Nuffield, William Morris of Cowley, but deleted the reference.

24 *Letters*, no. 135.

25 *Biography*, 163.

26 *Letters*, no. 98.

27 Ezard.

28 'Foreword to the Second Edition', *LotR*, xxv.

29 *Biography*, 124–5. Tolkien refers to the house of 'the White Ogre' (the miller's son). But the petrol station

was at former Sarehole Farm, home of 'the Black Ogre'.

30 Uglow, 257.

31 *Hobbit*, 13. There is disagreement over whether the end of *The Hobbit* (from the death of Smaug onwards) was written by January 1933, or was not completed until 1936. The fact that Bilbo returns to find nothing more bothersome than an auction of his property could (conceivably) support the earlier date. September 1933 was when Tolkien saw what had happened to Sarehole – the experience that shaped the hobbits' much more distressing return at the end of *The Lord of the Rings*.

32 *Lord of the Rings*, 1017.

33 Shippey, 171. Shippey further links Saruman with the mill's 'literally bone-grinding owner "the White Ogre"', relying upon Humphrey Carpenter's statement that the mill's 'chief work' was grinding bones for fertilizer (*Biography*, 20). Tolkien's own recollection that the mill 'really did grind corn' (Ezard) is confirmed by Wayne Dixon, current supervisor at Sarehole Mill Museum, on photographic and other evidence. He suggests that bonemeal production may have been an occasional sideline. Carpenter's probable source, a local history by John Morris Jones, depends on oral memories in the 1960s that may relate to the years after the Tolkiens had left. The sole documentary evidence for bone-grinding, from 1894, predates their arrival.

34 *Lord of the Rings*, 1013.

35 *Lord of the Rings*, 1018.

36 *Lord of the Rings*, 966; *Nomenclature*, 766. It was probably the Black Country that Humphrey Carpenter mostly had in mind when he said of Tolkien, 'Industrial Birmingham was something he hated. It does appear, I think, in his descriptions of devastated, frightening and even evil landscapes in Mordor.' He continued with a personal view: 'I think you can recognize something of industrial, smoky, desolate Birmingham, the kind of landscape that you see, for instance, coming out of the station and going from Birmingham to Wolverhampton' (*The Listener*, 30 June 1977, 853). The Black Country lies exactly in this area, and urban sprawl had increasingly blurred any dividing line from Birmingham.

37 Humphrey Jennings, *Pandaemonium 1660–1886: The Coming of the Machine as Seen by Contemporary Observers* (London: Icon Books, 2012), 165. An 1830 visitor was also reminded of volcanic desolation: 'The earth seems to have been turned inside out. Its entrails are strewn about; nearly the entire surface of the ground is covered with cinder-heaps and mounds of scoriae… The grass had been parched and killed by the vapours of sulphureous acid thrown out by the chimneys; and every herbaceous object was of a ghastly gray … Vulcan had driven out Ceres' (171).

38 F. B. Young, *Mr Lucton's Freedom* (quoted in Hall, 66).

39 *Lord of the Rings*, 924.

40 *Lord of the Rings*, 626; *War of the Ring*, 105.

41 *Letters*, no. 52.

42 *On Fairy-Stories*, 282. By the time Tolkien wrote 'The Scouring of the Shire' in 1948, in the aftermath

of the Second World War, a new wave of cheap housebuilding was in full swing around cities and towns everywhere, including Oxford. His Foreword to the second edition of *The Lord of the Rings* (1965) states categorically that this post-war wave of building had no impact on the ruin of the Shire. Indeed, this plot development had been projected as early as 1939–40. Yet it is hard to imagine him totally immune to the renewed urbanization as he wrote 'The Scouring of the Shire'. The Foreword is a forthright response to readers who seemed to ignore Tolkien's pre-war background and who insisted on reading *The Lord of the Rings* exclusively as social comment. It is not necessarily a full and fair view of his inspirations.

43 Patrick Curry, *Defending Middle-earth* (Boston: Houghton Mifflin, 2004), 15–16.

44 Lee, 212.

Appendix (pp. 187–8)

1 *Guardian* and *Telegraph*, 2 April 2013, www.theguardian.com/books/2013/apr/02/hobbit-tolkien-ring-exhibition and https://www.telegraph.co.uk/culture/books/booknews/9966793/The-Hobbit-ring-that-inspired-Tolkien-goes-on-display.html.

2 BBC News, 3 April 2013, www.bbc.co.uk/news/uk-england-hampshire-22008746.

3 en.wikipedia.org/wiki/Ring_of_Silvianus (accessed 5 May 2019).

4 J. S. Ryan (*In the Nameless Wood: Explorations in the Philological Hinterland of Tolkien's Literary Creations* [Zurich: Walking Tree, 2013], 93–135) sees the Lydney pilgrimage site as the inspiration for Aragorn as healer; nearby mines as the source of Moria and the treasure quest in *The Hobbit*; and Roman mosaics as the spark for Tolkien's 1960s Númenórean tile drawings. Helen Armstrong ('And Have an Eye to That Dwarf', *Amon Hen* no. 145 [1997], 13–14) argues that old mines at Camp Hill at Lydney, formerly Dwarf's Hill, inspired Moria, Celebrimbor of Eregion and the Doors of Durin in *The Lord of the Rings*, as well as the abduction of Lúthien by Celegorm and Curufin in the *Lay of Leithian*. Lyons, 49–74, thinks the mines gave Tolkien the idea for hobbit-holes.

5 Lynn Forest-Hill, 'Tolkien, Lydney and the Vyne: patterns of loss and discovery' (2013, available at Academia.edu).

6 *Hobbit*, 77.

7 *Lays of Beleriand*, 230.

8 Chaloner W. Chute, *A History of the Vyne in Hampshire* (Winchester: Jacob & Johnson, 1888), 8. The ring found at Silchester became part of the Chute family collection at their home, the Vyne. When it was put on show there by the current owner, the National Trust, news reports said that it was Mortimer Wheeler who had 'spotted the connection' between tablet and ring (*Guardian*, 2 April 2013).

9 'The Name "Nodens"', 182.

10 John D. Rateliff, 'To Recall Forgotten Gods from Their Twilight: J. R. R. Tolkien's "The Name

'Nodens"', in *A Wilderness of Dragons: Essays in Honour of Verlyn Flieger*, ed. John D. Rateliff (Wayzata, MN: Gabbro Head), 223–4.

11 *Shaping of Middle-earth*, 25.

12 Stefan Collini and Bernard Williams, 'Robin George Collingwood', *Oxford Dictionary of National Biography*, 2004/2008 (online). Collingwood took over the task of describing all British Roman inscriptions from F. J. Haverfield (d. 1919), who had already written about they Lydney curse and Vyne ring in the *Victoria County History of Hampshire* (London: Archibald Constable, 1900), 283–4.

13 R. G. Collingwood and J. N. L. Myres, *Roman Britain and the English Settlements* (Oxford: Clarendon Press, 1936; 2nd ed. 1937), vii. Phelpstead (77–8) argues that Tolkien contributed the Celtic insights to *Sir Gawain and the Green Knight* (1925), edited with E. V. Gordon at Leeds.

14 R. G. Collingwood, *Roman Britain* (Oxford: Clarendon Press, 1932), 137. Collingwood's visit to Lydney is mentioned in Jacquetta Hawkes's *Mortimer Wheeler: Adventurer in Archaeology* (London: Weidenfeld and Nicolson, 1982, 149) just before her reference to Tolkien's note.

15 *Letters*, no. 226.

16 Report of a conference paper as reported in Leonardo Mantovani, Valérie Morisi, Simone Ronchi and Tom Shippey, 'Tolkien and the Literature of the Fourth Age', *Amon Hen* no. 272 (July 2018), 14.

17 Jessica Yates, 'William Morris's Influence on J. R. R. Tolkien' (unpublished).

18 Holly Ordway, 'Tolkien, Morris, and the Dead Marshes', 19 November 2015, www.hollyordway.com/2015/11/19/.

19 There is no space here to pursue the obvious parallels in *The Roots of the Mountains* with Éowyn's story. Tolkien's Inklings friend Warnie Lewis (C. S. Lewis's brother) certainly recognized the similarities. He wrote that 'there are whole chapters of the new Hobbit in which Morris is beaten on his own ground – especially the journeys' (W. H. Lewis, *Brothers and Friends: The Diaries of Major Warren Hamilton Lewis*, ed. Clyde S. Kilby and Marjorie L. Mead [Harper & Row, New York, 1982], 206). This was in 1947, when the Inklings would have been listening to the Ride of the Rohirrim.

SELECT BIBLIOGRAPHY

Listed here are works cited several times in the Endnotes, where they appear by surname (and year, where necessary) or by short title. Also included are publications that I have found generally useful, even though they may not have been cited directly. Bibliographical details of other sources are given in the Endnotes.

Works by J. R. R. Tolkien

The Adventures of Tom Bombadil and Other Verses from the Red Book, ed. Christina Scull and Wayne G. Hammond. London: HarperCollins, 2014.

The Art of The Hobbit, text by Wayne G. Hammond and Christina Scull. London: HarperCollins, 2013.

The Art of The Lord of the Rings, text by Wayne G. Hammond and Christina Scull. London: HarperCollins, 2015.

Beowulf and the Critics, ed. Michael D. C. Drout. Tempe, Arizona: Arizona Center for Medieval and Renaissance Studies, 2011 (second edition).

Beowulf: A Translation and Commentary. London: HarperCollins, 2014.

The Book of Lost Tales, part one (History of Middle-earth, vol. 1), ed. Christopher Tolkien. London: George Allen & Unwin, 1983.

The Book of Lost Tales, part two (History of Middle-earth, vol. 2), ed. Christopher Tolkien. London: George Allen & Unwin, 1984.

Early Noldorin Fragments. Parma Eldalamberon, no. 13 (2001), ed. Christopher Gilson, Bill Welden, Carl F. Hostetter, and Patrick Wynne.

The Fall of Arthur, ed. Christopher Tolkien. London: HarperCollins, 2013.

Gnomish Lexicon (I·Lam na·Ngoldathon). Parma Eldalamberon, no. 11 (1995), ed. Christopher Gilson, Patrick Wynne, Arden R. Smith, and Carl F. Hostetter.

The Hobbit. London: George Allen & Unwin, 1978 (fourth edition). (For *Annotated Hobbit*, see Anderson, and *History of The Hobbit*, see Rateliff.)

The Lays of Beleriand (History of Middle-earth, vol. 3), ed. Christopher Tolkien. London: George Allen & Unwin, 1985.

The Legend of Sigurd and Gudrún, ed. Christopher Tolkien. London: HarperCollins, 2009.

Letters from Father Christmas, ed. Baillie Tolkien. London: HarperCollins, 2015.

The Letters of J. R. R. Tolkien ('*Letters*'), ed. Humphrey Carpenter and Christopher Tolkien. London: HarperCollins, 1995 (first published 1981).

The Lord of the Rings. London: HarperCollins, 2004 (50th anniversary edition).

The Lost Road (History of Middle-earth, vol. 5), ed. Christopher Tolkien. London: Unwin Hyman, 1987.

Lost Tales I: see *Book of Lost Tales, part one*.

Lost Tales II: see *Book of Lost Tales, part two*.

The Monsters and the Critics and Other Essays. London: George Allen & Unwin, 1983.

Morgoth's Ring (History of Middle-earth, vol. 10), ed. Christopher Tolkien. London: George Allen & Unwin, 1993.

Mr. Bliss. London: HarperCollins, 2011 (first published 1982).

'The name "Coventry"'. *Catholic Herald*, 23 February 1945.

'The name "Nodens"', in *Tolkien Studies* vol. 4 (2007) 177–83. Originally published in R. E. M. Wheeler & T. V. Wheeler, *Report on the Excavation of the Prehistoric, Roman, and Post-Roman Site in Lydney Park, Gloucestershire* (Oxford: The Society of Antiquaries 1932).

Nomenclature. 'Nomenclature of *The Lord of the Rings*', repr. in *The Lord of the Rings: A Reader's Companion*; see under Hammond.

On Fairy-Stories: see *Tolkien on Fairy-Stories*

The Peoples of Middle-earth (History of Middle-earth, vol. 12), ed. Christopher Tolkien. London: HarperCollins, 1996.

'Philology: General Works', in *The Year's Work in English Studies 1924*, ed. F. S. Boas and C. H. Herford. London: Oxford University Press, 1926.

Qenya Lexicon (Qenyaqetsa). Parma Eldalamberon, no. 12 (1998), ed. Christopher Gilson, Carl F. Hostetter, Patrick Wynne, and Arden R. Smith.

The Return of the Shadow (History of Middle-earth, vol. 6), ed. Christopher Tolkien. London: Unwin Hyman, 1988.

Sauron Defeated (History of Middle-earth, vol. 9), ed. Christopher Tolkien. London: HarperCollins, 1992.

The Shaping of Middle-earth (History of Middle-earth, vol. 4), ed. Christopher Tolkien. London: Unwin Hyman, 1986.

The Silmarillion. London: George Allen & Unwin, 1977 (first edition).

Sir Gawain and the Green Knight, Pearl and Sir Orfeo, ed. Christopher Tolkien. London: HarperCollins, 2006 (first published 1975).

Smith of Wootton Major, ed. Verlyn Flieger. London: HarperCollins, 2005 (extended edition).

The Story of Kullervo, ed. Verlyn Flieger. London: HarperCollins, 2015.

Tales from the Perilous Realm. London: HarperCollins, 2008.

Tolkien on Fairy-Stories, ed. Verlyn Flieger and Douglas A. Anderson. London: HarperCollins, 2014.

The Treason of Isengard (History of Middle-earth, vol. 7), ed. Christopher Tolkien. London: Unwin Hyman, 1989.

Unfinished Tales of Númenor and Middle-earth, ed. Christopher Tolkien. London: George Allen & Unwin, 1980.

The War of the Jewels (History of Middle-earth, vol. 11), ed. Christopher Tolkien. London: HarperCollins, 1994.

The War of the Ring (History of Middle-earth, vol. 8), ed. Christopher Tolkien. London: Unwin Hyman, 1990.

Words, Phrases and Passages in The Lord of the Rings. Parma Eldalamberon, no. 17 (2007), ed. Christopher Gilson.

Works by others

Anderson, Douglas A. (ed.). *The Annotated Hobbit*. Boston: Houghton Mifflin, 2002 (2nd edition).

Artamonova, Maria, and Nicolay Yakovlev. 'Tolkien's Oxfordshire'. Unpublished lecture.

Artist and Illustrator: see under Hammond and Scull.

Barnfield, Marie. 'The Roots of Rivendell'; in *þe Lyfe ant þe Auncestrye* no. 3, ed. Trevor Reynolds. Milton Keynes: Forsaken Inn, 1996.

Barton, Peter. *The Somme*. London: Constable, 2006.

Biography: see under Carpenter, Humphrey.

Blackham, Robert S. *The Roots of Tolkien's Middle-earth*. Stroud: Tempus, 2006.

Blunden, Edmund. *Undertones of War* (Chicago: University of Chicago Press, 2007; 1st pub. 1928).

Brace, Keith. 'In the Footsteps of the Hobbits.' *Birmingham Post*, 25 May 1968.

Brace, Keith. 'Perspective: Tolkien dismissed idea of a deeper meaning.' *Birmingham Post*, 27 November 2001, 11.

Bratman, David. 'In Search of the Shire', *Mallorn* no. 37. Tolkien Society, 1999.

Bridoux, Denis. 'Tolkien's Swiss Journey'. Unpublished talk, 2017.

Brookes-Smith, Colin. *Some Reminiscences of J. R. R. Tolkien*. Unpublished: Bloxham, 1982.

Burns, Maggie. 'A local habitation and a name', in *Mallorn* no. 50. Tolkien Society, 2010.

Burns, Marjorie. *Perilous Realms: Celtic and Norse in Tolkien's Middle-earth*. Toronto: University of Toronto Press, 2005.

Carpenter, Humphrey. *J. R. R. Tolkien: A Biography*. London: George Allen & Unwin, 1977.

Dickinson, Helen. *J.R.R.T.: A Film Portrait of J. R. R. Tolkien* (directed by Derek Bailey). London: Tolkien Partnership/Landseer, 1992.

Ekwall, Eilert. *The Concise Oxford Dictionary of English Place-names*. Oxford: Clarendon Press, 1936.

English School Association, Leeds. *Leeds University Verse 1914–1924*. Leeds: The Swan Press, 1924.

Ezard, John. 'Tolkien's Shire'. *The Guardian*, 28 December 1991 (www.guardian.co.uk/books/1991/dec/28/jrrtolkien.classics).

Family Album: see under Tolkien, John and Priscilla.

Fimi, Dimitra. *Tolkien, Race and Cultural History: From Fairies to Hobbits*. Basingstoke: Palgrave Macmillan, 2008.

Fisher, Jason. *Tolkien and the Study of His Sources*. Jefferson, NC: McFarland, 2011.

Flowers, Michael. 'Tolkien in East Yorkshire, 1917-18: A Hemlock Glade, Two Towers, the Houses of Healing and a Beacon', in Janet Brennan Croft and Annika Röttingger (eds.), *Something Has Gone Crack: New Perspectives on J. R. R. Tolkien in the Great War* (Zürich: Walking Tree, 2019)

Foster, William. 'An early history of the hobbits'. *Edinburgh Scotsman*, 5 February 1972.

Fussell, Paul. *The Great War and Modern Memory*. Oxford: Oxford University Press, 2013 (first published 1975).

Garth, John. *Tolkien and the Great War: The Threshold of Middle-earth*. London: HarperCollins, 2003.

Gelling, Margaret. *The Place-Names of Oxfordshire*.

Gilliver, Peter, Jeremy Marshall and Edmund Weiner. *The Ring of Words: Tolkien and the Oxford English Dictionary*. Oxford: Oxford University Press, 2006.

Hall, Michael. *Francis Brett Young's Birmingham: North Bromwich – City of Iron*. PhD thesis, University of Birmingham, 2007.

Hammond, Wayne G., and Christina Scull. *J. R. R. Tolkien: Artist and Illustrator*. London: HarperCollins, 1995.

Hammond, Wayne G., and Christina Scull. *The Lord of the Rings: A Reader's Companion*. London: HarperCollins, 2014 (second edition).

Hynes, Gerard. '"Beneath the Earth's dark keel": Tolkien and Geology', in *Tolkien Studies* vol. 9 (2012).

Kington, John. *Climate and Weather*. London: HarperCollins, 2010.

Lewis, C. S. *The Discarded Image*. Cambridge: Cambridge University Press, 1964.

Larrington, Carolyne. *The Norse Myths: A Guide to the Gods and Goddesses*. London: Thames & Hudson, 2017.

Lee, Stuart, and Elizabeth Solopova. *The Keys of Middle-earth*. 2nd edition, Basingstoke, Palgrave Macmillan, 2015.

Lord of the Rings Companion: see under Hammond.

Lyons, Mathew. *There and Back Again: In the Footsteps of J. R. R. Tolkien*. London: Cadogan, 2004.

Mabey, Richard. *Flora Britannica*. London: Sinclair-Stevenson, 1996.

McIlwaine, Catherine. *Tolkien: Maker of Middle-earth*. Oxford: Bodleian Publishing, 2018.

Nansen, Fridtjof. *In Northern Mists* (in two volumes). London: Heinemann, 1911.

Norman, Philip. 'The Hobbit Man', *Sunday Times Magazine*, 15 January 1967.

Orchard, Andy. *Pride and Prodigies: Studies in the Monsters of the Beowulf Manuscript*. Pbk ed. Toronto: University of Toronto Press, 2003.

Organ, Michael. 'Tolkien's Japonisme: Prints, Dragons, and a Great Wave.' *Tolkien Studies* vol. 10 (2013).

Phelpstead, Carl. *Tolkien and Wales: Language, Literature and Identity*. Cardiff: University of Wales Press, 2011.

Prest, John. 'City and University', in *The Illustrated History of Oxford University*, ed. John Prest. Oxford: Oxford University Press, 1993.

Rackham, Oliver. *The History of the Countryside*. London: Phoenix, 2000 (first published London: Dent, 1986).

Rateliff, John D. *The History of the Hobbit*. London: HarperCollins, 2007 (1st ed.)

Reader's Guide: see under Scull, Christina, and Wayne G. Hammond.

Resnick, Henry. 'An Interview with Tolkien', *Niekas*, no. 18 (1967)

Sabo, Deborah. 'Archaeology and the Sense of History in J. R. R. Tolkien's Middle-earth', *Mythlore* vol. 21, no. 1 (Fall/Winter 2007).

Scull, Christina. 'The Influence of Archaeology and History on Tolkien's World', in *Scholarship and Fantasy: Proceedings of the Tolkien Phenomenon*, ed. K. J. Battarbee. Turku: University of Turku Press, 1993.

Scull, Christina, and Wayne G. Hammond. *The J. R. R. Tolkien Companion and Guide: Reader's Guide*. London: HarperCollins, 2017 (2nd ed., in two volumes).

Sheppard, Thomas. *The Lost Towns of the Yorkshire Coast*. London: A. Brown & Sons, 1912.

Shippey, Tom. *The Road to Middle-earth: How J. R. R. Tolkien created a new mythology*. London: HarperCollins, 2005 (revised and expanded edition).

Simek, Rudolf. *Dictionary of Norse Mythology*, trans. Angela Hall. Cambridge: D. S. Brewer, 1993 (repr. 2000).

Tolkien, Hilary. *Black and White Ogre Country: The Lost Tales of Hilary Tolkien*, ed. Angela Gardner. Moreton-in-Marsh: ADC, 2009.

Tolkien, John and Priscilla, *The Tolkien Family Album*. Boston: Houghton Mifflin, 1992.

Uglow, Jenny. *The Lunar Men: The Inventors of the Modern World 1730–1810*.

ACKNOWLEDGEMENTS

The Worlds of J.R.R. Tolkien is part of a larger investigation of his creative processes that I began with *Tolkien and the Great War*, first published by HarperCollins in 2003, and continued more modestly in *Tolkien at Exeter College*, published by Exeter College, Oxford, in 2014. Much of the material emerged during research for another book on Tolkien – yet to be published – that I began during my year as a fellow of the Black Mountain Institute in Nevada in 2015–16; and I wholeheartedly thank the BMI for its generous support. Likewise I thank the Society of Authors and its Authors Foundation for a generous grant to help with work on that book, which has also indirectly helped with *The Worlds of J.R.R. Tolkien*.

The idea that I might write a book about places that inspired Tolkien was suggested by my former *Evening Standard* colleague Victoria Summerley, who helped bring her own publisher on board. I thank Andrew Dunn for his initial interest; and Philip Cooper, Nicki Davis, Emma Harverson and others at Quarto for working their magic on the book.

For permission to quote from Tolkien's works, to use his images, and to cite his unpublished writings, I am deeply grateful to the Tolkien Estate and Cathleen Blackburn. For facilitating research among Tolkien's papers at the Bodleian Libraries in Oxford, I thank Catherine McIlwaine and the staff of the Rare Books and Manuscripts reading room.

For all kinds of information, advice and support, I thank Douglas A. Anderson, Maria Artamonova, Marcel Aubron-Bülles, Nicky Balfour Penney, Jeremy Banning, John Barret, Bradley J. Birzer, Robert S. Blackham, Jane Chance, Janet Brennan Croft, José Manuel Ferrández Bru, John David Cofield, James and Jenny Curtis, Jenni Dixon, Wayne Dixon, Jenny Dolfen, Jeremy Edmonds, Jason Fisher, Michael Flowers, Lisa Garth, Suzanne Garth, Seamus Hamill-Keays, Yoko Hemmi, Neil Holford, Thomas Honegger, Daniel Joyce, Jonathan Kirkpatrick, Kristine Larsen, Alan Lee, Andrew McMurry, Nancy Martsch, Gergely Nagy, Charles Noad, Jenny Paxman (née Brookes-Smith), Tory Paxman, Carl Phelpstead, Ian Pritchard, Paul Readman, Alan Reynolds, Patricia Reynolds, David Robbie, Scarborough Maritime Heritage Centre, Christina Scull, Tom Shippey, Ollie Taylor, Morgan Thomsen, Adam Tolkien, Christopher Tolkien, Gene Webb, Scott Whitehouse, Victoria Whitworth and Jessica Yates.

My parents Jean and Roy Garth provided the peace and quiet in which to write the book. Portions were read in draft by Denis Bridoux, David Doughan, Megan Engel, Tom Hillman, Robin Darwall-Smith, Peter Gilliver, Michaela Hausmann, Mitchell Liddell, Robbie Park, Sally Pehrsson, Deborah Sabo, Kris Swank, and Edmund and Clare Weiner, all of whom offered valuable suggestions. My wife, Jessica Weinstein, also read and improved chapters in draft. With our daughter Lorelei Garth, she has borne the writing process with understanding and patience. I thank them all, as I also thank the wonderful photographers, known and unknown, whose images enrich this book.

Undoubtedly I have overlooked some debts; I hope I will be forgiven. Any errors, of course, are my own.

John Garth